Nobody Said It Would Be Easy

Nobody Said
It Would Be Easy

RAISING RESPONSIBLE KIDS—

AND KEEPING THEM OUT OF TROUBLE

Dr. Dan Kiley

HARPER & ROW, PUBLISHERS

 New York   Hagerstown   San Francisco   London

1817

To Mom for what she is,
to Dad for what he has become

FIRST EDITION

Designed by Sidney Feinberg

Library of Congress Cataloging in Publication Data

Kiley, Dan.
  Keeping kids out of trouble.
    1. Children—Management. 2. Problem children.
I. Title.
HQ773.K52   1978   649'.1   77-11821
ISBN 0-06-012369-9

78 79 80 81 82 10 9 8 7 6 5 4 3 2 1

Contents

Preface

After ten years of working with kids in trouble, I've written a book about what I do. If I've reflected on my work accurately, parents should be able to use my recommendations to sharpen their parenting skills. With added skills, parents can do a better job of helping their kids respect law and order. No one has to tell parents that crime and juvenile delinquency are major problems in our society. But someone needs to tell them how to reduce the chances of their kids adding to the problem.

When approaching such topics as sex, drugs, and vandalism, my style and subject matter create a stir. Parents react with fearsome dedication to their job, with the toughness they've developed during late-night worrying, and with a strong parenting ego that doesn't like to be wrong. Yet they seem to respect my attempt to merge the exactness of social-science research and the wisdom of my own experiences with down-to-earth explanations and recommendations. My specific objective is to help the science of human behavior make an impact on the social disruption that is invading every home and neighborhood. Parents don't mind if my recommendations take the form of ''street talk'' as long as they can understand what I'm saying and use it to keep their kids off the streets.

In writing this book, I've tried to avoid the impression that I have a blueprint to answer each and every parent's questions. In fact, to suggest that this is possible would be an affront to the uniqueness of the family and a slap in the face of ethical standards of professional conduct. Each child and parent brings a new challenge to the issue of raising kids. I've reduced the complexity and increased the relevance of my suggestions by narrowing my discussion to one topic: keeping kids out of trouble.

In reviewing this difficult topic, I've taken the side of the family, an entity greater than the sum of its parts. Without the integrity of the family, protecting kids from trouble becomes a nearly impossible task. This attitude places me in the corner that advocates the preservation of the family as the most basic element of society. I believe that the family is society's best bet for teaching respect for the law and reducing senseless social disruption. If the family can't or won't do it, then all of us are in for more trouble than we dare imagine.

Acknowledgments

There are many people whose help I wish to acknowledge. James Hoge of the Chicago *Sun-Times/Daily News* first recognized my potential and gave me needed encouragement. Herman Kogan, currently Field Enterprise's historian, helped me promote my work while making worthwhile criticisms. Lurton Blassingame, my literary agent, spent a good deal of time suggesting needed improvements. The support of Bernard Shir-Cliff of Warner Books was gratifying. The warmth and valuable contributions of Harper & Row editor Amy Bonoff were deeply rewarding.

The closer I moved to putting Protective Parenting into a workable format, the more I recognized the importance of my father and mother. They gave me a moral code that dictates respect, responsibility, and reciprocity while permitting tolerance for those who choose to live differently from the way I do.

Special recognition is given to the hundreds of families who trusted me and, through their successful application of my recommendations, share in the authorship of this book.

I owe countless thanks to my son, Patrick, who regularly

teaches me that love and involvement do not protect a parent from making mistakes.

The greatest portion of recognition goes to my wife, Nancy, who managed to make editorial comments refining both form and content while supporting me with unconditional love and devotion.

SPECIAL NOTE

The cases reported in this book are true. All names
and ancillary identifying data have been changed.
The information is presented so that parents may
change things before it's too late.

1

Introduction

Ten years ago, a sixteen-year-old kid walked into the clinic where I was working, slumped down in the chair across from me, and said, "Well, shrink, my probation officer told me I *had* to come to this hole; what's your excuse?"

Attempts to reassure him and help him to reflect on his hostility only resulted in sneers and grunts of disrespect. He finally replied to my probes into his motivation with, "Hey, I got nuttin' agin' you personal like, ya dig? But take your fancy words and concern to someone who gives a shit!"

Our "psychotherapy session" never got off the ground. This and subsequent experiences with troubled adolescents taught me that I knew very little about the life-style of kids who enjoy breaking the law. Yet their actions were so fascinating to my inquisitive and experience-hungry mind that I set about finding out what made them tick.

About a week ago, another smart-aleck kid plopped down in my office and said, "I don't need to be here. I ain't got no problems. You couldn't help me even if I did have problems."

This time, things were different. With a slight chuckle and an "Oh, really?" look on my face, I answered, "Man, are you messed up! No problems, huh? You gotta *big* problem and you don't even know it. You're in trouble up to your neck, and you're pretending to be cool. So quit the bullshit, fella, and let's get down to business.''

A decade of gut-level confrontation with troubled kids and hours of therapy with problem families have taught me many things. I quickly learned that 99 percent of all kids break the law at least once, but they lie about it and some parents believe the lies until it's too late. It took me longer to realize that, by age fifteen, kids who've had a lifetime of trouble see kindness as weakness. Any sign of understanding is taken as a license to continue social disruption.

When I first started working as a program director and superintendent for the Illinois Department of Corrections, I never realized I had so much to learn. I had many erroneous ideas. My biggest misconception was that only poor kids got into serious trouble. But moonlighting at a small sectarian college and a part-time private practice convinced me that no child is automatically protected from trouble and no parent is immune from suffering the bottomless pit of pain that accompanies a son or daughter getting into trouble.

I also learned that law-enforcement officials cannot prevent crime. Police departments, no matter how well staffed, can never prevent disrespectful and irresponsible kids from destroying property and violating the rights of others.

I saw that jail isn't a deterrent, either. It can be used to get some kids' attention, but only a small minority ever get that far. When they do, they are usually so numb to punishment that being in jail becomes a status symbol, not a reason to stop violating the law. If the problem of social disruption were as simple as keeping kids out of jail, then a book on the solution to crime and juvenile delinquency would contain only four words: ''Buy a good lawyer.''

In the past couple of years, as roving correctional consultant for special programs and serious cases, I've noted an alarming increase in the number of slashed tires, broken windows, damaged property, and shoplifted goods resulting from the activity of destructive teenagers. While I listen to parental concern for children, I still hear parents deny that their kids had any part in social disruption. They pretend that not getting caught releases their kids from responsibility.

Despite this attitude, there has been a shift upward in parents' awareness of what their children are doing. Ten years ago, I heard many parents say, *"It* can't happen to my kid." Today I hear, "I count my blessings that *it* hasn't happened to our family." But as many parents will testify, prayers, hopes, and dreams come to a violent, senseless end when a bundle of joy matures into a bag full of hate.

Counting one's blessings is not good enough. Parents must constantly be on the lookout for signs of social disruption originating within their own families. Only with this cautiousness can crime and juvenile delinquency be curtailed.

Trouble gets started in the home, and that's where it has to be stopped. Keeping kids out of trouble rests with parents, whether natural, foster, adoptive, or step. Parents must do many things, some of which they are not adequately prepared for.

In this book I intend to teach parents how to be better crime preventers. Authority figures from other domains may also find a tip or two that will work on their "turf." My crime-prevention approach covers definitions, explanations, insights, new perspectives, general strategies, and many recommendations for stopping trouble before it gets started.

This psychosocial conglomeration embraces what I consider to be the best that modern science and my experience have to offer. My thinking is guided by the theories and applied technologies of several outstanding social scientists.

The effectiveness of the Skinnerian behavior-modification approach is combined with the practicality of Dr. Albert Ellis's rational-emotive overview and the commonsense concepts contained in Dr. William Glasser's reality therapy. This psychological viewpoint is enhanced by Dr. Karl Menninger's concern for the rehabilitation of troubled youth, and the genius of Dr. Norval Morris's stance concerning the revision of juvenile law and corrections. This mixture combines with the conservative morality of a Midwestern farm boy who believed his mother when she said, "Son, if a person studies hard, remembers right from wrong, and learns from experience, the course of the world can be changed."

I doubt that I can change the course of the world, but I have been able to reroute the course of many kids' lives. The corrective measures I use are embodied in a group of child-rearing techniques that are bound together by a common purpose: to confront the factors that cause kids to engage in social deviance.

This foundation and superstructure of techniques contain enough innovative ideas and suggestions to qualify the resultant principles and actions as a new specialization in the child-rearing field. I call this child-care specialty *Protective Parenting*. Protective Parenting is a survival strategy for parents who are besieged by the self-centered antics of their childen. It is designed to redirect the energies of social deviance into the development of mature, socially appropriate skills.

The techniques of Protective Parenting can be used by people other than parents. Teachers, caseworkers, and ministers (to name a few) can use Protective Parenting to help kids stay out of trouble as well as to get them out after they have gotten into trouble.

There is nothing irreversible about a kid's getting into trouble. In fact, if handled honestly and aboveboard, trouble can bring parent and child closer together as well as teach the child how to avoid such problems in the future. Some of the most effective Protective Parents were once in trouble themselves.

Protective Parenting does not claim to be an all-encompassing guide to the secrets of raising a healthy, happy, normal child. Although the principles and strategies of Protective Parenting can be used in many situations, they are designed to be implemented when a child challenges, rejects, or violates parental expectations.

Protective Parenting covers only a part of the child-rearing scene. Parents seek professional help in solving many kinds of problems. Learning difficulties, specific academic problems, slowness in developmental processes such as walking and toilet training, stunted emotional growth in trust and love, mental retardation, low development of general social skills, problems of sexual adjustment, and other physical and emotional hurdles are all of legitimate concern to parents. However, these issues are not directly related to Protective Parenting, and in my experience, they rarely account for kids getting into trouble.

Kids get into trouble not because they lack certain mental or physical capacities but because they use whatever talents they possess for antisocial purposes.

Another view of Protective Parenting can be seen when one considers the prevention/cure dichotomy. Such exceptionally fine books as *How to Parent* by Dr. Fitzhugh Dodson and *How to Raise a Human Being* by Dr. Lee Salk and Rita Kramer[1] tell the parent how to prevent problems by doing things right.

Protective Parenting tells parents how to cure problems when things go wrong.

Those who wish to study this specialty should take note of the precautions I suggest throughout the book. Parents should be exceptionally careful not to jump to hasty conclusions. For the sake of examination and understanding, I bisected the parent-child interaction. In doing so, I left the impression that the child is an unabashed aggressor and his or her parents are the helpless victims of outrageous assaults. If one unsuspectingly accepts this false dichotomy, misleading interpretations could be made. For example, I've left the door open for some to conclude that

1. F. Dodson, *How to Parent* (Plainview, N.Y.: Nash, 1970); and L. Salk and R. Kramer, *How to Raise a Human Being* (New York: Random House, 1969).

kids *act* while parents *react*. Also, one could get the idea that kids operate independently of their parents when they get into trouble. These and similar conclusions are totally untrue.

In speaking of children's manipulative behavior, I've focused the spotlight on one link in the continual chain of parent-child interactions. This focusing is intended to simplify the problem, not make it simple to solve. Even the casual observer will note that a child's behavior depends in large part upon what the parent does, and vice versa. This interdependency can reach such proportions that only meticulous analysis can get at the heart of the problem. That is why I'm quick to remind parents that professional advice should be sought for difficult or long-standing problems.

One final precaution: while Protective Parenting can reduce a kid's chance of getting into trouble, it can't eliminate the possibility altogether. Nothing or no one can stop a kid from social disruption if he or she is bound and determined to cause trouble. However, if applied diligently, prudently, and consistently, Protective Parenting can change the course of many a child's life.

Before conception, prospective parents hope for a "perfect" child. Once the rabbit dies, they hope for a "normal" child. When their kid bops the neighbor's child over the head with a Barbie doll, they hope for a "well-adjusted" child. When the kid steals fifty cents from Grandma's purse, they hope for a "moral" child. But when the kid gets busted for smoking dope, parents give up hoping and scream for help.

Regardless of the amount of hoping or screaming, neither I nor any other professional can make parenting easy. Those who purposely or accidentally convince parents that raising kids is as easy as making them do a disservice not only to parents but also to the children, who ultimately fall victim to the all-or-nothing dictates of "parenting made easy."

I hope to avoid such a mistake during the course of this book. I'm not interested in telling parents how to raise kids who can dance well, find the differential exponent of the x factor, or carry on small talk at the junior prom. My goal is to help parents teach their kids how to live within the law and, no matter how it's sliced, that isn't easy.

2

Ambush

Two-year-old Christopher ("Butch") McDowell sat three chairs away from me, dressed in his Sunday best, ready to enjoy Christmas dinner with the relatives. Grandma carefully set a plate of turkey and mashed potatoes, a carrot salad, and a whipped-cream delight in front of Butch, cooing in his ear as she moved away. Little did anyone realize that Butch was about to embark on a mission of destruction.

Butch's mother encouraged him to exhibit his eating talents. "Show everyone how well you can eat, Christopher."

Butch reacted to his mother by flashing an angelic smile. While everyone congratulated Mommy and Daddy for raising a perfect child, I saw Butch's hand edge toward the mashed potatoes. I knew he was ready to spring his trap.

Before anyone could say another word, Butch had managed to put potatoes in his hair, and gravy down the front of Grandpa's new slacks.

Mommy lost her cool immediately. "Christopher McDowell! You cut that out or you'll leave the table."

Butch paused long enough to stick out his lower lip in defiance against a poorly contrived threat.

Then Daddy got in on the act. "Butch, mind your manners or you'll go to bed."

Butch didn't seem intimidated. He responded to his daddy's threat by sticking a piece of turkey in his ear.

Mommy was completely frustrated and demanded that her husband do something. So Daddy played the heavy, responding as if Butch had just jabbed his sister with a fork. "Butch, shape up right now or Daddy will spank!"

Butch reacted to this physical threat by throwing a blob of carrot salad on his sister. She started crying. In response to her tears, Butch gave out with his own. However, his screams were muffled by a mouthful of turkey.

Daddy looked madder 'n hell. He jumped up from the table, jerked the turkey out of Butch's ear, and scraped the potatoes from his head. That's when Grandma became a victim of Butch's trap.

"Is Grandma's little boy tired?" she said with a smooth purr in her voice. "Well, you're at Grandma's house, so you don't have to eat if you don't want to."

Mommy and Daddy slumped back into their chairs as Grandma stroked Butch and continued to pamper him with platitudes about being a "good boy." Butch's victory was complete. He celebrated the successful mission by sticking the cherry from the top of his whipped-cream delight up his right nostril. He turned to me, looking like a sloppy garbage collector, and gave me the old "ain't-I-cute" grin.

As I turned away so that Butch wouldn't see my laughter, I caught Grandpa's stare. My suppressed chortle reflected my belief that Butch was a human garbage disposal, but Grandpa's sneer suggested that he thought the kid should be returned to the zoo.

Butch McDowell is a fun-loving little boy. He didn't destroy his parents' authority on purpose. As his grandma often says,

"He might tear my house apart, but there's not a mean bone in his body."

Two-year-old children don't know how to plan or execute sophisticated attacks on parental authority. However, when their biological drive for immediate satisfaction is coupled with their uncanny knack for knowing when to interrupt adult activity, parental authority can quickly disintegrate. Butch is no different. He has energy galore, unbounded inquisitiveness, and more guts than sense. He puts his nose into everybody's business, and whenever he spends more than ten seconds in any situation, he demands that things go *his way*. He's a typical two-year-old kid.

His parents are also quite typical. They have a unique constellation of moral values, and they love their child, want him to have the best, and worry about his future. However, like most parents, they don't realize that Butch can turn concern into pity, freedom into tyranny, and love into hate. They don't know how to convert his impulsive defiance into respectful compliance. Their lack of knowledge could mushroom into more than an attack of mashed potatoes and carrot salad.

If Butch is allowed to continue his ways, he will gradually learn how to avoid responsibility, stockpile disrespect, and make a shambles out of household regulations. His parents will begin to lose their ability to influence his behavior, and he will fail to learn the techniques of self-control.

If ignored, Butch's disrespect for authority will move out of the home and into the classroom, public buildings, and places of business, where it will dominate his relationships with adults. He will probably exhibit his lack of self-control by violating the property or person of another and become one more nameless face in a growing crowd of teenagers who do what they damn well please, knowing that they run virtually no chance of getting caught.

If no one is able to teach Butch responsibility and self-control, he will be a kid in trouble by the time he is fifteen. And between the ages of sixteen and twenty-two, he will be a heartache to his parents and a pain in the posterior to society. Not only will he be unresponsive to familial and social laws, but he will also end up hating his parents and other authority figures, frustrated by his inability to comply with rules and regulations. Most likely, he will carry his belligerence into a family of his own, overreacting to his child's slightest prank with indiscriminate punishment. Unless someone turns the tide, his own children will react with defiance, having no respect for authority, either. The reason will be different, but the behavior will be the same.

When Butch plopped the mashed potatoes on his head and tossed a salad at his sister, he was declaring war the way a buck private might by throwing a rock at an enemy tank. As is the case with so many children, Butch's natural instincts teamed with a drive for independence, and he attacked the adult world around him. Butch's maneuvers represent an all-too-familiar example of how the seeds of deviance can sprout disruption within a simple and uncomplicated home setting. His parents called his antics "naughty," while his grandpa thought them uncivilized. Other parents label similar acts by their children as "disrespectful," "irresponsible," or "hell-raising." I call such an action an *Ambush*.

The Ambush is the key strategy used by children who are at war with their parents, and it highlights a child's rejection of parental expectations. It is this rejection—or rebellion, as many call it—which ultimately forms the foundation for deviance and a variety of disruptive acts. If not controlled, the Ambush leads to delinquency and eventually to hard, cold crime. Reduction of the breeding grounds of crime and delinquency demands a resolution of the war between children and their parents. This can happen through a complete understanding of the Ambush—the what, when, where, how, and why of this warring tactic.

In its simplest sense, the Ambush represents a child's attempt to get around the restrictions imposed by authority figures (usually parents). An Ambush begins when a child refuses to accept the lot that life presents. Through some type of manipulation, the child seeks the fulfillment of a wish *in spite of* what authorities say is right or wrong.

The fundamental logic of the Ambush is often hidden from conscious awareness. Somewhere inside a child's mind, the rationale for the Ambush goes something like: "Authorities tell me that some acts are prohibited. I don't like that. If authority is destroyed, the restrictions of life are lifted. If life has no restrictions, then I can do things my way. I like that!"

Although peculiarly logical, this reasoning is disastrous since always doing things "my way" puts a child on a collision course with society. When the dust settles, both sides have lost freedom, dignity, and self-respect.

All Ambushes involve some "hell-raising" designed to make the "don'ts" of life disappear. Even though most Ambushes are directed toward authority figures, the ultimate target is the dictum of reality that says: "You can't always have your way!"

An Ambush occurs as the child replies, "Oh, yeah? Wanna bet? *Watch!*"

An Ambush is stimulated by a "No," whether it is part of a parent's verbal response, a societal law, or an imaginary condition that the kid projects onto people or circumstances around him. When children hear "No"—or anything that even smacks of such a message—they often use an Ambush to try to make the "No" go away. In this way, an Ambush embodies a child's rebelliousness.

This rebellion against a "No" takes many forms. When kids rebel against parental attitudes while searching for their own moral values, the rebellion usually begins with caustic words, verbal threats, or other suggested retaliatory behavior ("You'll be sorry you said 'No'!"). At this stage, such verbal outbursts are nothing more than vocal exercise and should not be construed as dangerous rebellion. However, when kids use actions instead of words to Ambush authority figures, they have brought their rebellion dangerously close to serious trouble. Therefore, the words or motivations underlying possible rebellion are not as important as the disruptive behavior itself. Continual disruption, not loud words, constitutes serious rebellion.

Children who use Ambushes to rebel against a "No" are rebels with a cause. They want to destroy the restrictions that come with living. If successful, their Ambushes will intensify in frequency and escalate the parent-child war. If the war remains hot and heavy for the first ten years of life, the second ten will see the war move out of the house and into every major part of society.

During the teenage years, the war is often catastrophic. It reflects a monumental clash of values. Parents want their son or daughter to fulfill parental desires, hopes, and dreams (many of which grow out of parental frustrations). Kids tolerate talk of college, good grades, respect for adults, and being "good" so that they can enjoy what really turns them on: loud music, fast cars, wild parties, "liberated" sex, and constantly "copping a buzz" from pills, marijuana, and booze.

When the war is in full swing, a horrendous time lapse exists between parent and child. Parents want their teenagers to think of "tomorrow," while kids want to make sure that they use "today" to make fantastic memories of "yesterday." They are tens of light-years apart in thought. Teenagers want immediate pleasure gained from *now,* and parents know that too much "now" can result in the frustrated memories of tomorrow. If the war is nasty and ugly, children are unyielding hedonists while parents demand unwavering sacrifice. Under such hostile conditions, the Ambush takes on an angry, destructive, dangerous character.

The destructiveness of the Ambush and the parent-child war does not unfold overnight. It develops in two stages, one in childhood and the other during adolescence. At the outset, a toddler's demand to have things go *his way* is mostly a matter of biological programming. As time goes on, day-to-day exposure to adults teaches the child how to Ambush successfully. As the child watches other kids Ambush their parents and engages in trial and error, learning begins to play the major role in a kid's Ambush. In other words, the inclination to Ambush is gained from heredity; the actual techniques of the Ambush are gained through experience.

In the formative years, two factors must be present for an Ambush that can lead to trouble to take a shape. One is a child who is bound and determined to make life go his or her way. The other is a parent or other authority figure who acts as if his or her authority is perfect and beyond reproach. When parents act pompous, their offspring will attack in order to destroy what they mistakenly perceive to be a nearly impenetrable wall of perfection. The challenge is overwhelming. The kids fail to realize that, more often than not, parents who act as if they know everything really don't know anything.

When Butch Ambushed his parents, they were sitting close to him. He watched their reactions, discerned their weaknesses, and learned to narrow the scope of future attacks. When he enters adolescence, Butch will probably begin to Ambush life itself without using authority figures as intermediaries. This will serve to camouflage his deviance and make it harder for his parents to see trouble developing.

During adolescence, the development turns inward. Teenagers make value judgments about authority figures that depend on the nature of their childhood experiences. By age ten or eleven, kids have a vague mental picture of what an authority figure is and does. As time goes on, this image is sharpened and generalized to all authority figures and most situations. Thus, a kid who experienced a pompous parent during childhood will have a pompous-parent precept in mind during adolescence. This learned idea stimulates and guides the frequency and intensity of the Ambush.

The target of a teenage Ambush can be anything that even vaguely resembles the restrictions of life. The target can be parental values, society's laws, institutional regulations, or any material object made or maintained by authority figures. This is why an inert handful of sand fashioned into a window by society's adults can become the target of the warring antics of adolescents.

If parents exercise their authority with reason and thoughtful restraint during the kid's childhood, it is less likely that their adolescent will have the attitude that parents are too big for their own pants and deserve to be Ambushed.

After being repeatedly Ambushed by my own son and watching hundreds of kids Ambush all sorts of authority figures, I've concluded that an Ambush can occur just about any time or any place. It can begin soon after birth and last well into adulthood. It occasionally lasts an entire lifetime. Whether it is stimulated by parental "No's," societal laws, the double-dares of friends, revenge, pent-up anger, or the thousands of shades of emotional unrest, the Ambush always reflects the clash of two opposing forces.

The far superior, regimented, mature authority, made vulnerable by a lack of knowledge and a perfectionistic attitude, is bushwacked by unorthodox, rowdy, poorly organized rebels who use every sneaky trick in the book to destroy the power of the authority.

As I watch parents and children reenact the saga of cowboys and Indians over and over, I remain convinced that the only foolproof way to end this senseless destruction is for parents to take the initiative, spot an Ambush as soon as possible, and refuse to play the game. If parents are willing to face the fact that their child can be successful in defying their authority, they will learn to identify an Ambush and practice methods of avoiding the trap.

However, many parents are blind to their own weaknesses. They often refuse to believe that they are being Ambushed, even when faced with overwhelming evidence. For example, authors Bill Haney and Martin Gold conclude, based on fairly reliable data, that "Most teenagers and adults do not realize how rarely someone is caught for a delinquent act. In the Flint [Michigan] study, 433 of the 522 respondents admitted to 2,490 delinquent acts, yet only 47 adolescents and their 80 offenses made it into police records. That is, only three percent of the delinquencies committed were detected." [1]

Simple arithmetic shows that in one medium-sized city 2,410 delinquent acts committed by 386 teenagers were undetected by authority figures. My experience suggests that, if questioned, the parents of these 386 kids would sincerely believe that their children were innocent of any delinquent acts.

These same parents, and millions more like them, believe that an Ambush is effective only if an authority figure is a witness. However, Ambushes that aren't seen by authority figures are nonetheless real. Their path of destruction is also real. Authority figures do an injustice to kids and society by pretending that adolescent Ambushes aren't effective just because the kids don't get caught.

Children who use Ambushes to make life go their way usually don't consciously know why they do it. They fight a lonely war. While they may use a brother or sister as a pawn in carrying out an Ambush and, as teenagers, regularly receive tactical advice from friends, their Ambushes are solitary altercations between themselves and the restrictions that authority figures represent. Their Ambushes, then, represent a "me-against-the-authority" struggle.

Although this struggle may lead to mistrust, disrespect, and hell-raising in the home, an Ambush doesn't necessarily lead to trouble. However, all trouble begins with an Ambush. Whether or not kids are successful in using an Ambush to get into trouble depends on how effectively parents teach their children that making war will not make life's demands disappear. Parents don't have to fight with their kids just because their kids have

1. B. Haney, and M. Gold, "The Juvenile Delinquent Nobody Knows," *Psychology Today,* September 1973, pp. 49–55.

Ambushed them. If parents react to an Ambush by getting upset and returning the kid's fire, the war will intensify. It will move out of the home and into the streets. When the parent-child war spreads into the streets, there is no limit to the type of trouble that can develop.

If parent-child war is trouble, then society-child war is double trouble. An Ambush in society generates so many shades of disruption that authority figures often fight among themselves about the definition of "trouble." "Trouble" is one of those words that everyone can define, but few can agree on its meaning.

For the purpose of the present discussion, "trouble" is defined as a single disruptive act or a pattern of deviant behavior that leads—or could lead, sooner or later—to negative contact with a law-enforcement agency.

A child is in trouble or heading for it when he or she gets caught, could have gotten caught, or someday might get caught. Depending upon the nature of the child, family, and community, it may take ten seconds or ten years for a child to get into trouble. The longer a kid engages in troublesome behaviors, the harder it will be to change those behaviors.

There are as many different types of trouble as there are kids who experiment with raising hell. Parents don't have to understand all of them in order to confront trouble. It is sufficient to realize that, to one degree or another, all kids experiment with the Ambush, and thereby flirt with trouble. Trouble is like fire—all kids may play with it, but not everyone gets burned. A careless act, an impulsive thought, a dare, a joke, or an accident—all have the makings of trouble.

Trouble, therefore, is not necessarily one or two dumb things done by an unthinking kid looking for the boundaries to an exciting world. It is, however, a social problem to which parents, teachers, caseworkers, ministers, doctors, politicians, and other responsible authority figures in society must respond by providing as much protection to children as possible.

This protection must begin in the home and be spearheaded by parents.

Protective Parenting

Protecting children from all the types of trouble they can get into is a complicated business. If a child walks carelessly into the street, he or she must be protected if tragedy is to be averted. However, no one is going to protect a sixteen-year-old boy who's heading for drug addiction—no one, that is, but the kid himself. Protecting a young child and then gradually teaching the child to protect himself or herself is what I mean by the process of *Protective Parenting*.

Three years after I began treating delinquent adolescents in a residential setting, a local university group conducted a follow-up study of the sixty-six kids I had discharged. During the interview, each kid was asked, "Who do you turn to for help when you see trouble coming?" Sixty of the kids answered, "Myself." Teaching the child to identify trouble before it hits and to turn to one's "self" is the final objective of Protective Parenting.

As a child-rearing specialty, Protective Parenting represents a pragmatic system of problem-solving strategies designed to confront deviance and lead the child, family, and society down the path of living within the law while seeking a better life for all mankind. Viewed more simply, Protective Parenting is a method parents can use to turn the energies of the "Three D's"—disrespect, disruption, and detachment—into the constructive forces of the "Three R's"—respect, responsibility, and reciprocity. Most simply, Protective Parenting can be defined as a way for parents to keep their kids out of trouble.

Protective Parenting is a critical survival tool when sneakiness and deviance combine with rebelliousness to produce an Ambush, which becomes the central tactic in the parent-child war. The principles and techniques of Protective Parenting have cooled many wars and saved much heartache. But no matter how well trained they are, parents should always be prepared to protect their children, their family, and themselves from the unpredictable onset of the Ambush.

Some of the "best kids" get into serious trouble. Parents can avert such a family catastrophe by learning from even the smallest Ambush. If parents grow in knowledge each time they are Ambushed, the cure of one Ambush can mean the prevention of another.

For the most part, serious hell-raising begins with temper tantrums. Parents can stop some minor Ambushes from becoming major battles by making sure that the child understands that life won't bow to his or her every whim. The younger this happens, the better. Teaching a five-year-old that screaming won't get him a candy bar will make it easier to teach him that a six-pack of beer before school is not the way to handle "the crap they hand out in high school."

Protective Parents should understand that there are limits to the amount of hell-raising that authority figures should tolerate. No authority figure should automatically assume that kids will have sufficient common sense to know when enough is enough. Any parent who remembers his or her own adolescence will see the foolishness of assuming that a moral sense of right and wrong is somehow a natural product of heredity. Likewise, such an assumption is an abdication of parental responsibilities and an invitation to trouble.

Yet kids who get into trouble do have "common sense"— sense, that is, common to other kids. Unfortunately, this teenage common sense has little to do with a world of mature, self-controlled behavior.

Kids in trouble are the product of a war where both sides are fighting a losing battle. Deeply troubled kids see authority figures as the "enemy," someone to be defeated, and they fight with every dirty trick they can think of and with no appreciation of honor. They are warriors in the truest sense.

However, they have gorgeous big eyes and their smiles melt the coldest heart. Their dependency is often a pleasure. They are the joy of Christmas and the hope of the future. They are also sweet little deductions when April fifteenth rolls around. They might be warriors, but they are gentle ones.

Generation after generation, parents and other authority figures have faced, and will continue to face, the rebellious Ambushes of these gentle warriors. Only a precious few escape the battle. I have found two bits of food for thought very helpful to families who face the erosion of happiness that accompanies the parent-child war:

All of us have a streak of deviance running from the tips of our razor-sharp tongues to the ends of our sticky fingers; we're all warriors, but many of us aren't gentle anymore.

All people scream too much when faced with frustrations. Screaming, no matter how secret or sophisticated, leads to more screaming, which creates rejection by others, which leads to loneliness for the screamer. This creates more agitation, which stimulates more screaming. The psychological pressure of this vicious circle can and often does lead to physical violence, which is the loudest scream of all.

3

The Protective Parenting Questionnaire

Crime is only a whisper away from all kids, no matter how rich, handsome, popular, or well-bred they may be. But I constantly seem to listen to parents pretending that their children will be spared contact with crime. Such pretense is heard even when the evidence of trouble is overwhelming. I've come to understand that while parents care about their kids getting into trouble, they just don't know what to do when they see problems developing. So they pretend the problems don't exist.

Years of such pretense only deepen parental naiveté and prolong their dream of being perfect parents. But such dreams of perfection erode the mind's grasp of reality. In the end, many a parental dream world has been viciously smashed by the slamming of a jail door or a call from the police telling them that their child can't be found.

One way I fight parental pretense and ignorance is to tell horror stories about what has happened to other people's children. I try to be discreet in suggesting that such things could happen to anyone. Although some would rather be shocked than educated, many parents become sincerely concerned about the damage that troublesome behavior can do to their family as well as to society. I try to convince them that when children finally get into serious trouble, they are often in over their heads and it's too late for parents to prevent further problems from developing.

I always know when I've captured the attention of parents. Their genuine concern hits me right after a lecture and before I can get out the door. Two, three, or more parents corner me, and each push me for answers in turn.

The same message repeats itself: "How can I tell if I'm doing a good job with my kids? And don't tell me that I have to wait ten years to find out!"

While a "wait-and-see" attitude is the only absolute answer to this question, I am able to review a parent's protective role and give some general indication as to how he or she may be doing. This becomes impossible when six parents are standing around and eight more want an answer within five minutes. In response to such demands, I have developed an evaluation technique that permits parents to shed light on the question by way of self-examination. I call this technique the *Protective Parenting Questionnaire (P.P.Q.)*.

The P.P.Q. is a device with three purposes: to alert parents to some of the situations that call for Protective Parenting; to suggest the "best" solutions to these situations; and, most important, to permit parents to complete a self-assessment, within the privacy of their own minds, of their potential to enact the protective role—that is, to evaluate their Protective Parenting Potential (P.P.P.).

The P.P.Q. contains twenty situations that are critical to protective parents. These and similar situations have occurred frequently in the lives of the parents and kids who have sought my advice. Troubled families typically fail to solve these situations in a constructive manner.

For those who wish to evaluate their P.P.P., I offer the following instructions:

- Approach each situation seriously, as if it really happened.
- Put yourself into a "protective" role and stick with your "gut-level" reaction.
- Mark the answer that seems best to you.
- There may be other things you would do that are not listed. In that case, choose the alternative that comes closest to what you would actually do.

Protective Parenting Questionnaire

WHAT WOULD YOU DO IF:

1. Your twelve-year-old son, for the third time in a row, came home at 9:00 P.M. after being told to be home no later than 8:00 P.M.

   a. Confine him to his own yard for a week.
   b. Make him do three hours of menial labor to make up for his tardiness.
   c. Talk with him about the importance of being a good boy and what might happen if he doesn't follow the rules.
   d. Tell him he can't go to baseball practice for three nights.
   e. Give him a third and final warning that one more violation will mean a stiff penalty.

2. Your fifteen-year-old son said, "Why can't I have a ten-dollar-a-week allowance? My friend Mark gets that much."

   a. Say, "You're not Mark and you don't live where Mark lives, so don't expect to get what Mark gets."
   b. Say, "I don't care what you want; you'll be happy with what you've got!"
   c. Say, "If you were more responsible, I'd let you have it."
   d. Ignore his protest and repeat, "No more money!"
   e. Say, "Mark's parents don't care as much about him as we do about you."

3. Your thirteen-year-old daughter asked to go out with a seventeen-year-old boy.

   a. Say, "Yes, but only if you double-date with your older sister."
   b. Say, "Yes" and remind her that she'd better be good.
   c. Say, "No" and explain that you think she's too young.
   d. Say, "No" and explain that you think the boy is too old.
   e. Say, "I don't know," and ask your best friend's advice.

4. You discovered that your oldest child, a fourteen-year-old girl, had smoked marijuana.

   a. Try to understand her reasons and tell her never to do it again.
   b. Talk with her about the evils of drugs and then ground her for a month.
   c. Give her a booklet on drug abuse.
   d. Forget about it; she's just going through a phase.
   e. Seek the advice of a trusted friend or reputable professional.

5. Your eleven-year-old son's teacher told you that your boy, although a good student, was suspected of throwing spitballs and trying to get other students into trouble.

   a. Demand that the principal make the teacher quit picking on your son.
   b. Ground him for three nights.
   c. Talk with him about the necessity of conforming to classroom regulations.
   d. Tell him some of the "naughty" things you did at his age, but give him examples of the difference between fun and disruption.
   e. Spank him.

6. Your neighbor told you that he saw your seventeen-year-old son driving fast and weaving down Main street.

   a. Confront him with the facts and then suspend his driving for two weeks and tell him he hurt the family's good image in the neighborhood.
   b. Confront him with the facts. If he confirms them, suspend his

driving privileges for two weeks; if he denies them, suspend them for two weeks, anyway.

c. Confront him with the facts. If he confirms them, suspend his driving privileges for two weeks; if he denies them, forget it.

d. Confront him with the facts. If he confirms them, ask him what penalty he should pay, but don't settle for less than one week's loss of driving privileges; if he denies them, call the neighbor in for an open confrontation.

e. Confront him with the facts. If he confirms them, suspend his driving privileges for two weeks; if he denies them, call the neighbor in for an open confrontation.

7. Your six-year-old daughter continually failed to follow your orders to clean up her room (for example, put her toys away, arrange her drawers neatly).

a. Quit requesting this because it's too much for a six-year-old to do.

b. Warn her that if she doesn't change, you will spank her the next time.

c. Tell her that you won't do any of her favorite things (for example, taking her shopping, for treats, and to the swimming pool) until she starts following your directions.

d. Take away her favorite dress or most exciting toy for a week whenever she fails to put it away.

e. Yell at her, "Shape up right now or else!"

8. Your eight-year-old son got two "swats" in school for hitting another kid. After finding out what had happened, would you:

a. Remind him to respect other children and explain that he will get no more punishment because he has already received the school "swats."

b. Remind him to respect others and make him sit in a corner for thirty minutes.

c. Remind him to respect other children, ground him for three nights, and suggest that the principal find a new way to discipline your son.

    d. Remind him to respect other children, tell him he'll get no more punishment, and suggest that the principal find a new way to discipline your son.

    e. Demand a parent-teacher-principal conference and warn the school never to touch your son again.

9. Your five-year-old daughter said, "You can't make me," when told to quit biting her brother.

    a. Slap her across the mouth.

    b. Say, "Don't talk back to me," and sit her firmly in the corner.

    c. Bite her the same way she is biting her brother and say, "This is what biting feels like."

    d. Completely ignore her.

    e. Remove the brother to another room.

10. Your three-year-old son was crying over a broken toy.

    a. Say, "Crying is only for babies."

    b. Ignore him.

    c. Say, "It hurts to lose something you love, doesn't it?"

    d. Say, "Shut up or else I'll spank."

    e. Say, "Don't cry, I'll buy you another one."

11. Your thirteen-year-old daughter asked to go to a chaperoned boy-girl party the coming weekend. You have said that you want to call to make sure that the other parents will be home. Your daughter, obviously upset, says, "You don't trust me."

    a. Say, "No, I don't trust you; you're too young to go to a boy-girl party."

    b. Say, "Yes, I trust you, but I don't trust some of your friends."

    c. Say, "No, I don't trust you."

    d. Say, "Yes, I trust you in certain situations, but this is not one of them."

    e. Say, "Yes, I trust you, but trust is not enough."

12. Your ten-year-old son was caught shoplifting a small radio by a store detective.

    a. Suggest that he be taken to the police station and given a good lecture so that he realizes the seriousness of the situation.
    b. Make an agreement with the store manager that, under parental supervision, the boy will work off the price of the radio plus extra hours as a penalty.
    c. Tell the detective that you'll take care of it and then ground him for three weeks.
    d. Tell the store detective you'll take care of it and spank him when you get home.
    e. Give him a stern lecture about honesty in front of the detective and then forget about it.

13. Your two-year-old son ran into the street after being told to stay away from it.

    a. Immediately yell at him to get off the street.
    b. Run to the street and jerk him into the yard.
    c. Walk to the edge of the street and calmly ask him to get back in the yard.
    d. Walk into the street, spank him once, and say, "Don't run into the street."
    e. Tell his older sister to get him off the street.

14. Your six-year-old daughter said, "You told me that God loved everything. Why did he kill my puppy?"

    a. Say, "God has a reason for everything. He wanted your puppy in heaven."
    b. Say, "God didn't kill your puppy, Daddy (Mommy) hit it with the car."
    c. Say, "I'm not sure. You just have to have faith in God."
    d. Say, "Ask your daddy (mommy)."
    e. Say, "I'm not sure. Why do you think He did?"

15. You caught your seven-year-old son taking a dollar from your wallet in the same sneaky way his older brother had.

a. Give him a stern lecture about being a criminal and remind him that he could end up on probation like his older brother.
b. Jerk him away from the wallet and spank him hard, telling him that stealing is very bad.
c. Take away his favorite toys and keep him indoors for a week, explaining that you're not going to let him off as easily as you did his older brother.
d. After dinner, make him stand up and confess his theft to the entire family.
e. Tell him that because he stole the dollar he'll have no money for the carnival that weekend.

16. You found pornographic magazines in your fifteen-year-old son's closet.
    a. Don't say a word to anyone.
    b. Wait until everyone is gathered around and confront him with the material.
    c. Rip them up and leave them in a pile on his bed.
    d. Calmly and quietly confront him and then punish him by withdrawing his allowance for two weeks.
    e. Talk with your son about the importance of clean and healthy thoughts.

17. While grocery shopping, your four-year-old son screamed, yelled, jumped around, and created a verbal disturbance because he couldn't have a candy bar.
    a. Scream or yell in order to get his attention.
    b. Ignore him.
    c. Warn him to shut up; if he doesn't, leave the store.
    d. Spank him immediately.
    e. Buy him the candy bar if he promises to be quiet.

18. Your nine-year-old daughter emptied your most expensive bottle of perfume (aftershave lotion) on her doll.
    a. Lecture her about being less wasteful.
    b. Tell her that she shouldn't be playing with Mommy's (Daddy's) things.

    c. Ask her what she is going to do to pay for her mistake.

    d. Send her to her room for the rest of the night.

    e. Start to yell but forget about it because you remember what it was like to be an irresponsible child.

19. Your eighteen-year-old daughter told you that she thought she'd live with her boyfriend before marrying him because she didn't want to make the same mistake you had.

    a. Apologize for the unhappy home life and ask her to reconsider.

    b. Say, "Whatever turns you on is okay by me."

    c. Say, "I disapprove of that, and it will hurt me if you do it."

    d. Tell her you understand her pain and help her explore other alternatives.

    e. Say, "Married or not, you'll find out that a man will always get his way."

20. Your sixteen-year-old daughter asked to stay out until 1:00 A.M. to watch a monster movie at her boyfriend's house, and her curfew is 11:00 P.M.

    a. Say, "Absolutely not!"

    b. Say, "If you really want to watch the movie, you watch it here and have your boyfriend watch it at his house."

    c. Ask her what she intends to do to earn the extra privilege.

    d. Say, "Yes, but only if his parents will stay up with you."

    e. Tell her that both of them can watch the movie at your house.

P.P.Q. Answers and Discussion

The answers to the P.P.Q. are not complete without a discussion of all the alternatives. The letter after each number below is the answer that experience has taught me represents the best thing to do in the given situation. My selection of "best" answers came from parents who, faced with trouble, employed my recommendations and found that things got better. The four other actions are the most frequent alternatives that the parents were using when they first came to see me. The number after each letter represents the percentage of a trial group of 250 authority figures (mostly parents) who selected that alternative.

In order to be fully understood, each discussion must be placed within the context in which the answer developed. Recognition is given to the fact that some parents offset some poor decisions with two or three good ones. Also, many parents have found their own "best" answers by combining love with creative guesswork. These hardworking parents should not be dismayed if they disagree with me since their way, if successful, will rarely reach the ear of a professional.

As I review the situations and discuss the alternatives, the reader must remember that there are no absolutely right or wrong answers, only some that work better than others.

1. (b, 6 percent) Violation of curfew leads to troublesome behavior more often than any single rule infraction. Kids who eventually get into trouble do so after stretching a few minutes of tardiness into hours of unexplained absence. It is essential that a parent etch deeply into a youngster's mind the importance of following curfew regulations. This is best accomplished by devising a method of translating the absenteeism into a timed penalty. The menial labor will act as a cognitive acid, making an indelible mark on the kid's conscience. The three hours is a penalty that represents threefold retribution for the one hour of tardiness.

Two answers (a, 38 percent; c, 38 percent) don't represent a strong penalty. If at all possible, the constructive activity of playing baseball should be reinforced, not taken away (d, 9 percent). If a parent doesn't follow through after the first warning, subsequent warnings are bound to be ineffective (e, 9 percent).

This was the most difficult question. I can only surmise that parents don't take a tough enough stance about curfews (answers a + c = 76 percent) because they don't realize how dangerous its violations can be.

2. (a, 44 percent) Pressure from friends is overwhelming to adolescents. It can become so pervasive and constant that a kid may lose sight of his or her own identity. When this happens, a kid can end up in trouble and genuinely not understand how it occurred. Parents can relieve some of the pressure by helping their child remember the difference between personal identity and group conformity.

Expressing a lack of concern (b, 3 percent) stimulates revenge, while concern itself is not enough to battle peer pressure (e, 15 percent). Parents miss an opportunity to teach their children important lessons if they make general statements about responsibility (c, 15 percent) or repeat directives with an authoritarian attitude (d, 23 percent).

A fifteen-year-old must accept that what another gets to do is not a foundation upon which to base requests. If parents remember what it was like to be fifteen and to need friends desperately, special privileges can be permitted without violating rational guidelines.

3. (c, 72 percent) This is a situation in which a parent can quickly demonstrate that some requests are nonnegotiable. A thirteen-year-old girl has too much excitement to handle without adding the complex issues involved in unsupervised dating. Thus, for protective parents, thirteen is too young for dating. Period!

Saying "Yes, but . . ." (a, 6 percent) only sets the scene for arguing. Saying she should "be good" (b, 1 percent) is treating a thirteen-year-old as if she were three. Saying the boy is too old (d, 21 percent) creates more game-playing, and she'll simply look for a younger boy to date. Saying "I don't know" (e, 0 percent) is an abdication of parental responsibility. Saying "No" with a simple statement that she's too young will make the case open and shut.

4. (e, 15 percent) While it is true that most kids experiment with marijuana, it's nonetheless serious. If the girl is the oldest child in the family, it would be best if the parents consulted

with a trusted confidant. This confidant might be a friend who had a similar experience, a minister or another professional. This situation often causes a plethora of emotions in which parental actions and reactions are usually overdramatized. Objective consultation will give parents an opportunity to review the circumstances involved, set their emotions aside, and take whatever action is deemed necessary. In this way, the decision and discipline (if any) will be founded upon reliable family values and solid principles of parenting, rather than on an emotional reaction.

The girl needs to learn that she has broken a law that many people in the criminal justice system, whether rightly or wrongly, get very upset about. Depending upon the family, their moral values, and social attitudes, this lesson could take the form of reasoning, warnings, sharing thoughts and feelings, imposition of a penalty, or other disciplinary measures.

Understanding and warnings (a, 32 percent), fear (b, 1 percent), information without consultation (c, 36 percent), and ignoring the situation (d, 6 percent) are all possible courses of action. Some might be better than others. The only way to ensure the best is to seek trusted advice.[1]

5. (d, 11 percent) If an eleven-year-old boy is a normal, healthy kid, from time to time he will experiment with his capacity to disrupt the social order. If a teacher suspects him of engaging in minor acting-out and can't specify the problem, then a parent can conclude that the boy is having a lot of fun. Sooner or later, the boy will need help in distinguishing between fun and deviance.

Kids will always do naughty things, teachers will always try to put the blame on somebody, and parents will always be concerned that fun does not become troublesome. Therefore, in order to avoid being a tyrant (a, 1 percent), engaging in needless physical punishment (e, 1 percent), penalizing without rea-

1. This alternative read "Seek professional consultation," during the data-gathering process. Obviously, the rewording would have some effect on the normative data.

soning (b, 1 percent), or risking being irrelevant in mouthing the necessity for conformity (c, 86 percent), parents are well advised to confide in the child about their own "naughty" past. This will establish easy-flowing two-way communication in which the child has a chance to see Daddy or Mommy as a fun-loving child. In such an atmosphere, parents can do much to instill in their child an understanding of the thin line that separates personal excitement from social disruption.

6. (d, 41 percent) This is the best combination of many possible solutions. Several key lessons can be learned: many adults scrutinize the reckless driving of a seventeen-year-old; the time should fit the crime; self-punishment adds a special sense of seriousness to the violation of rules; even self-punishment must compromise with the reality of minimal penalties; and denial brings open, straightforward confrontation by the accuser.

Parents will regret any penalty that is couched in terms of the "family image" (a, 8 percent). If the accusation is denied, the two extremes of imposing a penalty without adequate proof (b, 17 percent) and dropping such a sensitive issue (c, 15 percent) should be avoided. Parents should give a child the chance to impose his or her own penalty whenever possible (e, 19 percent).

If the neighbor is truly interested in helping and not just carrying tales, his or her confrontation in itself will have a sobering effect on the boy. Such a confrontation would also tend to keep the neighbor honest.

7. (c, 49 percent) The definition of "authority figure" is best accomplished through action. A child needs to learn that an authority figure is the person who controls the goodies and expects some response from the one who wants the goodies. The quickest way to teach this invaluable lesson is for parents to graphically demonstrate to their children, at an early age, that the goodies of life have to be earned. If they have not done so before the child is nine or ten years of age, parents may find that their teenager neither respects authority figures nor exhibits responsibility.

Cleaning up a room is well within the reach of a six-year-old (a, 15 percent). Yelling (e, 4 percent) and threatening to spank (b, 6 percent) are unnecessary aggressive stances. Taking away a material object (d, 26 percent), while often a good alternative, isn't active enough in this situation.

8. (d, 24 percent) When a child hits another, it's time to take serious action. Parents will inevitably find that there was some type of provocation for such behavior. The child should learn that provocation is not cause for physical retaliation, except in cases of self-defense.

A few words about respect can be meaningful to an eight-year-old. The school system has already imposed its punishment, and it's unfair to double that punishment (b, 9 percent; c, 17 percent). However, it is barbaric, not to say irrational, for any authority figure to punish violence with more of the same. Parents who wish to have an impact on an archaic school system that punishes physical violence by striking kids are well advised to talk with, not fight against, school officials (e, 4 percent). However, parents should not let the situation drop (a, 46 percent). They should combine constructive criticism and group action in order to change school policy. This will provide better protection for their children during their time at school.

9. (c, 32 percent) Parents who get confused about discipline often do so because they deal with the wrong issue. "You can't make me" is a rational statement of potential independence. For the most part, it is healthy defiance. By biting her the same way she's biting her brother, a parent is saying to her, "You're right, I can't make you. But I'll let you know what it feels like to get bitten." In this way, the girl's independence is quietly acknowledged and she is taught, by the best of all possible instructors—experience—that the natural outcome of her act is not worth the act itself. The impact of empathy ("So that's what it feels like to be bitten") should never be underestimated.

Because some parents lack empathy or otherwise might use this "best" recommendation as a license to abuse their children, this alternative must be carefully considered before being implemented.

Attacking the girl's defiance (a, 6 percent; b, 38 percent) is overreacting to her efforts toward independence. The act is too aggressive to be ignored (d, 15 percent). Removing the brother (e, 9 percent) is avoiding the problem altogether.

10. (c, 78 percent) Parents who tell their children that rational crying is wrong do a disservice that will haunt the kids sooner or later. Allowing the boy to express his pain over a rational hurt (it's reasonable that a three-year-old will cry over a broken toy) will teach him how to be honest about his feelings. It's never too early to teach a child how to avoid keeping negative feelings inside. Bottled-up pain is food for adolescent revenge. Reflecting on pain also gives the parent a chance to avoid paying too much attention to crying, which in and of itself can become a method of manipulation.

Calling the boy a baby (a, 3 percent) teaches disrespect. Ignoring him (b, 8 percent) is inappropriate because the parent misses a chance to teach the child the benefits of self-expression. Threatening to spank him (d, 2 percent) is much too aggressive, while promising to buy another toy if he stops crying (e, 9 percent) is proposing a bribe.

11. (d, 42 percent) A chaperoned boy-girl party can be an excellent place for a thirteen-year-old to test some social skills. However, because of the complicated nature of the situation, the girl should be honestly told that since this situation is new, trust in her judgment has yet to be developed. If parent and teenager are to work together to avoid trouble, trust must be seen as a relativistic trait of their interaction.

Trust depends upon who, what, when, where, how much, how long, and what has happened in the past. The message of trust between a parent and an adolescent is this: "Show me that I can trust your judgment, and you'll earn more privileges; demonstrate faulty decision making, and I'll pull the reins of control tighter."

While thirteen-year-old kids are too young for unsupervised dating, they should be allowed the chance to go to supervised boy-girl parties (a, 4 percent). Parents should always avoid setting themselves against their kids' friends (b, 22 percent). A simple statement of no trust is not sufficient (c, 4 percent), while saying that trust is not enough (e, 28 percent) invites a knock-down, drag-out fight.

12. (b, 24 percent) It's never too early for a child to learn that there are other authority figures to be reckoned with besides parents and teachers. The manager of a store has authority over the behavior of its patrons. The manager should be involved in this situation immediately. A workable schedule of retribution should be devised that both fits the physical and emotional capabilities of the ten-year-old and closely relates to the crime (for example, dusting off all radios, TVs, and stereos in the store). The task should be supervised by an adult and be of sufficient length to teach the child that the length of time fits the extent of the crime. If this is done carefully, he will learn to respect the boundaries of authority.

Whenever possible, law-enforcement officials should be kept out of any type of discipline in a child's life (a, 30 percent; d, 24 percent). They tend to overextend their law-enforcement responsibilities and dabble in the affairs of a judge, prosecutor, moralist, social worker, or other social-welfare agent. Once a child is caught, lectures (e, 2 percent) are meaningless and penalties unrelated to the crime (c, 20 percent) lack sufficient impact. Instead, the child should be placed in the hands of his or her parents (or guardian) and the appropriate authority figure whose territory was invaded by the child's misbehavior.

13. (d, 58 percent) This is one situation in which spanking should be used. One good swat on the rear in the middle of the street plus the verbal admonishment can be an excellent teaching experience. It is an acceptable way to dramatize the dangers of playing in the street. However, spanking cannot be effective if given within a punishing atmosphere. That is, spankings and

verbal rebukes lose their meaning when they are the dominant theme of parent-child interaction. This is why I always caution the prospective spanker to offset the violence of hitting a child with the warmth of a gentle touch. My exact prescription is this: For each time a child is spanked, he or she should be touched gently three times. This should occur within a few moments of the spanking, when the child is playing appropriately again.

Parents can use this prescription whenever they spank their child. It is especially helpful when parents hit their child in order to relieve their own frustrations. In these cases, parents can take constructive action once they regain their senses and the child resumes appropriate behavior.

If a child is spanked once for going into the street, he should be touched gently three times as soon as he returns to appropriate play in the yard. This same formula can and should be applied to yelling or screaming (verbal spanking). That is, for each harsh word or phrase, the parent should give the child three words or phrases of endearment after appropriate behavior has resumed.

Once again, yelling (a, 4 percent) and such impulsive physical acts as jerking (b, 6 percent) won't teach the child necessary caution. This situation is too dangerous to ask an older sister to do the work (e, 2 percent). Being calm is good, but a little more intervention than just talk is needed (c, 30 percent).

14. (e, 28 percent) Religious beliefs often form the foundation for a mature moral character. However, they can also form the basis of antisocial revenge behavior designed to "get even with God." The difference between the two outcomes of religious faith rests with the degree to which the beliefs are internalized. If adopted into conscious awareness as a chosen way of life, religion can become a constructive force in a child's and adult's life; if imposed upon the person or cloaked in secrecy, it loses its relevance and, depending upon other circumstances, fades into oblivion or gnaws at independence and a sense of well-being.

A six-year-old should have the opportunity to talk out her confusion, pain, misunderstandings, and disgust when it comes to any topic, but especially issues as hard to comprehend as God and supernatural intervention. Vague restatements of theological doctrine (a, 30 percent; c, 11 percent) prohibit personalization. Reality (b, 30 percent) is good, but the confusion still needs to be expressed. Pushing responsibility onto the other spouse (d, 1 percent) is admitting that there is only one parent in the home.

15. (e, 66 percent) The natural consequences of an act have more impact on the future occurrence of that act than anything an authority figure can pull out of a hat. While it is sometimes impossible to allow the natural consequences to take their full effect (for example, the natural outcome of swimming inappropriately would be drowning), parents should take every plausible step to see that the child's experiences provide every ounce of learning possible. Experience is the best teacher only if someone ensures that the child can make a connection between his or her behavior and the consequences suffered or enjoyed.

The lesson to be taught in this situation is simple: If you steal money, you'll lose money in the future. The sooner parents begin this disciplinary measure, the greater their chances of teaching an enduring lesson. The older a child becomes, the less control parents have over the things that the child considers important.

Taking away privileges and/or toys (c, 8 percent) is often a good alternative but not best in this case since it doesn't relate to the crime. Confession in front of the family (d, 4 percent) would most likely stimulate the growth of revenge or guilt, neither of which is desirable. Lecturing (a, 18 percent) often falls on deaf ears; anyway, the seven-year-old may idolize his brother and want to be like him. There are many things a parent could do in this situation, but spanking (b, 4 percent) should not be one of them.

16. (a, 32 percent) Parents should keep their noses out of a

kid's closet. If they meddle in their kid's private life, they should be prepared to keep their mouths shut.

Exploring sexuality from all possible perspectives is crucial to the psychosocial development of a teenager. It is inevitable that pornographic literature will become part of that search for self-identity in many kids. Parental intervention via warnings, information-giving, or reminders should occur only when kids request it, their behavior interferes with the rights of another, or their action seriously violates the family's moral code.

Confronting a fifteen-year-old with porno material in front of others (b, 2 percent) is quite disrespectful. Ripping up the material and leaving it on the bed (c, 9 percent) is asking for revenge. Quiet confrontation and punishment (d, 13 percent) could be implemented if the boy ever used the material to be disruptive. Talking to a teenager about "clean" thoughts (e, 44 percent) serves only to communicate parental hang-ups.

Nude pictures kept in an out-of-the-way place should not interfere with any sensible person's rights. If parents consider such literature a serious violation of the family's moral code, they can rest assured that their kids will take their inquisitiveness into the streets.

17. (b, 34 percent) Ignoring a screaming four-year-old is a challenge to any parent. Doing it at home is difficult; in a social setting, it is almost impossible. However, ignoring screams of disappointment and frustration, especially in public, is crucial to the future reduction of such disruption. A parent in a grocery store has to withstand not only the vocal attack of childish displeasure but also the self-doubts that accompany the real or imagined looks of others' annoyance.

Moms and dads regularly add to their child's temper tantrums by castigating themselves for what they believe to be parental failure. "I'm not as good as that parent because my kid is screaming and his (or hers) isn't," they lament. Parents who judge themselves through the eyes of other parents are abandoning their own values and beliefs in favor of the dictates of parental peer pressure. Screaming, designed as a temper tantrum, should be ignored if at all possible.

Screaming and yelling (a, 1 percent), while good for parental tension, does not teach a constructive lesson. A warning, followed by leaving the store (c, 32 percent), could work, provided the boy liked to shop. If he did, such action might make him quiet next time. Unfortunately, most parents find grocery-shopping financially painful, so it's small wonder most kids don't like it, either.

Spanking a candy-bar Ambusher (d, 25 percent) is asking for trouble. Next time, he'll scream louder than hell and make sure the parent can't catch him. Promising a treat in return for the cessation of disruption (e, 8 percent) is bribery. A candy bar can be used to establish peace and tranquillity. However, it should not be given until *after* peace has set in. This makes candy an incentive, not a bribe.

18. (c, 46 percent) Sometimes, dealing with the simplest issue of an infraction is best. How's, what's, where's, and why's, while often important, can be overemphasized. When this happens, motive-guessing, mind reading, and unnecessary complexity result. A child misusing another's property constitutes a situation for which a simple solution is tailor-made. "You made a mistake, and now you pay for it." That's all!

Lecturing (a, 6 percent) and issuing shouldn'ts (b, 37 percent) muddy the water by adding needless complications to a cut-and-dried misbehavior. Introducing self-punishment will strengthen the girl's awareness of the importance of self-control. Too much understanding is a dangerous thing since it can become an excuse for the lack of discipline (e, 10 percent). Sending a nine-year-old to her room (d, 1 percent) usually isn't much of a penalty because most kids have more entertainment available in their rooms than anywhere else.

19. (d, 74 percent) This daughter is attempting to use the best authority-eroder on the disruptive market: guilt. She is ob-

viously unsure of herself and wants to put the blame for her uncertainty on the parent. There is but one thing any parent could do to influence the decision of such a young woman: avoid feeling guilty and help her struggle with responsibility by talking it out.

Apologizing for unhappiness may have its place (a, 8 percent), but not when the issue is a kid's uncertainty. Also, such apologies can lay the foundation for guilt. Some parents, in the name of being "modern," forget to be parents. Giving a confused daughter an "I-don't-care" message (b, 2 percent) is not modern, it's an avoidance of parents' responsibility for guiding their children. Admitting to being hurt (c, 15 percent) is okay, but in this situation the issue is the daughter's pain, not the parent's. The last alternative (e, 1 percent) is an unnecessary projection of parental attitudes, whether correct or not.

20. (c, 8 percent) Most parents get upset with such requests because they find it difficult to accept the fact that they can't control what their kid does when he or she is outside the home. The best answer in this case embodies compromise, a key strategy in any network of self-protective activities. "I'll give you this if you give me that" teaches a kid the art and science of give-and-take with authority figures.

Making the girl come up with an acceptable trade-off will alert her to parental concern and the seriousness of the situation. Nonnegotiable stances (a, 13 percent) should be kept to a minimum. The second alternative (b, 11 percent) contains the implication that the parent suspects some improper sexual activity. Being sneaky about legitimate concerns will backfire on the parent because the girl will choose dishonesty in the future.

"Yes, but . . ." (d, 13 percent) is a sloppy comment because once the girl hears the "Yes," she will work hard to circumvent the "but." Trying to make her watch the movie at home (e, 55 percent) is a devious way of saying "I don't trust you." If trust is the issue, it should be dealt with openly, not hidden by a recommendation.

This situation has generated more heated arguments than all the rest combined. Parents, especially mothers, don't like to think of their daughters being alone with boys. When they do, fears and frustrations pop up all over the place.

Rating the P.P.P.

A person's potential to enact the protective role successfully can be rated by totaling the number of agreements with my answers and placing the score within one of the five categories I've developed over my years of working with parents.

0–3 You're making a lot of Protective Parenting errors and need a complete reexamination of your attitudes concerning keeping kids out of trouble. You might falsely believe, *"It* can't happen to my kid."

4–7 You're doing some things well. Some of your day-to-day disciplinary measures need changing. You might be trying to make Protective Parenting too easy with oversimplified notions, such as, "All it takes is love, correction, and a lot of prayers." You have to remember that love can be an excuse for laziness, correction often falls on deaf ears and padded rumps, and God helps those who help themselves.

8–11 Your score is average. You make some errors, but you do a good job overall. You profited from the discussion and would like to learn more. You probably realize that your kid is quite capable of breaking the law but believe that he or she does it in fun and with no malicious intent.

12–15 You're doing an above-average job with your kid(s). You're not afraid to admit mistakes, and such honesty, especially in front of your kids, teaches them self-control and respect for authority.

16–20 Your score is fantastic! You've got to be one of three things: a behavioral scientist with all the right answers, an excellent quiz-taker, or that rare breed of parent who's already well-versed in the art and science of Protective Parenting.

If your P.P.P. was higher than you expected, congratulate yourself; but remember that cockiness can be a parent's downfall. If your score was lower than you expected, keep in mind that there is plenty of room for disagreement in the assessment process. P.P.Q. ratings are indeed relative.

The P.P.Q. is designed to prepare the reader to examine the protective strategies discussed in the next twelve chapters. If you disagree with my position, you aren't necessarily wrong, but you're not necessarily right, either. There are no *right* or *wrong* answers.

My recommendations are open to question, especially by parents who use their creative common sense to find innovative answers to troublesome situations. If during the course of the book you find yourself at odds with my strategies, follow this simple advice: put disagreement aside and try the things I suggest. If they work, use them; if they don't, forget them. But don't waste precious time getting upset about my recommendations. Save your emotional energy; you'll need it for coping with your kids.

4

The Protective Role

Parents play many roles. Among the more traditional ones are provider, teacher, and disciplinarian. Each role embodies different expectancies. A teaching role involves actions that are noticeably different from those of a provider. Yet each role parallels the other. Mommy or Daddy is the same parent whether putting dinner on the table or reviewing a child's homework. So it is with the many other roles parents play each day.

Parents play some roles better than others. Some excel at the expression of physical love, while others have endless patience. Some parents are outstanding at setting a good example, and others could win awards for their understanding. Most parents cancel out the negative effects of their weak points by excelling at their good ones. However, one role shakes this delicate balance: the protective role.

When asked to describe the most difficult part of the parenting character, a majority of parents invariably mention something about "protecting my children from trouble." When pushed to define the protective role, each one gives a different definition. Parents have a hard time agreeing what "protection from trouble'' means, but they all affirm that it is one of the most important things parents do.

Despite this commitment to the job, parents still have many problems with the protective role. In fact, they are *so* dedicated to doing a good job protecting their children that no one thinks to ask one simple question: "Do you know exactly *how* to protect your children from trouble?"

The answer is usually "No." Parents want to protect their children, but they rarely know the exact words and actions to use. Faced with disruption, the need for protection, and the lack of specific recommendations, parents ad-lib. They make up their protective role as they go along. Faced with Ambushes that never seem to end, parents go to one extreme or another in an exasperated attempt to find an effective solution to their problem. Yet extremes create more problems than they solve.

The lack of specific protecting techniques is compounded by the absence of reliable reference points for determining what is trouble and what is not. Parents look to others to discover the "norm" of protection. Since this reference point relies on the public behavior of other children, it changes from day to day. What is "child's play" one day might be seen as trouble the next. To combat this unreliability, parents need a tool to help them determine when child's play becomes trouble. With such help, the family becomes its own reference point.

I've developed a procedure that alleviates much of the guesswork associated with the protective role. The procedure acts as a prompter, enabling parents to resolve two of the biggest challenges presented by the protective role. The prompter permits parents to diagnose the degree of trouble, using the family as the reference point, and suggests a general course of treatment that allows for the expression of each parent's personality. The focal point of this prompter is the technique I call the *ABC Assessment*.[1]

1. The ABC Assessment is used in Protective Parenting as a result of my ten years of clinical experience with juvenile offenders. However, the ABC orientation to behavioral

The ABC Assessment is a three-part analysis of a situation. It focuses on a child's behavior *as it occurs* in and around other people, especially parents. Correct use of the ABC Assessment permits parents to make a movie of their child's behavior.

The "A" stands for *A*ntecedents, or what comes before the child's behavior. The antecedents represent the setting in which the behavior occurred, including who did or said what prior to the child's actions.

The "B" represents the child's *B*ehavior. The behavior, in the simplest terms possible, is what the child said and/or did in reaction to A.

The "C" is the *C*onsequence, or aftermath, of the child's behavior; that is, how the world reacted to the child's behavior.

Most parents find that they must put the ABC's on paper when first learning how to use this technique. A piece of lined paper with three columns marked "A," "B," and "C," respectively, does the trick. Since the interaction between a child and the world can be mind-boggling, parents are well advised to fill out the three columns as if they were taking pictures of a situation. Putting the pictures in sequence makes a movie. As parents evaluate different frames of this movie from differing perspectives, the protective role emerges.

The cue for initial action is that sense of uneasiness parents get when they suspect that something is going wrong in the family. Parents can use the ABC Assessment to scrutinize this feeling to see if they have any legitimate reason to worry about potential trouble. The first time they're used, the ABC's should be focused on *one* situation where parents believe emotions between them and their children run hot and heavy. For example, parents may decide to study the dinnertime situation because

---

description has been in the public domain for at least twelve years. Although somewhat different from the current use, it was described by Drs. Sarah Ross and Dale Bond in *Synopsis and Leader's Guide,* "Introduction to Behavior Modification," Tape 1, Behavior Modification Principles, produced by the Illinois Department of Mental Health, PACE Adolescent Unit, Decatur, Illinois, 1971.

it is there that tempers flare and trouble seems to be brewing.

Parents should put their heads together when they can find time to quietly examine the situation. (After the children are in bed and the TV is off works best.) At this time, parents should write down as many ABC's as they can remember, including brief descriptions of everything they can agree upon.

Since a child's disruptive behavior is easiest to remember, parents should start their ABC Assessment with "B." If son Bill throws peas at his sister, a simple statement should be written in the middle column under the heading "B"; that is, "Bill threw peas at Sally."

After a few moments of reflection, the parents may decide that Column A should read: "Dad said, 'You'd better eat,' and Sally repeated the warning." This, then, represents the antecedent of Bill's pea-throwing.

It is relatively easy for parents to remember what was said or done after the behavior. Thus, the C, or consequence, might read: "Sally screamed, Mom warned, and Dad ignored."

Once this picture of the ABC's is written down, it becomes a reference point. The ABC's of the situation grow up around it. Parents can then move in chronological order forward and backward, writing down each behavior of the child they can remember, *good as well as bad.*

Parents find that the more ABC's they write down, the easier the process becomes. Eventually they should find that they have gathered fifteen or twenty examples of the child's behavior in the given situation. With such a list, parents have a graphic description of what occurred. After a few nights' practice, parents can make this "movie" with little difficulty.

Parents should not be surprised if there is some overlapping of the A's and C's. The consequence of one ABC can easily become the antecedent of the following one. With Bill's pea-throwing, the C, "Sally screamed, Mom warned, and Dad ignored," will become the A of the following picture. Thus, on the next line, the A will be identical to the previous C. Then, the B might read: "Bill stuck out his tongue"; and the C: "Mom slapped Bill's mouth."

This chain reaction, with one entry becoming the antecedent of the next, might continue for several lines. The chain is broken when silence prevails for several minutes, the topic changes, or the situation ends. Several chains of ABC's encapsulate the complicated nature of the family interaction in the situation, and the movie is complete.

Once the parents have reduced the situation to the ABC's, they should review all the B's and mark them "+," "−," or "0," indicating that they considered the behavior to be positive, negative, or neutral. This simple exercise provides a solid foundation upon which the protective role can continue to function.

After making this moral judgment, parents are ready to draw a conclusion as to the presence of trouble. They must summarize the ABC Assessment so that they can answer the question: "How often did the child fail to comply with authority?"

To answer this question, parents must obtain a percentage of noncompliance. They must determine how many times the child did not follow a request, directive, warning, rule, or other expectancy that was delivered to or clearly known by the child. ("Eat your peas" counts as a directive. "I had a bad day at the store" does not.)

Parents must watch one pitfall when making this tabulation. There may be some noncompliant behaviors that seem to come out of the thin air. For example, a pea might fly across the dining room just after Dad has said to Mom, "Honey, want to go to the movies this weekend?" In such cases, the noncompliance was stimulated by something the boy said to himself, not what an authority figure said to him.

In this case, pea-throwing is still a failure to comply, even though no clearly visible A preceded the behavior as an expectancy of compliance. Pea-throwing is unacceptable (at least, in most homes), and Bill knew it. However, he created his own A by saying something to himself like: "I'll show Mom and Dad that I don't have to eat my peas." In such instances, Column A should still read just as it happened, with an asterisk (*) indicating that another, invisible A was present. This reminds parents to count these situations as noncompliances.

Parents must then pick out all the plus and minus B's that have to do with compliance. They must separate the compliant B's from the noncompliant ones. A simple fraction stating the relation of noncompliance to the total behaviors will yield the percentage that answers the key question: "How serious is my trouble?"

At this point, parents have enough information to decide whether or not they have a problem brewing in a situation they suspect of being troublesome. All they need is some method of comparing the level of noncompliance in the situation with society's tolerance for disruption.

After ten years of studying the millions of shades of trouble that kids generate with their Ambushes and working within the criminal justice system in the disposition of juvenile offenders, I have developed guidelines for helping parents decide what is trouble and what is not. I have determined that any noncompliance greater than 50 percent should be considered troublesome. Although I use 50 percent as the absolute cutoff in terms of noncompliance, I try to convince parents to lower this tolerance to 25 percent. Thus, 75 percent compliance is acceptable. This level assures adequate conformity but leaves room for occasional hell-raising, experimentation, creativity, and the disruption that can result when a child has had a "bad day."

Since trouble starts in the home and moves outward, I've categorized troublesome behavior to show parents how trouble can grow if noncompliance is allowed to flourish. I have delineated five levels of trouble.

Level 1 More than 50 percent noncompliance with parental directives, requests, demands, rules, or warnings.

Level 2 In addition to Level 1, more than 50 percent noncompliance with similar expectancies at school.

Level 3 In addition to levels 1 and 2, more than 50 percent non-compliance with similar expectancies in the community; that is, in stores, restaurants, recreation facilities, and so on.

The percentages mentioned in the first three levels must be based on some type of time-lapse observation. For example, compliance in the home could represent seven days of observation; compliance at school could represent five days of observation.

Level 4 Violations such as shoplifting, petty theft, breaking and entering, vandalism, truancy, running away, and the abuse of drugs, including alcohol.

Level 5 A deepening of deviance, resulting in one of four outcomes, in which a child:

- pledges allegiance to counterculture, antiestablishment, destructive-minded groups such as warring gangs, drug communes, revolutionary bands, and other counterproductive organizations.
- is lost in a purposeless and drifting state of mind, moving aimlessly from one fad to another.
- cavorts irresponsibly about the country with total disrespect for the law or earning a living, unthinkingly maligning property or person.
- commits one severely disruptive act or repeatedly commits illegal acts and is confined in a penal institution.

While it is necessary for a child to pass through Level 1 to reach Level 2 and through Levels 1 and 2 to reach Level 3, many kids experiment with disruption and unintentionally reach Level 4 without passing through Levels 1, 2, or 3.

With quick and prudent action, a child can be removed from Level 4 trouble with relative ease. However, except for a rare, violent, and unpredictable act, Level 5 trouble is the result of a child's passing slowly but surely through the first four levels.

Once parents make a preliminary decision about a heated situation, they may choose to broaden their evaluation. Using the

ABC Assessment, they can see how much trouble is present in the home and how much, if any, is spreading outside the home.

To study noncompliance in the home (Level 1), the ABC's of two or three situations *in addition* to the one used in the original evaluation should be gathered. Noncompliance at school can be studied by asking the teacher to gather the ABC's of at least three different situations (for example, recess, lunch, math class). Level 3 noncompliance can be evaluated by parents if they have sufficient opportunity to observe the child in a variety of community settings.

After gathering information on several situations, parents should take an extra, time-saving step. They should reflect on the ABC's and group the B's into categories. Grouping behaviors saves time and energy but doesn't hurt the protective role. It would be great if parents could handle each behavior separately, weighing the circumstances of each ABC. But it's just not possible.

Categories of problem behaviors are obtained by picking out all the noncompliant/compliant B's and grouping them according to topics or themes that repeat themselves in different ABC's. If a behavior doesn't seem to fit into a group, it should be treated as a category in and of itself. For example, Bill's "food abuse" might include throwing peas (observed in the home), squishing potatoes in his fingers (observed at home and in a restaurant), and sticking carrots in his nose (observed at school). However, if Bill confined his noncompliance to pea-throwing, the problem category would be "pea-throwing."

When categories of behavior have been written down, parents can then compute percentages of noncompliance *for the categories*. These percentages will guide them in selecting the one category that should receive their time and concern.

Unless they have a particular bias, parents should concentrate their protective role on the category that represents the highest percentage of noncompliance. If Bill's "food abuse" comprises 62 percent noncompliance, his "obscene language" 38 percent noncompliance, and his "resistance to going to bed" 90 percent noncompliance, the parents should work on Bill's bedtime behavior first.

However, if one or both parents are horrified by "bad language," it might supersede bedtime behavior in importance. It's a decision that parents can make by simply weighing the relative importance of the percentages and their personal tolerance of certain behaviors.

Once a category is selected, the protective role enters its critical period. Parents are now ready to protect their child by reducing the Ambush and, with it, the child's chances of getting into more serious trouble. Once parents commit themselves to the next step, there's no turning back.

To get the ball rolling, parents have to state their trouble in positive terms, so that instead of a "problem" they have a "goal."

The goal of the food-abuse problem is "food appreciation"; of obscene language, "appropriate language"; of resistance to going to bed, "compliance with bedtime rules." When the category of problem behaviors is stated in positive terms, the protective role is completely activated.

When parents reach this stage in the science of Protective Parenting, they sometimes get sidetracked. They've completed a rough diagnosis of the trouble, evaluated their tolerance for trouble, made decisions about acceptable limits of noncompliance, pinpointed problem behaviors, categorized them, elected one as most important, and set a goal for change. It is at this point that parents tend to relax momentarily and reflect on the "why?" of their problems.

This burning question cannot be contained any longer. "Why does my child do what he (or she) does?" Finding out why their child throws peas consumes them. It also takes them off the main track and leads them down a blind alley.

There is no simple answer to the "why" question. Social scientists spend countless hours and millions of dollars trying to determine the cause of disruption, trouble, crime, and delinquency. Even when I spend hours getting to know a family, I often find that I can't fully comprehend the cause of a certain pattern of disruptive behavior.

In the hundreds of cases I've handled, I've found familiar problems playing a major role in deviance: peer pressure, school adjustment, TV violence, misuse of pornography, bad examples set by parents, and many other complicated social-psychological variables.

If parents feel they *must* have an answer to the question, I give them an oversimplified but workable solution.

"What causes kids to get into trouble?"

Kids do! They take their limited freedom of choice and choose to raise their own brand of hell, using whatever disruption is at hand.

I sometimes think that the widespread preoccupation with the causes of crime—TV, parents, peers, pornography, maladjustment in school, sex, violence, poverty—is actually a grand scheme devised by bright, conniving teenagers to take the heat off the real culprits: themselves.

Obviously the answer to "Why?" is more complicated than simply saying, "The kid did it." However, it is the right place to start and usually satisfies the parents' thirst to know the cause.

What is important at this point is the most challenging question of Protective Parenting: "What exactly do I do to keep my child out of trouble?"

This question puts parents back on the right track. It also takes them back to the ABC Assessment. There, they must study the ABC's from a new perspective. They must study the relationship between the antecedents and the consequences of compliant and noncompliant behaviors. In other words, they need to know what difference existed between the A's and C's when the child complied and when he or she did not.

When parents look at the ABC's of compliant situations, they find that their successes tell them what they should do about their failures. If parents think the A was most important, they may spend more time convincing the child of the value and beauty of doing things correctly. They may say, "Peas are wholesome food, and wholesome food is good." Or, "Little boys need peas. Peas should be eaten, not thrown." Such an orientation sets a scene that encourages the child to comply at point B.

If parents think that the consequences had most to do with the behavior, they turn their attention to reward and punishments. Since consequences usually *do* have a great impact on behavior, parents are wise to concentrate their efforts at point C. Also, effective, well-timed consequences will reinforce the beliefs laid down in A and make them mean more than lecturing, preaching, and complaining.

Concentrating on consequences helps parents realize that kids will work for good things and try to avoid bad things. Thus, a food abuser may have to pay for the food thrown, and a food appreciater may get a special dessert.

Since the C of one interaction can become the A of the next, parents find that the best method of reaching their goal is to use some combination of A and C. Thus, they might say, "Peas are wholesome food. If you eat them, you'll get dessert; if not, you'll lose part of your allowance."

Implementing a combination of this type brings controversy to the protective role. Experts disagree about the relative importance of imparting values via talking, increasing some behaviors with rewards, and decreasing other behaviors with punishments. Some say that taking positive things away (including attention) is the most effective punishment. Others say that giving negative things makes punishments more active. Still others say that taking away a good thing *and* giving a bad thing is the most comprehensive action.

Other issues such as the timing of punishment, how many

times a child should be warned before being punished, and how to determine the most effective rewards and punishments are hotly contested by experts and parents alike. Even well-designed research has yet to answer these questions satisfactorily.

The protective role that I espouse treats these issues quite practically. I believe in an "if-it-works-use-it" approach. I advise parents to search the ABC Assessment, find the most effective combination of rewards and/or punishments, and do more of what proved successful in the past.

The easiest place to start is for parents to encourage their children to comply because it is the "good" or "right" thing to do. Parents can promote this antecedent by using love to stimulate compliance. However, if the Ambush is deeply ingrained, love alone won't have much impact.

Parents usually find that they must back up their love with some consequence signifying that they mean business. Rewards for compliance and ignoring for noncompliance should be the first choice. If this doesn't seem to work, a reward should be taken away and not returned until compliance is reestablished. If this still doesn't work, the parents are going to have to get tougher.

If after the parents have tried the first two steps the child's level of noncompliance hasn't changed, a reward should be taken away and a negative consequence given. This double-edged punishment usually works. If it doesn't, the child is probably listening to inner voices of rebellion. The parents will probably need professional help in finding a solution.

When searching for the right combination of value-giving, rewards, and punishments, parents should keep two helpful hints in mind:

First, punishment won't make a child do the right thing; it can only stop him or her from doing the wrong thing in a specific situation. Unless a child knows what the right thing is, punishment will only create anger and resentment. Therefore, the use of punishment should *always* be accompanied by something that tells the child what he or she is supposed to do.

Second, parents should pay close attention to what they do after a child complies. In looking back over the ABC's, parents may find that when their children comply, they ignore them, thereby inviting disruption as an attention-getting device. If a child complies, "Thank you" can work miracles.

As parents apply their disciplinary strategies, they must expect their children to raise a stink. They will moan, cry, throw tantrums, and engage in all sorts of back talk. While it is a source of irritation and legitimate parenting concern, back talk is inconsequential. Protective Parents keep their eyes on compliance, not complaints.

This subtle emphasis can mean the difference in a child's avoiding Level 5 trouble. Parents can highlight this distinction by saying to the child, "I'll tolerate some back talk as long as you do as you're told."

Parents have told me that tolerating back talk is the hardest part of the protective role (and, for that matter, the hardest part of parenting). I've developed special recommendations to help parents around this difficult obstacle.

The best thing to do about back talk is ignore it. Parents should keep telling themselves, "Compliance, not complaints."

If this doesn't calm them, they can engage in "active ignoring." This occurs when parents repeat the directive several times, pretending that the child's back talk is nonexistent.

An even more active posture is taken when parents give the child an ultimatum concerning the reluctance to comply. For example, "If you don't do as I ask within one minute, you will lose telephone privileges for the rest of the night." This is a threat of punishment that focuses on noncompliance, not back talk.

If this doesn't work, parents may choose to make a frontal assault on back talk. This is done by threatening punishment for back talk rather than noncompliance ("If you continue this back talk, you'll lose the car for a week").

No matter how active parents become in dealing with back talk, they must follow a cardinal rule: Don't talk back to a child's back talk.

Parents who feel affronted by a child's back talk should consider one final thing: very few children enjoy becoming "mature." Therefore, parents can expect to hear moans and groans from children about doing things they don't want to do. Parents must decide if a child's compliance is worth listening to some back talk. Parents who don't know how long they can tolerate back talk should remember that the more a child complies, the less he'll complain.

Once parents have settled on a disciplinary strategy, they should stick with it for at least two weeks. Consistency in applying the strategy is an absolute necessity. Parents can't move to the final step of the protective role—evaluating the results—until their consistency is very clear to the child.

If parents change their disciplinary strategy right in the middle of a two-week period, they should give their new strategy another two weeks before evaluating the results. If parents find themselves changing their strategy every day or two, they may be forced to consider that the problem rests with themselves, not with the child.

Once the parents have applied the desired protective role for at least two weeks, they must employ the ABC Assessment one final time. They should complete the ABC's of the preselected situations as a spot check to see if their strategies are working. Like a physician who checks the patient's temperature after giving medicine, parents must recheck the level of noncompliance to see if it has been reduced to acceptable limits.

Using the same procedure as before, parents should compute the percentage of noncompliance in the target category. If the percentage is acceptable, the protective role was successful. If it has improved but is still unacceptable, the protective role must continue on the same course. If it is unchanged, the parents should reevaluate their disciplinary strategies.

Depending on the outcome of the evaluation, parents may decide to do several things. They may ease their concentration, happy with their success. They may select another problem category, realizing that the protective role will be easier next time. They may forget about the written paper and the ABC's, enacting the protective role without additional prompting. They may choose to take several weeks off from thinking about trouble and relax. They may look at their situation and decide they need to seek outside help.

It sounds a bit bizarre, but some parents may ask their disruptive children for suggestions on what they should do next. The insight a gentle warrior can have about his or her disruption can be amazing. I've seen cases in which the child has gone so far as to describe the nature of the real problem and what the parents should do to change it. It never hurts to ask.

Even when parents realize that they have reduced trouble and decide to quit worrying, the protective role should not be put in mothballs. Some parents solve one situation only to find that another problem pops up in its place. Others find that when their child is nine everything is beautiful, and then one day, five years later, the kid acts as if he or she has had no training whatsoever. Once the protective role is understood, parents should never allow themselves to get out of practice. They never know when trouble will appear on their doorstep.

Like all parenting techniques, the protective role is best enacted by two parents. However, if a single parent is willing to work extra hard, especially during the gathering of ABC information, the protective role can work. The most difficult challenge is faced by those parents whose spouses are unwilling to help in the protective process. These parents have to face not only the warring antics of their children but also the cold-war resistance of wives or husbands who don't care enough to help.

When properly employed, the protective role is no more complicated than such roles as teacher or provider. ABC Assessment, tabulation of noncompliance and percentages, determination of the degree of trouble, categorization of behaviors, goal selection, pragmatic use of values, rewards, and punishments, and evaluation of results are the pieces to be fitted together. They are surrounded by the cautions of avoiding too much "Why?" and not getting boxed in by back talk. The role is stimulated by never-ending Ambushes and trouble that acquires energy from poor impulse control, low frustration tolerance, and a variety of temper tantrums.

The hardest part about the protective role is convincing parents that they should take the time to learn it. Even at the outset it takes only thirty minutes a day. Later on, it may take only three or four minutes to enact. But parents concentrate so hard on making things go right, they don't want to think about things going wrong, let alone practice for such an unthinkable event. Yet the unthinkable is happening to more and more families, and parents find themselves ill-prepared to protect their children.

Once parents know how to enact the protective role, they feel much more confident in their parenting and much less frightened about their child's being victimized by the world. Best of all, they are able to teach their child the protective role. That's the greatest accomplishment of all.

Prelude to the Case Histories

The science of Protective Parenting is the foundation for learning the protective role. Finding the right combination of values, rewards, and punishments to protect a child from trouble while accommodating an individual family's strengths and weaknesses is an art. While the science can be assimilated in a matter of weeks, it takes months and even years to master the refinements of saying or doing the right thing at the right time.

The rest of the book is dedicated to the art of Protective

Parenting. I start by reviewing a general strategy for simplifying the protective process. I call this strategy the *Kiss*.

Armed with a firm but loving Kiss, the reader can examine the one hundred–plus cases in the eleven chapters that follow. The cases are separated into ten age units so that parents may see how the variations in the Ambush theme develop during different time periods.

If you see that your nine-year-old's behavior looks more like that of an eleven- or thirteen-year-old, don't be surprised. Remember that each child is cut from a different mold, and each parent must find a unique way to survive the attacks of these gentle warriors.

Each down-to-earth case review is intended to give more insight into the question: "What exactly do I do to protect my child from trouble?" The first age unit is infancy to two years. I start early since the job of keeping kids out of trouble begins as soon as things don't go the way they are "supposed" to; that is, shortly after the baby comes home from the hospital.

5

Keep It Simple

During my years of trying to sort out the problems of distraught, anxious parents and hell-raising kids, I've often found myself overwhelmed by highly complex situations. For example, when I'm faced with the sophisticated Ambush of a bright, power-seeking sixteen-year-old who thinks he knows everything and is willing to suffer in order to look "cool," complexity is unavoidable.

Parents' reactions to adolescent Ambushes prove especially perplexing ("Should I?" "Could I?" "How about . . . ?" "What if . . . ?" "But that means that I . . . doesn't it?" "My God, I'll never understand why . . . !"). When I first faced these murmurs of bewilderment, I often had the feeling that my training and experience were inadequate to deal with the endless problems of troubled families. In short, I felt stupid. After realizing that my stupidity resulted from trying to solve too many puzzles, I adopted a preference for simplicity. I found that keeping things as simple as possible was the best way to arrive at workable solutions to supposedly insurmountable problems. It also made me feel better.

When parents detailed a complicated, long-standing problem

with their child and the son or daughter wailed at life's inequities and complained about parental domination, I would repeat over and over to myself, "Keep it simple, stupid. Keep it simple, stupid." When I followed my own advice, I discovered I was able to cut through much of the complexity and help both parent and child reach mutually acceptable solutions.

As time went on and the complexity of troubled families seemed never-ending (in fact, it gets worse each year), I concocted a handy little word that abbreviated my "keep-it-simple-stupid" approach. When overwhelmed with complexity and feeling stupid, I would repeat, *"Keep It Simple, Stupid.* K.I.S.S. Kiss."

The Kiss still doesn't get rid of an occasional feeling of stupidity, but it does tend to minimize it. For those who might wish to reduce complex situations to a manageable size and feel better about it, I recommend the Kiss approach. Here's how it works:

Mindy's mom sounded cold and aloof over the phone. She asked for an appointment as if she were placing an order with Sears, Roebuck. She said she wanted to discuss a slight problem she was having with her daughter. It sounded more than "slight," so I told her to come in immediately.

After the usual social amenities, I asked her to tell me what was wrong. She tried to keep her defenses intact, but they cracked into a thousand pieces as tears streamed down her face.

"Mindy . . . Mindy . . . was arrested . . . last night . . . for possession of marijuana. I . . . I don't know why . . . why . . . I don't know what to do. She's not a bad girl." She paused briefly to wipe mascara from her cheeks. "Her father and I have tried to be the best . . . the best of parents. She's had everything she . . . she . . . could possibly want. She's a cheerleader and . . . and . . . and on the honor roll. We . . . we don't . . . she doesn't run around . . . too much."

For the next twenty minutes, Mindy's mom poured out hundreds of disjointed details about her life with Mindy. She was overwhelmed with confusion, and thus a prime candidate for the Kiss. In preparation for the Kiss, I questioned her intensely, reconstructing the nature of her day-to-day interaction with Mindy. I interpreted the marijuana bust as a sign of a fundamental breakdown in the protective process. I employed the ABC Assessment by asking, "What did you say? What did she say? What did you say back?," making a movie of a typical conversation. In this way I put their interaction under a microscope and discovered the nuts and bolts of their problem.

Later in the day, I met with Mindy. Once she had aired her complaints about the inequities of life, I cross-checked the conversation, using the same technique. After a total of three hours of questioning, I had obtained an accurate replay of an encounter that occurred frequently. This is what had happened:

Mom was moving briskly about her middle-class kitchen trying to clean up breakfast dishes and prepare dinner at the same time. Shopping, lunch with the girls, and eighteen holes of golf had disrupted the housekeeping schedule expected by her husband. It was approximately 5:30 P.M. Her husband was due at 6:00 P.M. She was in no mood for an interruption.

However, as she was in the midst of scrubbing egg yolk from her stoneware, Mindy walked into the kitchen and asked, "Mother, can I have a new dress for a dance?"

Without looking up from the sink, Mom replied, "Why?"

"Jim asked me to the Sweetheart Dance next weekend, and I absolutely *have* to have a new dress."

Mom turned from the sink, planning to initiate a situational analysis, but had no chance to speak.

"Everyone is getting a new dress. Do you think we could go shopping Saturday? Or would Friday night be better?"

"Hold your horses, young lady!"

"I'm just trying to make it easier for you, Mom. I just need a new dress. You understand that? Right? I'm just trying to make it easier. . . . Which would be better for you? You have to see—"

"Hold on just a second," Mom interrupted. "What do you mean you need a *new* dress? What happened to the old dress?"

"Mother, which one are you talking about?"

"The one you had a few weeks ago. Just a couple . . . a few weeks ago."

"What did it look like?"

Mom dropped the scrub brush, somewhat distraught. "The one you had for . . . whatever it was . . . a couple of months ago. Whatever it was . . ."

"Do you remember what it looked like?" Mindy remained calm during her cross-examination. "Do you?"

Mother was beginning to feel a familiar sense of frustration. "That doesn't make any difference. What makes a difference is that you just had a new—"

"It doesn't make any difference!" Mindy was threatening anger while looking out the window, her hands clenched tightly at her sides. "Obviously, the problem we're having right now is that it doesn't make any difference to you. Okay? It makes a *big* difference to me. Anyhow, I've worn that dress before, and you don't remember what it looks like, but I *do!* And you—"

"Ahhh, is that the one that's so revealing? The one I didn't want you to get in the first place?"

"Ahh, come off it, Mom. Mother, if—"

"No decent boy in the world would look at you twice if you wore that dress!"

"Don't hand me that crap!" Mindy sat down abruptly, slamming her elbow on the table. "Are you telling me that Jim's not decent? Are you cutting down my friends now?"

Mom sat down next to her. "I'm just saying that you don't need a new dress when you had one that was. . . . And they're getting worse all the time. And you simply don't need a new dress. That's what I'm saying." Mom was talking like an auctioneer by now.

"I don't really care what you're saying," Mindy replied in a cool, collected manner. "Now . . . I . . . I need a new dress.

Karen, my best friend, is getting a dress. . . . I could go shopping with her if the problem is you don't want to go shopping.
Okay? If you're busy or gonna go away—"

"The problem is that I just don't see that you need a new
dress. You just had one, and I don't see why. . . . We're not
going to spend more money on a new dress."

"Mother, the one I had is a Christmas dress. Okay? This is
spring. This is the Sweetheart Dance. Okay? Mother, c'mon
. . . I can't wear the same thing again. Everybody's seen me in
it. Do you know what they're gonna say if I wear the same
dress?"

"When I was a young girl, I didn't care about all that stuff.
And—"

"Fine, Mother! Don't care about it! Obviously you don't care
about it now, either. Look at the dress you've got on now."
After this shot, Mindy leaned forward with a little more concern. "You really don't understand how important it is to me.
You don't understand me. You don't understand how important
it is that. . . . I know I had that dress. You're right. I had it
four or five months ago, and you guys spent a lot of money on
it, and I appreciate that. But you don't understand me."

Mom calmed down a wee bit. "What you don't understand is
that . . . how we're supposed to come up with the forty or fifty
dollars."

"Mother, it's really important to me. You don't understand
that. Everybody else is getting one. Everybody else has seen me
in that dress. The same people are going to the dance . . . the
same people are going to see me again."

"There's too much of that going on nowadays. And I *do* understand what you're saying . . . but there's too much of
that—"

"*What?*"

"That . . . that 'everybody-else-is-doing-it' stuff. Everybody else is doing it—that's the reason you do it. Because everybody else is doing it. That's not a good enough reason."

"Mother, you don't understand. That's not why I'm doing it. I'm doing it because I want a new dress and I need one. You don't understand me."

"Well, what about the money, then?" Mother remembered feeling quite frustrated when introducing this concept. "Your father can't be just giving out money all the time. Have you got the fifty dollars?"

"It's not going to cost fifty dollars."

"The last dress cost forty, and they're going up all the time. Have you got the forty dollars?"

"If you guys can go out and spend money on drinking and taking all your friends out to dinner and to bowling and golfing and . . . c'mon, you can spend all that money—"

"Your father—"

"You guys go out to eat and spend forty bucks a night when you go out to dinner."

"Your father works hard and goes out . . . and it's his right to have that . . . and it's my place to be with him." Mom was getting redder by the minute. "He earns the money and he has a right to spend the money that way."

"That's right! And he would want to have his daughter look the best . . . you always—"

"You don't understand—"

"Every time I go to church, you're always saying, 'We want you to look the best, we want you to look the best.' I'm not going to look 'the best' if I don't have this new dress. That's what you want me to be. You want me to be 'the best' . . . I'm gonna let down your friends."

"Yes, but . . . can't you be the best without having a new dress?"

"No!"

"Can't you be the best in terms of being a nice girl—"

"No. You know the Johnsons down the street? You're always telling me, 'Be like her daughter.' Her daughter is getting a new dress."

There was a long pause as Mom went to the sink for a drink of water and Mindy sat stoically at the table, realizing she had found a sensitive point.

"Yes, but her daughter doesn't get new dresses every few months. Furthermore—"

"Oh, Mother, you don't *know* that."

"I know . . . I know that Mrs. Johnson and I were both girls, too, once."

"Oh, you make more money. Oh, *you* were a girl once? *Big deal!*"

"And . . . we . . . didn't—"

"Didn't *what*, Mother?"

Mom started pacing around the table, trying to look concerned and adult. "What kind of dress do you want?"

"One that's different from the one I already have."

"That's *different* from the one you already have?"

"The one I have is a winter dress. I want a summer one. I want a halter dress. That's cut down in front and straps in back. I want a halter dress with a little jacket. So that—"

"That's much too revealing! You can't. . . . I . . . honey, you can't do those kinds of things."

"What kinds of things?"

"Those are much . . . too . . . those are . . . those dresses are much too . . . stimulating!"

"What? Stimulating for whom?"

"Honey, you know what I'm talking about."

"No. What *are* you talking about?" Mindy had a smug look on her face.

"Just . . . *toooo* . . . stimulating . . . *for Jim!*"

"Oh, you mean you don't wear dresses that stimulate Daddy?"

"That's different."

"How's that different?"

Pausing and then responding with an air of superiority, Mom said, "We're married!"

"*Mother!* What does that have to do with Jim being attracted to me?"

"That's fine. But there must be some limits. Now, you agree with that. There have to be some limits. There's a law—"

"Fine! I'm not gonna go out naked. What I'm asking is no big deal. I just want a new dress. I don't understand what you're all hassled about."

With an air of finality, Mom blurted out, "Have you got the money?"

"I've got some of it."

"How much?"

"I have about twenty dollars. I'll pay for—I'll pay half of it."

"What happened to all your baby-sitting money? What have you done with that?" Mom recalled feeling as though she were winning a major victory at this point.

"What money is that, Mother?"

"The money you've been making from baby-sitting the last few months."

"I spent it."

"You've spent it already?"

"Uh-huh."

"What did you spent it on?"

With a hint of soft sarcasm, Mindy leaned forward and replied, "I bought you a Mother's Day present and some clothes for school."

Mom remembered stammering and feeling a twinge of guilt before saying, "See? You have to choose how to spend your money. So do your father and I. We have to make decisions about where to spend our money."

"Fine. One of your decisions should be to buy me a new dress."

"What about the vacation we were going to take this summer?"

"Oh, c'mon. You gonna tell me that forty bucks means we

can't go on vacation? C'mon, Mother, you guys blow that in a weekend. Don't give me that!''

"That's not—''

"Are you telling me to get a certain kind of dress? Fine. We'll go shopping and we'll agree on something. Okay? Now, what are you telling me, Mother?''

"I don't know why you have to have everything you want right away.''

"I didn't say 'right away.' Today's Monday. I said Friday or Saturday we'll go get it.''

"Every time you want a new dress, don't you ever . . . ever . . . think about that maybe . . . maybe . . . somebody else doesn't have . . . maybe you shouldn't have as much as. . . . You can't have everything you—''

"Oh. Should we send a dress to the poor kids in China, Mother? Should we do that?'' Mindy was getting vicious now.

"Yes! I mean . . . I . . . You're making fun of me. I don't understand why you have to make fun of me. But I think you should have a little compassion for other people that don't have anything.''

"I do.''

"Everybody has to have a new dress . . . *Everybody?''* Mom was screaming now.

"All the people that are important to me are.''

"That's another thing . . . about some of your friends. Some of Jim's friends are . . . are . . . highly questionable.''

"What does that mean?''

Mom began to sound overly righteous. "That's exactly what it means. They're highly questionable.''

"In what way, Mother?''

Mother leaned backward slightly as she pointed the fateful finger of parenthood at Mindy. "I think they smoke marijuana . . . and . . . drink . . . and run around, and I . . . think Jim probably goes with them. I don't want any daughter of mine hanging around with that kind of person.''

"So what you're saying is that because some of Jim's friends might smoke dope, I can't have a new dress. C'mon, Mother! C'mon, give me a better argument."

"You accuse me of not hearing you. I . . . I think you don't understand *me*. I don't think you've heard a thing I've said."

"I've heard everything you've said, Mother. You said that you and Daddy don't have the money for a new dress. Yeah, and I told you that you go out and blow it every weekend. You said you wanna spend money on vacation, and I *know* we're gonna spend four thousand dollars on vacation. Then you tell me that I haven't heard a thing."

"You don't know everything you think you do, young lady. You just don't know everything!"

"Okay, *fine!* Then enlighten me, Mother." Mindy was glaring across the table.

"I've got to get busy with the dishes. . . . I don't have. . . . Your father is going to be home any minute. This is leading nowhere. I've got—"

"It's not leading anywhere because you don't want it to. You are—"

"You don't have one respectful tone in your mouth. Not one respectful tone."

"You're right. I don't respect you right now because you're not listening to me and you don't understand me. And you think it's more important to get the dishes washed so that my father can't see that you were playing around all day instead of doing what you're supposed to be doing. You gotta get the house clean so Daddy won't be pissed! So you don't listen to your daughter."

There was a long pause as Mom looked away and sighed deeply.

Mindy continued, "It's more important that Daddy not yell at you than that you listen to me. This is important to me. This is—"

"Now you're acting childish. You want me to tell your father that you were acting childish? To use your famous word, *c'mon!*"

"Fine. Go ahead. He'll be here any minute. You'd better hurry up and clean up over there or he'll see it. Mother, you know you were out today with the girls, and you know that Daddy doesn't like that. Dinner's not even ready!"

"Now you're acting like a little baby. You don't want me to talk to your father about a new dress and have to say that his daughter was acting like a little baby, do you?"

"Fine. Go ahead. You can—"

"You want me to talk to your father—"

"Fine. Go ahead!"

"I'm too busy to talk to you about it right now. I'll think about it, and I'll speak to your father about it. Maybe we do have the money. I don't have time to talk to you about it right now."

The conversation lasted about twelve minutes. In such a short time Mindy was able to carry out an Ambush that would have awed General George Patton. As her mother told me about it, she was more upset with Mindy's lack of respect than her request for a new dress. Mindy, on the other, believed that Mom had made a big deal out of nothing. She wanted a new dress and saw no reason why she shouldn't have it. (By the way, she got the dress the following Friday evening.)

Mindy and Mom had three or four such "discussions" per week. They happened each time there was the slightest hint of conflict between them. Mindy had learned how to use disruption to good advantage. She organized her Ambush strategies so that she usually got what she wanted when she wanted it. Mom had a hard time seeing the relationship between the weekly arguments and Mindy's trouble. Once I finished the following analysis, Mom saw the above conversation as a full-scale battle, merely one scene from a feature-length war.

Mindy initially tried to get her way with a simple, matter-of-fact approach. She placed her mom in a limited-choice situation (*either* Friday *or* Saturday). Feeling squeezed, Mom reacted with an authoritarian response ("Hold your horses. . . ."). By doing this, she unintentionally threw the first bombshell and indicated her willingness to fight.

The conversation quickly became irrelevant. As Mindy pursued every side issue imaginable, Mom reacted with increased frustration, digging herself deeper and deeper into a hole. The only way she could keep the walls from caving in was to cover her frustration with authoritarianism. This was an indication of weakness and gave Mindy more ammunition. As Mom became unnerved, Mindy grew calm and confrontative.

Mindy carefully ignored, interrupted, or avoided any reality issue (for example, money). When faced with rational points, she neatly dodged her mother's confrontation by introducing sensitive and emotionally laden issues. One technique of disrespect was the regular use of the word "okay," said in question form, but intended as a put-down. She was treating her mother like a kindergarten student who had to be taught the alphabet one letter a day.

Mom didn't realize that she was getting noticeably upset. Her voice became high-pitched and her speech rapid (she even got this way while repeating the story). As Mom lost emotional control, Mindy calmed down, talked softly, and showed how "mature" she was in the face of her mom's "hysterics." This caused Mom to become more upset, to which Mindy reacted by becoming more aggressive. Mindy engaged in unnecessary brutality in making the wisecrack about her mother's dress. Not wanting to get the "enemy" needlessly upset, she gracefully backed away.

Mindy's key Ambush strategy was a mixture of relating peer pressure and provoking maternal guilt for her mother's failure to understand. Each time Mom went off on a tangent that Mindy didn't want to follow, Mindy returned to the dress issue. Each time Mom talked of money, Mindy blitzed her with "Everybody else will have a new dress'' or ''You just don't understand me.'' In this way, Mindy kept the conversation jumbled, muddled, and bogged down in the vagueness of triple meanings. In other words, she made sure the dialogue went *her way*.

Mom made a crucial error in asking questions, the answers to which she probably already knew or should have known (''What did you do with the money you earned?''). This was a poorly designed revenge tactic. She further demonstrated her lack of awareness by referring moralistically to marijuana, drinking, and unfit companions. This was an empty cannon and proved only that she didn't know what was going on in her daughter's life. Mom lost her head, an event that all gentle warriors count on.

Mindy didn't hesitate to jump on Mom's display of weakness in order to finish her off. Mindy's comments about the household schedule, Mom's ''playing with her friends,'' and Dad's potential anger forced Mom to realize that the longer she argued with her daughter, the less she would get done in the kitchen. If she continued to argue, she'd never get the work done. It was too late to say ''No'' to the original request and she couldn't say ''Yes'' without checking with her husband. Any way she turned, she was trapped. She had been backed into a corner, and her weapons had been rendered useless. She had to surrender. The Ambush was successful.

Mindy's mom was not doing well as a Protective Parent. She was making a difficult job impossible. She was allowing herself to be regularly sucked into a battle she could not win. I showed her how she could employ the ''keep-it-simple'' philosophy to Kiss off some of the confusion. It would take four steps:

1. She would have to admit that, no matter how hard she tried, she'd never be perfect at Protective Parenting. Faced with Mindy's disruptiveness, she could not avoid a certain degree of fallibility. Instead of worrying about perfection, she had to admit that she would necessarily be imperfect and concentrate her efforts on reducing her mistakes.

2. She would have to learn how to dissect a conversation and list the issues involved.

3. She would have to learn the fine art of issue elimination. This entails refusing to permit irrelevant and tangential issues from creeping into a task-oriented discussion.

4. Finally, she would have to learn how to make a decision. Within the Kiss approach, this involved three separate steps:

   a. Deducing several courses of possible action.

   b. Projecting the probable outcome of each action.

   c. In keeping with personal and familial values, selecting a course of action that has a high probability of generating the desired outcome.

On the following day, we completed this four-step process. With the 20/20 vision of hindsight, Mom was able to reduce the problem to a workable size. This is how we applied the Kiss approach to the above conversation.

1. We spoke at length about her desire to be a perfect mother. She realized that while perfection is an admirable goal, it is unattainable. She understood that it is self-defeating to feel guilty about not being perfect. No matter how hard she tried, she'd always be faced with some mistakes. She temporarily released herself from guilt, and we moved on.

2. With her concurrence, I listed all the issues that had crept into the conversation:

Mindy's desire for a new dress	rebelliousness
Mom's need to be understanding	close-mindedness
the value of money	Mom's marital relationship
peer pressure on Mindy	both parties' revenge
parental authority	Mindy's false concern for Mom
Mom's guilt	analysis of motives
Mindy's impulsiveness	Mom's frustration with her own
Mindy's childishness	adolescence
boyfriend's expectancies	recreational values
Mindy's compulsiveness	delay of gratification
Mom's inquisitiveness	parents' drinking behavior
sexual mores	Mindy's hostility

femininity versus masculinity
paternal domination
Mindy's rejection of parental
   control of her rewards
dress code
social influence of drugs and alcohol
social acceptance
Mom's fear of failure
Mom's fear of Dad
housekeeping standards
Mom's personal appearance

Mom's supposed lack of empathy
standards of decency
Mom's embarrassment at "sex
   talk"
Mom's defensiveness
parental need for achievement
peer pressure among parents
religion
socioeconomic values
value of self-sacrifice
Mindy's lack of compassion
freedom of choice

When I showed this list to Mindy's mom, she damn near fainted. Yet, reviewing the conversation, she was able to see that each of the above had been involved to one degree or another. Helplessly bogged down in the muck and mire of an overwhelmingly complicated situation, she was more than ready to Kiss off much of the confusion. She desperately wanted to believe that this conversation didn't *have* to be so mind-boggling.

3. We went down the list and started to eliminate issues. By avoiding talking about decency and morals, she was able to eliminate sexuality, boyfriend's expectancies, freedom of choice, dress code, and a raft of other issues. This elimination didn't bother her in this instance because she really wasn't worried about the kind of dress Mindy bought. By eliminating any reaction to Mindy's attack on her own and her husband's recreation, she could do away with issues such as parents' drinking behavior, religion, parental peer pressure, and other tangential issues. She was content with this elimination since these things, while important at other times, didn't have anything to do with a request for a new dress.

We continued to eliminate issues that she decided had no relevance to the conversation. We finally arrived at two central issues that seemed crucial: the request for a new dress and the value of money.

4. We generated five possible answers to the problem raised by the discussion. For each answer, we projected the outcome in terms of what Mindy would learn.

- *The most complicated answer:* Deal with all forty-four issues and receive an exceptionally nagging headache. Mindy would learn that getting things from authority figures necessitated a long, tedious battle, bringing in every conceivable issue. Eventually she would become such a pest that she would get what she wanted.
- *A simpler answer:* Eliminate extremely tangential issues such as religion and socioeconomic class. If she got the dress, Mindy would learn not to bring in quite so many tangential issues; if she didn't, she would work a little harder and longer in preparation for battle.
- *An even simpler answer:* Kiss off all the issues except the need for a new dress, the value of money, peer pressure, and paternal domination. If Father said yes, Mindy would learn to get rid of much of her manipulation and deal only with restricted issues. If Father said no, Mindy would learn she had to find new techniques of bringing critical issues to Daddy's attention. She probably would not waste time arguing with Mom.
- *The simplest answer:* Kiss off everything except the two key issues: a new dress and money. We role-played how this might sound:

  MINDY: Mom, can I have a new dress?
  MOM: Have you got the money?
  MINDY: Not right now.
  MOM: I guess we'd better talk about some kind of loan.

- *An oversimplified answer:* Don't deal with any of the issues; just say "No." Mindy would learn that she must circumvent her parents' authority altogether. Instead of asking for help, she would use dishonesty, lying, and cheating to get what she wanted.

After we had generated this wide spectrum of potential solutions, Mindy's Mom chose the simplest answer. Once she had committed herself to a course of action, our Kiss was complete. I encouraged her to practice the Kiss approach every time she felt Ambushed, assuring her that the more she analyzed the situation *after* a confusing interaction, the more she would be able to do it *during* a confrontation.

When I finished my pep talk, I expected to see some sign of confidence. Instead of looking hopeful, she appeared befuddled.

"You're educated and experienced, and it took you almost two hours to do this Kiss thing. How in the world am I supposed to do it by myself?" she asked.

Realizing she needed more than another appointment, I shared with her the plight of another mother, whose daughter's behavior made Mindy's antics seem like child's play.

I told her of an eighteen-year-old girl who had been caught prostituting herself in a nearby town for twenty-five dollars a man. She smoked marijuana without restraint and complied with parental requests only when she felt like it.

This situation was so filled with disappointment, revenge, anger, and despair that I had had to apply the Kiss in stages. It was too late for moralizing, preaching, or mother-daughter "talks." Thus, the first stage concentrated on issues that should ensure success. The issues were the mother's love for her daughter, the daughter's love for her mother, and their mutual desire to see things change for the better. In short, I asked them if they wanted to relate to one another. (If I couldn't find positive results at this level, there was no need to proceed.)

The second stage was a natural consequence of the commitment they finally made to each other in Stage 1. In this stage, I forced the mother and daughter to choose two things they wanted most out of their relationship. The mother wanted her daughter to protect herself against an arrest and to have sexual relations with boyfriends only. The daughter wanted less complaining and more understanding from her mother.

The third and final stage was most difficult. They had to put their words into action. Each time they found cause to criticize each other, they were instructed to return to the agreement they had reached in stages 1 and 2. Slowly but surely, they focused their attention on the strength that comes with mutual respect and love. With less complaining and more understanding from her mother, the daughter found a boyfriend, smoked marijuana only in her bedroom, and even helped with the dishes a few nights a week. She still wasn't an angel, but she wasn't in jail, either.

After finishing the details of this three-staged, seven-month Kiss, I waited for evidence that Mindy's mom saw some light at the end of the tunnel.

Finally, she cracked a bit of a smile and said, "It's not going to be easy, but I'm willing to try. I'll need your help, especially at first."

After further assurances that hard work would eventually pay off, Mindy's mom started to leave, feeling some confidence that she could improve her Protective Parenting. Halfway out the door, she suddenly turned to me and, with a horrified look of regret, said, "Oh, my God, we still haven't solved the marijuana problem!"

I told her not to worry about it. I had neither the heart nor the energy to explain that she didn't have to do anything about the arrest. It was water under the bridge. Mindy's father had already applied the Kiss strategy by giving a lawyer five hundred dollars to "take care of things." It would only be a matter of time before a judge would rule in favor of releasing Mindy to the care and custody of her father. Mindy's Ambush would have succeeded.

As I closed the door and returned to my desk, I couldn't help but feel compassion for Mindy's mom. The lady clung to the thought that the only problem was that her daughter had smoked a joint and gotten caught. The Kiss would change that. Mother would realize that day-to-day little problems were gradually growing into big ones. Now that Mindy had been busted, her mom wanted me to make her guilt go away by magically changing Mindy from a reefer freak into a choirgirl. Impossible! Only Mom, with help from a Kiss, could make amends for the times she had been too busy, too tired, or too preoccupied to deal with the obnoxious behavior of a gentle warrior.

As parents, we often find it easy to ignore minor disruptions. Our personal needs limit the amount of time and effort we can give to our kids. Children's obnoxious behavior doesn't get our undivided attention until it reaches such aggravating proportions that someone else starts to complain (hopefully not a cop). By that time, the horse, so to speak, has left the barn.

Most parents are genuinely shocked when their child gets into trouble. Their typical reaction is something like, "Well, he's a normal kid . . . has a few problems like all kids . . . but, not *this!*" Years of daily contact blur their vision. They've gotten used to tolerating their child's deviance, never realizing that someday someone else won't. When another authority figure "busts" their kid, the protective wall of "It can't happen to me!" comes crashing down on top of them. They feel like hell but don't understand how it happened.

When parents finally face this experience, they generally fail to realize that the immediate problem is only the tip of the proverbial iceberg. Beneath the surface are countless bad habits of living that have produced innumerable Ambushes. Parents who wish to dive beneath the symptoms and search for the causes of trouble need a life-support system. So that children and parents don't suffocate each other, I advise the inclusion of the Kiss survival kit in the "hunting" gear. However, Kissing is not as easy as Mindy's example might suggest.

The major drawback in the Mindy story is that it tends to make Kissing a problem look easy. Most issues of Protective Parenting are much more difficult than a request for a new dress. Problems like dating, drinking, sexuality, and peer pressure are much harder to simplify because there are more issues involved.

Parents can feel comfortable Kissing their kids as long as they manage to stay somewhere between the two extremes, the Overkiss and the Underkiss.

The Overkiss

Parents tend to Overkiss when they pretend to help their child, but are really madder 'n hell at them, trying to get revenge, or don't give a damn about them in the first place. Overkissing parents either dump their frustrations on the kid without being concerned about the long-term effects or reduce the issues to absurdity in order to save time or make fun of their child. At this extreme, the Kiss approach becomes suffocating and engenders hate and revenge in the kid. Here are a few examples of the Overkiss:

> "What you think doesn't make a damn bit of difference."
> "Don't be a baby. You don't need a new toy."
> "Wanting to go steady is immoral and can only lead to sin."
> "What type of dumb talk is that? What type of bike your friend has doesn't make any difference to me."
> "I've had it with your disrespect! It's none of your business why I won't let you go out this weekend."

Name-calling and errant emotionalism dominate the Overkiss. Parents who oversimplify a problem are letting themselves in for hassles later on. Those who suspect that they might be Overkissing their children should remind themselves not to talk to their children about complicated situations when they're upset or too angry to be objective.

The Underkiss

For a variety of reasons, parents may find themselves in a situation where they are unable or unwilling to reduce the number of issues involved in a discussion. Mindy's mom was a perfect example. The stage is set for the Underkiss when a parent feels guilty about not being perfect.

Underkissing is usually the result of an Ambush and embodies the parent's reaction to being pressured. Here are some Ambush intros that often lead to Underkissing:

"Face it, Mother, you really don't understand me."
"C'mon, Dad, you know it's not that easy."
"You might deny it, but you just don't want me to have fun."
"You're not being fair. I thought we were all equal in this home."

These comments are word games, designed to skirt reality and get the parent on the defensive. If a parent is sucked into playing these games, Underkissing can result. Here's my way of responding to the above one-liners:

"I might be able to understand you better if you dealt with reality."
"It may not be easy, but I'm gonna make it simpler for both of us."
"I'd appreciate it if you didn't try to read my mind."
"What does fairness have to do with you using the car? I own the car, pay the unkeep, gas, and insurance, and you want to use it whenever the mood strikes you. That doesn't sound fair to me, either."

If parents can handle the opening salvo, the ever-dangerous back-against-the-wall position can be avoided. Shedding guilt and a fear of failure is the quickest way to initiate the Kiss. Once started, the simple approach reinforces itself and grows stronger.

However, the simple approach can be misapplied. Unless fully understood, the Kiss approach can be used to justify the extremes of child abuse/neglect and overindulgence/permissiveness. The Kiss should not be mistaken as an easy way for tired or unwilling parents to shun their responsibility.

In the final analysis, you who are parents (or someday might be) will forever be examining your child-rearing values, questioning and requestioning your motives and actions, as well as reviewing all the facets of your parenting life. Examination of your conscience will most likely go hand in hand with pacing the floor, wringing your hands, and wondering why you became parents in the first place.

You will probably ignore your children when they need you the most, and pay attention to them when they should be ignored. You will make mistakes of discipline and unintentionally teach them many of your bad habits. You may even spank or hit them in a completely inappropriate manner. Yet when push comes to shove, all these concerns and worries can be blown away with a breath of fresh air if you remember one simple thing: No matter how much complaining, moaning, hollering, or screaming you do, make sure you Kiss your child as often as you can.

6

Infancy to Two Years: Start Early

There's nothing so gentle as the softness of a baby's skin and a child's capacity to give love so freely. Conversely, there's nothing so warlike as the harshness of an infant's screaming for a clean diaper, a bottle of milk, or your undivided attention. Unbelievably, the gentle softness and warring harshness are wrapped in the same small bundle. Most parents are too busy enjoying the warmth and ignoring the harshness to realize that one of the two will dominate their child's life within a few years.

Parents who start early to socialize their child have fewer problems in later childhood and especially during adolescence. Many parents don't realize it, but socialization begins immediately after birth, with or without their help.

I begin my case analyses of Protective Parenting problems with children from infancy to two years because it is during these years that the capacity of all humans to be warriors is most readily apparent. It is also a time during which parents can begin the arduous task of shaping their children's gentleness into a dauntless spirit of determination that ultimately will provide them with the power and courage to banish their violence into oblivion.

Patience is a fundamental skill. Here are three boys who needed to wait awhile.

SITUATION: Billy's mom complained that her five-month-old son spent 90 percent of his waking time screaming, fussing, and crying. No toys seemed to interest him. The physician said that there was nothing physically wrong with him.

REACTION: No matter what she was doing, day or night, Billy's mom ran to pick her son up as soon as he started crying. Billy was spending most of his waking hours in his mother's arms.

By the time she sought my help, the mother was holding Billy while she cooked and did the laundry and mended. The situation had reached the point where Billy interrupted his mom and dad's attempts to make love, even in the middle of the night.

INTERPRETATION: While babies find screaming the most efficient way of gaining attention, Billy had to learn other methods. Teaching Billy that cooing, jabbering, or simply being quiet would get him attention was critical. If screaming remained Billy's major technique of attention-getting, he would have learned his first lesson in disruption.

In order to teach Billy other methods, Mom had to reduce her fear of doom and rid herself of guilt. She had to take care of her own needs as well as Billy's.

RECOMMENDATION: We first talked about her worry and fear of something horrible happening to Billy. She had heard that every time a baby screams, he wants something. She felt guilty about not giving the baby what he needed. Her physician told her that babies sometimes scream for attention and reassured her that she was taking good care of Billy's physical needs.

With her husband's help, we charted Billy's screaming and discovered that he would yell for twenty-five minutes before shutting up. Thus, when his physical needs were met, Mom had to wait twenty-six minutes before picking Billy up. This way, she reinforced Billy's being quiet and playing with the toys in his crib instead of screaming.

It didn't take Billy long to learn that, when he was not in physical pain, the best way to get Mom's attention was to coo and babble. Mom helped matters by stopping her work and spontaneously picking Billy up when he wasn't making a sound.

LESSON: Teach a child that screaming for attention results only in a sore throat.

SITUATION: During a marriage-counseling session, the wife complained that her husband was insensitive to her problem with their seven-month-old son, Peter. Peter's mom said that her husband didn't realize how "wild" Peter was becoming. She explained that Peter threw his food around the kitchen every time he was placed in his high chair to eat.

REACTION: The husband laughed as he told how his wife chased food all over the kitchen while yelling at Peter to "stop it this instant." Peter would laugh, wrinkle his nose, and look for something else to throw. Each time Mom gave him something to eat, Peter would shove part of it in his mouth and throw the rest in any convenient direction.

Mom would get more upset, and Peter would giggle loudly, obviously enjoying himself. Finally, Peter would get yanked out of the high chair and set firmly in the playpen.

Typically, Mom and Dad would then engage in a heated argument about Peter's right to throw food around the kitchen.

INTERPRETATION: Peter was having a ball, playing "watch-mommy-chase-the-food." He engaged in a simple Ambush. Mom said, "Eat," and he replied, "No, I want more play." By returning the food, Mother gave in to Peter's wishes. Peter had no reason to stop his game or to believe that what his mom was saying meant anything. Her behavior told the story.

This situation might have been exasperating to Mom and funny to Dad, but to Peter it was one of his first successful experiences in making the world conform to his wishes.

RECOMMENDATION: Peter needed to understand through *actions* that there was a limit to his game-playing. Not only did Mom have to change her chasing but I suggested that Dad stop laughing and start helping his wife.

The key to the change was that both parents had to realize that Mother's actions said "Yes," even though her words said "No." Peter was paying attention to the actions, not the words.

Once they understood this, it was simple for them to decide not to give Peter any food when he threw it. They were also to stop yelling because it was only music to accompany the tossing of food.

LESSON: One action is worth a thousand reprimands.

SITUATION: I was sitting in a luncheonette when the two-year-old in the booth next to mine decided he wanted more ketchup on his hot dog. He reached across his mother, knocking a French fry from her hand. She said, "No more ketchup, Brian." He kept reaching and struggling against his mother's arm, repeating over and over again, "More. More."

REACTION: Over the top of my magazine I saw Brian get "More"—more of his mom's hand than he had bargained for. Without warning, the lady hit Brian in the mouth so hard that his head snapped back against the wall. He screamed, started crying, and pounded the table. His mother returned his screams, threatening to send him to the car. Her final shot was nasty: "You'll get lost and I won't even care."

INTERPRETATION: There was little doubt that Brian's pushing and shoving was bothersome. His mother had rejected his bid for more ketchup, and he didn't accept it. At this young age, he was using his limited vocal powers to express his displeasure.

The mother would certainly have further trouble with Brian if she overreacted to his demands in the future. She set herself up for a revengeful Ambush by getting upset over a limp, skinny piece of meat by-products and a glob of red sauce.

RECOMMENDATION: When similar situations arise in my lecture-discussions, I usually take a strong stance in favor of employing the Kiss. In this particular situation, the lady would have been miles ahead if she had said to her son, "Brian, you can have all the ketchup you want *after* you calm down and wait quietly for one minute.''

LESSON: When push comes to shove, a child should be Kissed.

Brian, Billy, and Peter demonstrated the strength of a child's desire to seek complete satisfaction. Young children are willing to risk physical assault or fall over in exhaustion in pursuit of that famous four-letter word, *more!* Parental reaction to this pursuit will depend upon the situation. In Brian's case, the amount of ketchup he wanted was not worth his mother's getting so wrought up. While she could have taught him prudent use of a condiment, her lack of patience and potential explosiveness made her incapable of doing so. In this case, she should have let it go.

However, since demanding attention is crucial to the concerns of Protective Parenting, Billy's and Peter's mothers needed to overcome their internal tensions and deal with the screaming and food-throwing.

In the three situations described, Billy and Peter, more than Brian, needed to learn the meaning of a six-letter word, *enough!*

''Enough is enough'' applies across many situations. Jackie and Charlie stretched a good thing too far and demonstrated their need for protection.

SITUATION: I received a call one evening from my cousin during which she asked for some advice for a neighbor. From what she said, the two-year-old daughter of the lady was about to drive everyone in the neighborhood crazy, including my cousin.

The situation was somewhat complicated but boiled down to this. Two-year-old Jackie was ''cuter than a bug's ear,'' but her incessant talking made people forget about her big brown eyes and long curly hair and try to get rid of her. She would walk into a neighbor's garden without a stitch of clothing on and babble about ''Captin' Kan-a-rroo'' or interrupt a dinner party in order to be a ''Good naber like Misser Robgers said.'' My cousin said that Jackie had stood in front of her car for fifteen minutes that day repeating the same story about a ''munkee.''

REACTION: My cousin chuckled as she told me of Jackie's verbal plague, but the strain in her voice told me that she no longer thought it humorous. Jackie's mom was begging for help since her warnings and "No's" were being ignored by Jackie. Likewise, the neighbors thought Jackie was too cute and young for them to do anything about her disruption. Therefore, when Jackie babbled, all the neighbors clenched their teeth and were attentive and pleasant to her.

INTERPRETATION: Jackie was fascinated with the world of words. Being able to understand children's TV shows and use her memory to recall exciting visual and auditory experiences had enabled her to share in her mother's world. However, if she weren't taught some limits to her self-expression, her mouth might get her into trouble someday.

RECOMMENDATION: I told my cousin to explain my interpretation to her friend as best she could. Then I suggested that she help Jackie's mom arrange meetings with key people in the neighborhood for the purpose of systematically eliminating some of the hassle that Jackie presented.

The neighbors were to be told the following: "If Jackie's talking bothers you or if she talks too long, too loud, or at the wrong time, explain the circumstances and ask her to leave. Then ignore her. If she keeps talking, walk away and continue to ignore her. However, if you feel like talking with her sometimes, do so and then explain that you like to talk to her sometimes." I assured my cousin that if everyone were trained to act the same way, Jackie's obnoxiousness would soon subside. I cautioned her to make sure that Jackie had ample opportunity to talk without censure.

LESSON: If a two-year-old can drive the neighborhood crazy with words, think of what she will eventually do with actions.

SITUATION: I was ambling about a hardware store in search of a funny-shaped thingamajig to fit my strange-looking whatchamacallit so that the gismo in my office would work. I was examining a doohickey when I saw a woman checking out a pile of thingamabobs. Her son was standing up in the shopping cart trying to reach a string of multicolored lights. His eyes were as big as grapefruits, and his face was beaming with excitement and anticipation. The lady must have been more perplexed than I by the variety of goods because she didn't see that her son was about to topple out of the cart and onto the concrete floor.

REACTION: I didn't want to barge up to the lady with dire warnings (after all, maybe she knew something that I didn't). Yet I couldn't just walk away. So I dropped seven or eight doohickies on the floor, creating an appropriately loud, attention-getting racket. She wheeled around and grabbed her son and yelled, "Charlie, you sit down or Mommy will spank." With the help of her heavy hand, Charlie sat down. The lady turned back to her examination, and Charlie immediately resumed his pursuit of the lights.

This time, without my help, the lady caught Charlie as he was about to fall headfirst into a bin of bolts. She repeated her threat, turned away, and five seconds later, Charlie was back at it. This time he wasn't so lucky. I stood in awe as Charlie lunged for the lights, grabbed onto a supporting beam, and hung there as his mother screamed at him. She jerked him into her arms and beat his bottom soundly. She set a teary-eyed Charlie in the cart and strolled away.

INTERPRETATION: Charlie couldn't have been much more than eighteen months old. He was obviously alert and inquisitive. He had an impulse to get to the lights and didn't know how reaching for lights could cause a sore head. He probably had already had painful falls in his year and a half of life, but he wasn't experienced enough to connect leaning out of a cart with a nasty bump on the noggin. His mom needed to protect him from his impulsiveness and, simultaneously, teach him the rudiments of self-protection. Taking Charlie into her arms and hitting him just after he'd been frightened was an inappropriate use of spanking.

RECOMMENDATION: The best way Charlie's mother could have handled this situation would have been to prompt Charlie to ask for assistance (depending upon how well he could talk) in examining the lights ("You want to see the lights? Okay. Say, 'Let me see the lights, Mommy' "). Once he had complied, she could easily have lifted him to the lights, explained their function, and placed him back in the cart. Not only would he have been satisfied, he'd also have learned to think ahead enough to ask for help in doing something beyond his capabilities.

I was tempted to tell the lady to stroke Charlie at least three times within a few minutes to offset her ill-timed physical assault. However, I had my own problems trying to find the right doohickey.

LESSON: In a fascinating world that is often out of reach, children need to be lifted up, not beaten down.

Jackie's uncontrollable babbling to the neighbors and Charlie's unceasing grab for the bright lights both needed parental intervention. They had to be taught that there are limits to their exploration. Neither child was capable of understanding the consequences of those actions. Nor did either child know what he or she was doing—and had no business doing it. In all such cases, parents can help everyone involved if they take time to admit that their flesh and blood find it easy to get in over their heads. They must be willing to rise above parental pride and find innovative methods for harnessing the energies so readily apparent.

The next two warriors would convince anyone that the dinner table is the toughest battlefield of all.

SITUATION: I was sitting in the local burger palace trying to give myself a break when four kids and two mothers sat down in the booth next to mine. I decided to observe the tribe, knowing an Ambush couldn't be far off.

It wasn't five minutes before the youngest, about two, started the attack. It happened to be St. Patrick's Day, so when Mom brought the burger and fries to the table, she also set a strange-looking green milkshake in front of the young warrior. Her admonition was a prediction of things to come: "Now, Shane, be careful and don't spill."

No sooner had she set the food in front of her son than he proceeded to "do his thing." First, he tore the hamburger apart and plopped his hand in the ketchup and pretended that he was in his sandbox. Then he dashed a ketchuped French fry toward his sister as if he were a knight at the Round Table. He topped off his act by turning his green milkshake upside down on top of his head.

REACTION: As the green goop limped from his ears onto his fancy playsuit, Shane's mother let out three screams, two hollers, and a bellow. The other mother stood by with a smirk of self-satisfaction on her face as if to say, "Can't keep your kid in line, huh?"

INTERPRETATION: I returned to my office and talked to myself for at least twenty minutes, trying to decide why parents have so much trouble with kids at the burger palace. It finally dawned on me that Shane's mom had set herself up for a battle by placing her son in a situation in which having fun is ten times more important than eating. She had been indirectly Ambushed by advertising because TV commercials tell young children that being at the burger palace is more fun than the circus, a sandbox, or a new toy. This mother had to learn not to compete with a hero in clown's clothing, a spine-tingling burger-ler, and a fat but happy double-decked bun.

RECOMMENDATION: Shane's mom would have had a much better time if she had realized that taking her son to the burger palace is like going on an adventure to a new playground. She shouldn't have concentrated her effort on Shane's eating; he wasn't really interested in that. He wanted to share in the excitement promised by television. The lady could have bought Shane the same meal and let him enjoy himself. However, he should have worn different clothes—the same ones he wears in the sandbox.

LESSON: If a parent really wants a "break," take the kids to Grandma's and go out for a steak.

SITUATION: My wife and I invited a couple who were good friends of ours for dinner one evening. Lamenting the sudden defection of their babysitter, they showed up with their two-year-old daughter, Kristen.

Five minutes after sitting down to dinner, Kristen began playing with her food. She jabbed the peas with her knife, pushed the chicken around her plate as if it were a motorboat, and stuck a spoonful of mashed potatoes in her drinking water.

Halfway through the meal, Kristen was wandering around the dining room, seeing how many fingerprints she could leave on the furniture and wallpaper.

REACTION: In addition to embarrassment, our friends were obviously displeased with their daughter. They tried to coax, cajole, and order her to behave. They threatened reprisals and promised treats if she would be a "good girl."

In an act of desperation, the mother grabbed Kristen and took her into another room, where I could hear some spanking and crying. Kristen reappeared with tears in her eyes and sat quietly at the table. About ten minutes later, her hand edged back toward her plate and she began to play with her food again. This time, we were finished eating and left the table. Kristen joined us after a cleaning session in the bathroom.

INTERPRETATION: Kristen was learning the rudiments of several behaviors that often lead to disruption. She was impulsive, ignored warnings, did not follow rules, and exhibited disrespect toward parental wishes.

This situation, in itself, was not serious. However, it did represent a classical example of how children learn, at an early age, the basics of deviance, which often compound themselves into social disruption and trouble.

RECOMMENDATION: I did not feel comfortable approaching the man or his wife about Kristen's deviance. If I had, I might have suggested that a special effort could be made to entice Kristen to exhibit appropriate table manners. For example, Mom might have said, "Kristen, see if you can eat the way Mommy does. You don't want to spill food on your new dress, do you?"

For those kids who say "Yes" to the last question, parents may have to take a firm stance and remove the child to another room or place a cookie on the table and say, "Once you've eaten, you can have the cookie."

LESSON: The stairway to trouble is steep; most kids take their first step up when they learn to walk.

The dinner table is usually the first major battleground of parents and their gentle warriors. Kristen and Shane demonstrated how kids find the jugular vein of young parents' authority. Their food abuse and poor table manners strike at the heart of such family values as cleanliness, wastefulness, and social manners. The tension of the two situations was heightened by the fact that eating in public and with friends is usually a mechanism by which parents want to show off the product of their work.

The best way for parents to survive food Ambushes is to be less concerned about how their child looks when he or she eats and to concentrate their efforts on the legitimacy of and compliance to their requests. To a child, eating can be an exciting time, epecially when reluctance to eat or fussing with their food causes Mom and Dad to lose control of themselves.

The next three kids literally walked or ran into trouble.

SITUATION: During a group discussion I was having with parents, a woman described a problem she was having with her year-old daughter, Tanya. It seemed that the little girl loved to walk and was very interested in exploring the places that her newfound ability would take her.

However, in her parents' home were many fixtures, figurines, and other expensive decorations, all of which Tanya wanted to play with. If not watched constantly, Tanya would pull something off a shelf, upset a lamp, or knock over a figurine. Her mother was getting worried about the imminent destruction of the interior of her home.

REACTION: A typical encounter between mother and daughter saw Tanya move toward something of value, and, as she came within a few feet of the object, Mother would yell, "No!" This was followed by Mother's running to Tanya, jerking her into the air, and setting her in a "safe" corner of the room. Tanya would soon abandon her toys in search of more exciting adventures, moving once again toward a valued object. In the same semihysterical manner, her mother would interrupt Tanya's maneuvers, returning her to the toy corner. This activity was repeated several times until, finally, Tanya was jerked roughly off the floor and placed in the playpen.

INTERPRETATION: Tanya was obviously a bright, inquisitive child, wishing to explore the strange new things in her world. She not only received pleasure from searching but also was delighted to play a rather novel game with Mommy. She wasn't about to take "No" for an answer, especially when "No" really meant "Not now." However, Tanya's mother was hypersensitive to the value of her decorations and was not dealing with her daughter's need to explore.

RECOMMENDATION: I suggested that the mother use the following procedure to teach her daughter safe exploration of new things. When Tanya approached an object, she was to join her, take her hand, and, as she reached out, allow her to touch the object gently. Meanwhile, Mom was to explain what Tanya was touching and why she should only touch it. Tanya was to be helped in a similar manner to approach everything in the house, accompanied by the warning that some things should only be touched, while other things can bring pleasure and enjoyment during play.

With such a young child, a few things can be "off limits" (stove, heater and so on), some things can be touched, and many things can be played with. Tanya would learn to discriminate among looking at, touching, and playing with things in her world.

LESSON: If everything in a home is "to be seen, not touched," then the home is actually a house where children don't belong.

SITUATION: Twenty-two-month-old Mike's father brought up an interesting situation during the course of a parent conference. He noted that his son, a dauntless explorer, was not afraid to walk down any hall, into any building, or up any staircase. Unfortunately, during his adventures, Mike constantly bumped into walls and other large obstacles.

REACTION: The father explained that Mike would fall down, usually bruise a part of his leg, cry a little, and move on. His father would say something like, "See what happens when you're not careful? Now, don't do that anymore." However, within a few minutes, Mike would run into another barrier, hurt himself, and receive another parental warning. Mike's father ended his story by saying, "Mike will eventually learn to watch where he's going."

INTERPRETATION: I quizzed the father at length and found out that Mike ran into things because he was too busy gawking at the world to watch where he was going. I cautioned him to take the situation a bit more seriously. At some point, Mike must learn to pay attention to the little things, or someday he might stumble into trouble and wonder how it ever happened.

RECOMMENDATION: I suggested that Mike's father simply take Mike by the hand and walk about, looking at the beautiful sights. In this way, Mike could continue to explore but would also be subconsciously learning psychomotor coordination. The better his coordination became, the more his father could withdraw his hand.

LESSON: Parents sometime make a molehill out of a mountain.

SITUATION: Eighteen-month-old Chris's mom brought up a fundamental issue in Protective Parenting. She noted that Chris loved to wander around outside, but if she didn't watch him constantly, he would run recklessly into the street.

REACTION: Whenever this happened, Mom would run into the street, screaming all the way, and jerk Chris back into the yard. Once in a while she would give him a light pat on the rear as she set him on the ground. However, as soon as her back was turned, Chris would make a beeline for the street. Finally, she would have to take him inside. She was so exasperated by Chris's antics that she jokingly said, "I think I'll put him on a chain like the dog."

INTERPRETATION: Chris had found a simple game of Ambush that not only proved exciting to him but also drove his mommy crazy. He loved the game of "watch-mommy-chase-me," not realizing it could be deadly. It was clear that Chris had to be taught that running into the street without looking for cars or other dangers was absolutely prohibited. This case called for the prudent use of physical punishment.

RECOMMENDATION: I outlined the following program for shaping Chris's walking outside. Mom was to take Chris for a walk three or four times per day, walking close to his side down the sidewalk near the street. She was to carry a flexible, thin piece of tree branch (like a weeping willow branch). Chris was to be allowed to wander on the grass, but as soon as he began to step off the grass and onto the curb or street, she was to tap him lightly on the rear with the branch—hard enough so that he felt it but not hard enough so that he yelled. Each time she struck him, she was to say, "No, stay on the grass."

She was to do this for a couple of blocks and then approach a crosswalk. Then, dropping the stick and grabbing his hand, she was to say, "We're going to cross the street. But first, we must look for cars. Do you see any cars?" After engaging in this kind of limited participation, Mom and Chris were to cross the street and do something that was fun (like playing on the park swing or getting an ice cream cone). Then the entire process was to be repeated on the other side of the street. Eventually, Mom would be able to walk with Chris and use the verbal command "No" instead of the branch.

LESSON: Punishment does not have to be abusive or harsh to be effective.

Mike, Tanya, and Chris had their own individual ways of stumbling into trouble. They all could put one foot in front of the other, but they had not yet mastered the "psycho" part of psychomotor coordination. They needed help in developing their ability to think while they were walking. Their plight reminded me of a sixteen-year-old boy named Mark who had never learned to think ahead of where his feet took him. Mark liked to steal cars. After careful assessment, I discovered that Mark always stole cars from the same lot. Simply by teaching Mark to walk home using a different route, I significantly reduced his temptation to steal. I used this success to build other positive traits and helped Mark work himself out of trouble.

The last two cases suggest that parents use extreme caution before hitting children.

SITUATION: I was looking for shoes in a large department store when a mother and her two daughters stopped in the aisle across from me. While the mother and older daughter looked at shoes, the younger girl, who was about eighteen months old, started whining about wanting some candy. When the mother told the little one to wait, the girl stuck her tongue out at her.

REACTION: Without one word, the mother slapped the girl across the mouth and screeched, "Don't you ever stick your tongue out at me or you'll get more of the same." She backed off briefly and then added, "If you don't like to shop with Mommy, you can go sit in the car."

INTERPRETATION: The mother overreacted to a rather typical act of defiance. Her reaction was an example of "overkill," in which grossly exaggerated physical punishment is used to handle a mild form of deviance. The threat to make the child sit in the car was empty and will undermine the mother's authority in the future.

RECOMMENDATION: The mother could simply have ignored the defiant gesture. She also could have explained to her daughter what she was looking for and asked for her help, little as it might be. If the daughter's defiance escalated beyond tolerance, removal from the store would be warranted.

LESSON: Physical punishment and idle threats make a parent feel better but rarely help a child.

SITUATION: Doug's parents consulted me regarding their two-year-old son's defiance. To make a long story short, Doug rejected almost every request made by his parents. He usually refused to eat, go to bed, dress himself, or stop a disruptive behavior. In response to his parent's request, he would say "No," "No, I won't," or "Not me."

REACTION: Doug's parents, believing that they should take immediate, concrete action, employed such punishment techniques as spanking, slapping his mouth, standing him in a corner, sitting him in a chair, and yelling at him. None of these punishments appeared to work since Doug's defiance seemed to be growing in frequency and intensity. They wanted a new punishment technique that would prove effective.

INTERPRETATION: These parents were overreacting to Doug's defiance. In doing so, they forgot to try to use words to shape Doug's compliance. Furthermore, they were giving him so much attention because of his negative responses that he had no good reason to change. Their punishments far outweighed their rewards, and he was learning that saying "No"—the primary technique of deviance—was the key to receiving attention from authority figures.

If this trend were not reversed, Doug's "No" would soon turn active and he would initiate disruptive behavior.

RECOMMENDATION: I established a simple program in which sensitive issues (eating, sleeping, dressing) were introduced by asking questions that ensured a "Yes" answer but included compliance with previously problematic situations. The list of questions included such things as:

"Do you want ice cream after you finish your beans?"
"Do you want me to read you a story before you go to sleep?"
"Do you want me to get you a popsicle while you get dressed?"

Compliance with certain problematic situations automatically brought a goodie. We ensured that saying "No" was completely unprofitable by introducing a program whereby any "No" was absolutely ignored.

Doug's parents quickly saw that their son was easily manipulated into a positive frame of mind once he received ample opportunity to respond positively.

LESSON: If punishment is the parents' first choice, a kid will make them wish it had been their last.

Punishing a child means doing something painful to the youngster. While there are times when punishment is an effective tool, parents should not be too hasty about inflicting pain on their child, especially in response to simple acts of defiance.

There were many positive things the parents involved in the two cases outlined above could have done before inflicting pain on their kids. Explaining the situation, removal, using an incentive, and ignoring come to mind. The creative genius of parental concern can generate countless strategies. Hitting a kid should remain last on any list of potential disciplinary actions.

Parents must be willing to tolerate some signs of defiance.

Kids will always test limits, not the least of which is parental patience. Parents are asking for trouble if they communicate to the child that limits are so rigid that physical gestures and verbal defiance immediately result in physical punishment.

Some professionals don't help parents learn patience. In *Dare to Discipline,* Dr. J. Dobson gives parents a free pass to punishment when he says, "When a youngster tries this kind of stiff-necked rebellion ('I will not,' or 'You shut up!') you had better take it out of him, and pain is a marvelous purifier." [1] Dr. Dobson fails to note that inflicting pain on others is the hallmark of criminal activity and there's no greater teacher than experience.

As kids begin their journey through life, physical punishment should be kept as far from their path as possible. If parents start early with realistic expectancies and constructive follow-through, spanking and hitting can fade from the punishment scene by a kid's fifth birthday. The slow but sure construction of a pathway of rational rewards and well-timed penalties will strengthen reason and nourish self-control. If this route is mapped out by age two, kids will be well on their way to the most important destination of their whole life: self-protection.

1. J. Dobson, *Dare to Discipline* (Wheaton, Ill.: Tyndale House Publishers, 1970), p. 27.

7

Three and Four: Testing the Limits

If you tell a three-year-old he can have two lollipops, he'll grab six; tell him he can play in the yard, and he'll end up two blocks away; remind him to eat his beans, and he'll scatter them all over the floor; tell him you love him, and he might say, "I hate you!" While these acts are definitely disrespectful and irresponsible, they are actually the result of a kid's exploring the unknown.

When a parent makes a request, dictates a rule, gives an order, or issues an ultimatum, a warning boundary is established. This boundary supposedly separates "safe" from "dangerous" territory. Protective Parents must set these boundaries if they are ever to help their child learn the difference between deviance and creative conformity. However, it is good to remember that setting such boundaries is not unlike telling a mountain climber that he or she is not permitted to scale a newly discovered peak.

At or near the age of three, children begin a more active investigation into the who, what, when, and where of their world.

While their ignorance caused them to stumble into trouble a year before, they now fall in because of their inquisitiveness. "No's" and "Don't's" represent a challenge to investigate what lies beyond. The motivation for this search seems to be a combination of many things, one of which is peering into a hidden world of danger, and the second of which is a voice of pride that says, "I can survive when everyone else can't."

In applied child psychology, this activity is usually called "testing the limits." It's a phenomenon that begins early, grows steadily during childhood, and flourishes during adolescence. If a child receives careful instruction and the adolescent learns to define his or her own boundaries, then testing the limits will follow a socially acceptable pattern during adulthood.

An adequate explanation of this lifelong activity is yet to be made. When it is, it will emerge from some complicated biosocial, physioecological, and psychophilosophical analysis of man's behavior. However, no matter what the verdict, it will never fully explain that mysterious inner force that defies reason and drives me back to the hors d'oeuvre table, saying, "If two felt good, four should be dynamite!"

The first two cases tell a story that never seems to end.

SITUATION: A typical socialization problem was outlined during a group discussion. Three-year-old Stella and her favorite playmate, three-year-old Tracey, get together when their mothers have coffee in the morning. Stella is a little more aggressive and regularly takes Tracey's toys away from her and starts playing with them. Tracey immediately screams, interrupting the mothers' Kaffeeklatsch.

REACTION: Tracey's mother yells, "Play with something else and let Stella have that." Stella's mother, not wishing to be outdone, demands, "Give that back to her and don't take it anymore." After this, the two kids usually resume playing and the mothers return to their coffee. Within a few minutes, the entire scene is replayed.

INTERPRETATION: This was not a serious situation as outlined to me. However, it is one to which the mothers should pay more attention. There will always be a difference in assertiveness among kids, and when they get together, there will be conflict.

This is a situation in which Stella and Tracey could be taught the rudiments of the most important of the Three R's: reciprocity. They should realize that compromise means rewards for both of them, while fighting results in the loss of mutually desired objects.

RECOMMENDATION: The easiest way for these mothers to deal with this bickering would be to employ a clear-cut *win-lose* proposition. That is, the girls should be told, "If you play together quietly and share your toys, you can both have some ice cream. If you continue to fight, you'll lose the toy you're fighting over."

The limits should be very clear, and, of course, the rewards or penalties must be delivered as promised.

LESSON: Cooperative play is a giant step toward reciprocity.

SITUATION: I was asked to consult with Leon's parents by the director of the day-care center where the four-year-old child attended three hours of pre-kindergarten activities. The problem appeared to be rather serious. Each time Leon was asked to do something, he broke down and sobbed uncontrollably. Situations such as snack time, rest period, and structured activity (coloring) stimulated the crying. Leon didn't make much noise when he wept; rather, giant tears streamed down his face as he sat motionless in his seat.

REACTION: In an effort to make an accurate assessment, I decided to observe the problem myself. Sure enough, as soon as the teacher said, "Let's eat our Twinkies," Leon started crying. He was a sorry sight. In fact, he looked so pitiful that the teacher held him on her lap, the aide whispered words of endearment to him, and the other kids offered him bites of their Twinkies.

Leon gradually stopped crying and started munching soggy Twinkies. Although no one else paid much attention, I observed that Leon played happily and appropriately when no one structured his time.

INTERPRETATION: Leon had obviously found a very effective means of avoiding the authoritative demands inherent in structured activity. He had also discovered a potentially disastrous tactic for reacting to school.

Conversations with his mother revealed that she rarely made situational demands on Leon, and, when she did, similar crying occurred. Leon's father and mother were separated, so this Ambush was further complicated by feminine overprotection and attempts to compensate Leon for the "loss" of his father and not enough contact with male authority figures.

RECOMMENDATION: I suggested that Leon be ignored when he sobbed and that he not be given treats, privileges, or special attention when he cried. Coupled with this was to be all sorts of recognition when he played appropriately. I also gave the teacher the name of a college professor who gave a course in child psychology in which students were expected to gain some on-the-job experience. It was quite possible that a male student could be assigned as a special aide/Big Brother for Leon.

Finally, I instructed the boy's mother to carry out a similar program at home. Also, I suggested that she seek out counseling for herself so that Leon wouldn't have such a handle on her heart.

LESSON: Don't judge a problem by the size of the tears.

Stella, Leon, and Tracey found unique ways of reacting to the pressures of new social situations. Stella grabbed, Leon sobbed, and Tracey screamed. Warnings and sympathy didn't deter them from their behavior. The respective authorities should have implemented disciplinary measures that coupled words with actions in defining the limits of the situations.

These kids needed to learn a lesson in losing. Stella and Tracey wanted a toy, while Leon craved attention. All three had to be taught that their behavior went beyond acceptable limits and would cost them the very thing they were working so hard to get. Parents should not be afraid to take the necessary tough line in taking things (including attention) away from their children in order to teach them the negative side effects of raising too much hell.

The next three cases demonstrate that parents have to make sure they have a kid's attention before they implement protective measures.

SITUATION: The mother of a four-year-old boy was referred to me by her family physician. Four-year-old Jimmy was the only child of a business executive and his college-educated wife. Like most children in similar situations, Jimmy had every new toy available, attended most G-rated movies, slept in his own double bed, and ate what he wanted.

Jimmy usually complied with requests made of him. However, whenever he failed to comply, his mother would yell at him. When this or similar conflicts over noncompliance arose, Jimmy would make a beeline for his bedroom and start banging his head against the wall.

REACTION: Jimmy's mother had become so sensitive to the situation that as soon as he dashed for his room she ran after him and struggled with him to keep his head from hitting the wall. She would pull him into the living room and talk gently about "not doing such naughty things." As soon as she thought everything had calmed down, she'd return to her work. The moment her back was turned, Jimmy would let out a war whoop, head for his room at a gallop, and start banging his head on the wall. This chain reaction would continue until his mother took Jimmy outside to play or to the store for a treat.

INTERPRETATION: Jimmy was punishing his mother for yelling. He had found a tactic that was creative, effective, and highly dangerous. Further examination revealed that Jimmy didn't pull this stunt with his father. Besides, he never had time to hit his head against the wall more than three or four times before his mother stopped him.

There were several things that had to be done to settle this problem. Most important, Jimmy had to learn that extreme forms of disruption don't halt the unpleasant aspects of life. Mom was boss, and even though he didn't like some of the things she did, head-banging was no way to react. If Mother didn't take immediate action, there would be no limit to his disruptive potential.

RECOMMENDATION: I set up a multipurpose program for Jimmy's family. The list I gave to his mother looked something like this:

1. Find other alternatives to yelling.
2. Buy a small football helmet.
3. Whenever Jimmy starts to bang his head, *walk* to his room, allowing him time to experience how a sore head feels.
4. Gently but firmly place the helmet on his head and then tell him that he may continue to hit his head against the wall if he wishes.
5. Stand and watch him, not saying a word.
6. When he stops, ask him if he's through. If he says "Yes," remove the helmet and talk with him about cooperation and helping each other with problems. If he says "No," say "Okay" and leave, allowing him to bang his head until he gets tired and quits.
7. Make a special effort to say something nice to Jimmy when he complies with a request without fussing.
8. Avoid speaking to Jimmy about his head-banging.

FOLLOW-UP: Jimmy's head-banging increased a little the first few days, then slowly decreased over the following three weeks. After a month, it ceased altogether. Thus, the helmet idea worked like a charm on this Ambush, except that Jimmy's hard head and persistence caused a large hole in the wall next to his bed—a small price to pay for parental victory, however.

LESSON: Parents must use their heads when a child abuses his.

SITUATION: Vickie, a neighborhood cutie, had a propensity for getting lost. It didn't make any difference where she was, she still could get lost. Her father told me that she had gotten lost in church, in a department store, in a supermarket, and in a neighbor's basement. Recently, she had been lost for ten minutes in a funeral parlor.

REACTION: Vickie's brother usually brought the situation to his mom's attention by saying, "Vickie is lost again, Mom." Mother would immediately stop what she was doing and begin a frantic search for Vickie. When found, Vickie would be told, "Stay put and don't do that again." But as soon as Mom's back was turned, Vickie would wander off again.

INTERPRETATION: Vickie was demonstrating her detachment from the physical boundaries imposed by her mother. Not only was she Ambushing her mom by disregarding the "No," she was also having a lot of fun exploring the new and exciting things in her world. If not checked, Vickie could be well on her way to deviance.

RECOMMENDATION: Vickie's mother was to make a special effort to accompany her daughter on some of her searching expeditions. Active involvement in shopping would help, as would some type of penalty imposed on Vickie when she left without permission (for example, having to stay indoors, not being allowed treats, or not being allowed to play with a friend).

LESSON: If parents lose sight of their kids, the kids may get lost forever.

SITUATION: Across the street from my office is a restaurant with the best pizza in town. They also have old-time movies, which prove a delight to my son as well as to other children.

I had taken an early dinner break one evening, and the silence of the dining room was shattered by the explosive entry of a four-year-old boy, followed closely by his young parents. He ran to the table directly in front of the movie screen and demanded, "We're sitting ober here. Ober here!" His parents, attempting firmness, said, "No, Jeff, that's too close."

REACTION: Jeff continued his demands, increasing the intensity of his screams and the level of his agitation. His antics centered on wanting to sit "ober here." He started crying, manifesting a full-blown temper tantrum. His parents appeared stunned as they moved toward the front table. They sat down with Jeff, and I heard them tell him, "If you're quiet, maybe we'll stay here." In fact, they stayed and watched the movie with upturned heads as Jeff ran around the dining room raising more hell.

INTERPRETATION: It was obvious that Jeff had no respect for his parents' wishes. He tied them into knots with his temper tantrum and forced them into bribing him to be quiet.

This situation is repeated millions of times each day in homes and places of business. This and similar examples of bribery are the most frequent errors that parents make. They lead to a multitude of disruptive behaviors. Reversing a bribe and making it a constructive disciplinary measure is a fairly simple maneuver.

RECOMMENDATION: Jeff's parents could have taken a simple approach. They should have said to their son, ''Jeff, if you continue screaming, we're leaving. If you calm down, we'll stay.'' Of course, they would have to follow through.

This type of choice would probably ensure Jeff's conforming to their expectancies instead of their giving in to his demands. By withdrawing their objection in order to secure Jeff's silence, his parents were bribing him to be quiet.

LESSON: To a four-year-old, raising hell is sometimes more important than ice cream and pizza.

Jimmy, Vickie, and Jeff were wreaking havoc with parental authority. They paid no attention to the limits imposed by their parents. Each of them demonstrated one of the Three D's of deviance: Jimmy was extremely disruptive, Jeff disrespectful, and Vickie detached. Preventive discipline was in order.

I never cease to be amazed at how difficult it is for some parents to get tough without becoming brutal. Parental compassion is a marvelous trait, and many parents need more of it. But compassion dominated by sympathy becomes overprotection. And misplaced compassion that prevents firmness spawns eventual disaster.

Jimmy, Jeff, and Vickie needed to control their demands. Danny and Sherry needed to control their mouths.

SITUATION: An embarrassed mother confided to me that she couldn't control the ''naughty talk'' of her three-year-old son, Danny. At various times throughout the day, Danny would sit in a corner of the kitchen and repeat over and over again, "Shit, damn, hell, son of bitch."

REACTION: The mother said she had tried everything. She had slapped him, washed his mouth out with soap, spanked him, set him in a corner, taken his toys away, and yelled at him. She was at her wits' end.

INTERPRETATION: As all children will do when they first learn to talk well, Danny was experimenting with words. From my observation, it seemed that Danny received a lot of attention when he recited his litany of obscenities and was usually ignored when he played quietly.

Danny was not making moral judgments about his language; his mother was doing that. She was getting upset about what she thought was immoral language. Mother's uptight attitude made her an easy target for an Ambush.

RECOMMENDATION: As soon as Danny began his profanity, his mother was to walk away and not return until Danny had started doing something more appropriate. She was to avoid any reference to "naughty words." Danny was too young to understand what she was talking about.

LESSON: Parents should not teach their children that certain words have magical powers.

SITUATION: Four-year-old Sherry was a very shy little girl. She had a sister ten years older and therefore was being raised as an "only" child. The problem, as presented by Sherry's mother, was that Sherry was often observed talking to herself.

She carried on two- or three-party conversations, using her dolls to represent other people. In addition, she often made comments as if to monitor her own behavior. For example, she would say, "You're a good girl, Sherry," or, "You sure are cute, Sherry."

REACTION: Sherry's mother was quite upset about the situation. She was unable to make Sherry stop talking to herself. She tried to shame her daughter by saying, "Only babies talk to themselves," and threaten her by demanding, "Stop that or I'll spank."

When these tactics didn't work (in fact, Sherry would go to the closet in order to play), the mother wrote the newspaper and talked to her minister in an attempt to make her daughter "normal." The result of all this was that the mother was getting more tense around Sherry, convinced that the problem was severe.

INTERPRETATION: Children Sherry's age, especially if they are bright and creative, have many innovative and heartwarming ways of examining their place in the world. When there is no playmate readily available, children like Sherry will simply create a friend or two through role-playing.

Sherry's capacity to explore different roles will fluctuate for several years and finally stabilize later on in elementary school. The critical issue here was that her mother needed to stop paying so much attention to Sherry when she was talking to herself.

RECOMMENDATION: I suggested that Mom talk with someone about her own self-confidence, especially as it applied to motherhood. Most important, she was to stop trying to prevent Sherry from talking to herself. Mother was to play with Sherry if time allowed; even better, she might try to find a friend with whom Sherry could play regularly.

LESSON: Talking to yourself is not only fun but also psychologically healthy since, in a world filled with poor communication, misunderstandings, and lack of empathy, you are probably the only one who really understands you.

Danny and Sherry were both exploring the wonderful world of words. They were on the verge of learning that words hold magical powers. They saw that a certain group of words caused their mothers to give them special attention. Punishment was self-defeating in that it would eventually force the behavior to disappear from the home, only to be seen again in another setting.

Too many kids like Danny and Sherry grow into adulthood believing that saying it makes it so. I've seen many nineteen- and twenty-year-olds who are shocked to learn that things don't happen when they mouth the words of good intentions.

I recently visited a sixteen-year-old jailed on auto-theft

charges. He was dumbfounded as he tried to reconcile the disparity between his strong desire to lead a straight life and the fact that he had been caught red-handed behind the wheel of a stolen car. This kid, like so many others, had a misguided faith in the power of words. He honestly believed that actions flowed automatically from words. No one had taught him that there is no such thing as "word magic." He had yet to realize that his will to *do* was the key to making his actions speak louder than his words.

The next two warriors showed how the mouth can be used to Ambush parents without uttering a sound.

SITUATION: Three-year-old Diane's parents were quite affluent, highly conscientious, and spent a lot of time developing and maintaining social contacts. The problem, which came to my attention during a garden party, was that Diane liked to spit on furniture, rugs, lamps, statues, and any other interior decoration within range.

REACTION: According to her father, her mother usually caught Diane in the act of spitting and slapped her mouth, telling her never to do it again. However, Diane was becoming adept at avoiding getting caught and driving the family crazy. When Mother and Father found evidence of her clandestine Ambush and confronted her with it, Diane innocently denied any knowledge of the misdeed.

INTERPRETATION: Using her mouth in an inappropriate manner, Diane was seeking revenge on her parents. She was making fun of and expressing anger toward the sterile environment generated by parental preoccupation with material goods.

The prim and proper furnishings and the "don't-touch" attitude of her parents were targets for Diane's Ambush. It was quite possible that she was getting the idea that the material goods in her house were more important than she; hence, the revenge. Diane's disrespect had to be handled differently, or else she was heading for trouble.

RECOMMENDATION: The slapping had to cease immediately. Because the mother was quite nervous, it was necessary that she seek some help with her own problems. I recommended a colleague who might possibly give her a tranquilizer to see her through the tense time.

I then suggested that she spend a lot of extra time with her daughter doing things that were fun. Within this atmosphere, Diane's spitting could be punished by setting her in a corner for five minutes each time she did it. I also recommended that Diane have more access to furnishings upon which she could play.

LESSON: Parents must respect their kids more than any material object; if they don't, kids will use materialistic means to make them wish they had.

SITUATION: The mother of four-year-old Virginia brought up a novel problem during a discussion session. She complained that every time her daughter sat on her lap, she was the victim of a nasty bite.

REACTION: Each time this happened, Mom would slap Virginia's mouth. Virginia would then begin to cry, wiggle away from her, and run to her room. Mom would follow, feeling guilty. She would then make up to Virginia with kind words and special treats.

INTERPRETATION: Virginia was clearly violating the limits of appropriate use of her mouth. While it was not a serious problem, it did call for remedial steps.

Virginia's mom was the victim of a two-pronged attack. Not only did she have tooth marks on her arm from a "playful" daughter; she also had the scars of a guilt-provoking Ambush on her conscience. She needed a double-edged solution.

RECOMMENDATION: One-half of the solution involved judicious use of physical punishment. I suggested that Virginia's mother gently but firmly return the gesture each time Virginia bit her. Mom's bite was to be just hard enough to demonstrate to her daughter what it feels like to get bitten. When Virginia cried and ran off, Mom was to take a few seconds to explain the situation and then ignore her.

The other half of the solution had to be implemented before any biting occurred, if possible. I told the mother to play a new game with her daughter. This game involved kissing instead of biting. As soon as Virginia sat on her lap, the mother was to begin the game by saying, "See if you can kiss two of my fingers." The interchange of kissing a preselected number of fingers was to go on until Virginia could sit on her mother's lap and make love, not war.

LESSON: Limits must be imposed on "bad-mouthing" others.

It was understandable that Diane and Virginia explored other uses of the marvelous tool right below their noses. After all, their mouths had been an instrument of pleasure for over three years. Sucking had brought nourishment, cooing had resulted in love and attention, eating meant satisfaction, and kissing and talking brought a variety of rewards. How were they to know that spitting and biting were beyond the limits of acceptability? Certainly their parents' behavior didn't help matters. In fact, parental reaction suggested that spitting and biting were excellent attention-getters.

These two case histories represent situations in which a clear line can be drawn between right and wrong. For example, making a distinction between the appropriateness of kissing and the inappropriateness of biting will prove beneficial in preparing the child for the more complicated discriminations necessary for adolescent survival.

The last two cases only scratch the surface of the hundreds of ways three- and four-year-olds can test limits.

SITUATION: I was standing in the checkout line of my favorite discount store when I witnessed an Ambush. A girl who appeared to be about three years old was crouched beneath her mom's shopping cart, riding atop the frame, the same place where I was toting twenty pounds of charcoal briquettes.

She had a package of red licorice in her hand, and each time we took a step toward the cashier, she ripped another piece of the wrapping from the candy with her teeth. Somewhere around the third or fourth rip, her mother, bending over to check her out, caught her in the act.

REACTION: The mother immediately assaulted the kid with harsh words: "Krissy, you cut that out. Give me that candy right now. You know better than to use your teeth like that. Anyhow, you never asked for that candy. Now *give it to me!*"

The girl held the candy close to her chest and curled up like a kitten with a ball of string. The mother continued her demands, but the girl never moved.

The mother's attack was temporarily interrupted by another step forward in line. The entire process was repeated each time there was a lull in our movement toward the register. Finally, Krissy got the package open and started nibbling away. As the mother reached the checkout point, she bent over, yelled another threat, turned to me with a "Well, what can I do?" look, and said to the cashier, "My little girl has a package of candy I have to pay for."

INTERPRETATION: This mother could be heading for big problems, and her daughter for trouble. Krissy's candy-snitching was the foundation upon which a superstructure of social deviance could be built.

This type of evasiveness is particularly distressing because it represents lying through action. It demonstrates how kids learn the benefits of hiding the truth without the use of words. This type of sneakiness, if unchecked, can lead to lying with words.

RECOMMENDATION: Several different things could have been done with Krissy. The mother could have taken the candy from her daughter when she first discovered the theft and returned it to the proper place, saying, "If you steal, you won't get any."

The mother could have taken the candy and said, "You can't have the candy until tomorrow because you took it without asking."

My favorite suggestion for situations like this takes more time and effort but has a higher payoff. The mother, when spotting the candy, could have said, "You want the candy?" Once she had received an affirmative answer, she could have said, "Then you'll have to pay for it by helping Mommy carry out the groceries." The payment would have been easy enough for Krissy to manage (carrying a small bag of vegetables, for example).

No matter which suggestion she followed, the mother should have talked with Krissy about the negative side effects of trying to take things without permission. She could have ended this encounter by saying, "You don't have to be sneaky around Mommy."

LESSON: Honesty may not always be the best policy, but every kid should know how it's done.

SITUATION: I was drinking coffee at the corner doughnut shop when my neighbor and his three-year-old daughter sat down at my table. She was carrying a giant chocolate candy bar and several lollipops. I had always been enraptured by Renee's beauty, this day being no exception. Long, flowing brown hair, a soft smile, and big brown eyes gave Renee the power to melt the coldest heart.

As soon as her Coke was set down before her, she began to open the candy bar. Her father said, "Renee, I told you that you couldn't eat that until after dinner."

REACTION: Renee pulled an Ambush that was absolutely astounding. She immediately dropped her head so that her chin touched her chest. Then, slowly and dramatically, she raised her head. Her eyes widened beyond belief and seemed to challenge: "You don't really mean that, do you?"

About a third of the way up, she cocked her head sideways, peered out from beneath her eyelashes, and slowed her ascent. From my vantage point, I could see that her father was watching her every move, anticipating the explosion of joy and pride that would fill his heart when her eyes finally met his. When Renee's head ascension reached the three-quarter mark, her father caught the full blast of her heart-stopping beauty and sighed, "All right, you can have some . . . but don't spoil your dinner."

INTERPRETATION: Renee was quickly learning how to use her beauty to make the world go her way. She had developed a simple game to carry this out: "Daddy says 'No,' I work him over with my cute little act, and I get what I want."

The Ambush was simple and obvious, but so pleasing to her father that he relented to her wishes as if to reward her for being cute. It wouldn't take long for Renee to widen, perfect, and strengthen this skill.

She could easily become a very hateful young lady once she realized that people were treating her like a doll—plastic and beautiful on the outside but full of stuffing on the inside. The opening lyrics of a once-popular song encapsulate my view of Renee's Ambush: "Pretty girls just seem to find out early, how to open doors with just a smile."

RECOMMENDATION: This was one of the few situations in which I had a chance to demonstrate how to counteract an Ambush. After her father rescinded his original directive, I said, "Renee, show me your trick again." She willingly obliged, not the least bit bashful about showing off. She dropped her head and raised it again, this time fixing her eyes on me.

Once I had recovered from the blast of gentleness coming from her eyes, I said, "Do it again, just once more." She complied. I had her repeat the same act four or five times and then said, "Gosh, you sure are good at that—I bet you could get anything you wanted, couldn't you?" As her head indicated the affirmative, I saw her father's grin turn to a sheepish smile as he finally understood how Renee was using her natural beauty to get things she wanted.

I told my friend to repeat my approach each time Renee Ambushed him. Several repetitions would give a chance to prove to his daughter that her "act" wouldn't work, besides giving him a chance to recover from the numbing effects of Renee's beauty.

LESSON: A smile can open many doors, but one of them may lead to trouble.

Renee and Krissy are only two of the millions of kids who experiment with deception every day. Crouching beneath a shopping cart and hiding behind gorgeous eyes are only a couple of the many possible examples of sneaky behavior. Since sneakiness has purposes other than disruption, it doesn't necessarily lead to trouble. However, when it fosters self-deception, a crucial ingredient of deviance comes to life.

Lying to one's self gives deviance its roots. If children become proficient at lying, they slowly begin to believe that what they think is the absolute truth. In turn, they tend to impose their personal reality on the world around them. Changing the world is simply a matter of creating a new set of lies.

The logical end of this self-deception is detachment. Children who make their own reality and then live as if it is *the* reality grow into adolescents who say, "I don't have to live by the same rules as everyone else. I'm special. I can justify whatever I do; after all, I create my own laws."

Under these circumstances, testing the limits of authority becomes a purely academic issue, since there are *no* limits to be tested. This dissocial stance is more common than one would believe. It develops all too easily. All it takes is a streak of stubbornness (which comes naturally), a dab of creativity, and parents who look the other way.

8

Five and Six:
Choice, Not Chance

It may be tough to be a five-year-old, but it's tougher to be the parent of one. Somewhere around this age, the child enters one of the two critical stages (the other is ages fourteen to sixteen) in his or her struggle to avoid becoming civilized. The crisis hits when Mom and Dad realize their baby has the potential to be a scheming, conniving little deviant and Baby starts practicing elaborate forms of Ambush.

It is during this time period that children should begin to recognize the connection between their behavior and the things that happen to them. If they learn that they have some control over the consequences of their actions, they'll begin to exercise their free will. This will be the first step down the road to the lesson that, within limits, a person's life can be run by choice, not chance.

This realization is often confusing. The child recognizes that the limits upon the process of choice fluctuate from situation to situation and, for the most part, appear to be boundless. The parents, meanwhile, are faced with the double bind of controlling the exercise of free will while sowing the seeds of independence. For the children, it's kind of like walking down a narrow, dimly lit hallway for years, only to be thrust one day into an open-air arena where hundreds of people sit on the edge of their seats, waiting to be entertained. Kids suddenly face many new powers, but don't know what to do with them. They experience:

- improved self-confidence coming from successful social adjustment at school
- an increase in verbal ability, especially in confronting others
- a reduction in fear of reprisal by adults for misbehavior
- a sharpened awareness that parents are faulty *plus* the ability to graphically point out those faults
- a heightened sensitivity to approval by others
- an increase in introspection accompanied by the realization that they are very important to their parents

These things come together in varying mixtures at approximately the same time. The resultant pressure forces the child into occasional frenzies, and the parents begin to wonder why they ever became parents. The antics of a five-year-old can be sidesplitting, but the humor can quickly dissipate when one ponders the effects of failure at this age level.

The best overall strategy for parents during this difficult time is fourfold. First, worry about the nitty-gritty, day-to-day mistakes a child might make should be reduced to a minimum. Second, concern about budding values is premature. Third, a child's free will should be exercised across a wide variety of situations. Fourth, the child should learn that the choice process is limited by the number of *realistic* alternatives the brain can generate in any given situation. Thus, emphasis must center on the development of basic skills rather than on success or failure in any one situation.

The complexity of problems and potential solutions skyrockets at this age level, compared to those previously reviewed. To give the reader a feel for the possible complications, I have outlined the situation and reactions of the first case in story form. This is how I saw it:

SITUATION: A disheveled, apparently overworked (and none-too-affluent) woman struggled in the door of a large supermarket with a baby under one arm and a five-year-old boy tugging at her other hand. The five-year-old was protesting the fact that his mother had just yanked him away from his favorite TV show, "Gilligan's Island." The kid made a frontal assault, screaming a war whoop as soon as his mother put her purse in the shopping cart: "I wannaaa candeee barrr." His drawn-out request was ignored as his mother prepared for the torturous job of trying to find something to eat that wouldn't wreck her budget. The war whoop grew louder and stronger: "I wannaaa candeee barrr!" Mom gasped at the price of milk and addressed her son out of the corner of her mouth: *"No!"*

REACTION: As soon as his mom gave him the "No," the kid's face filled with anguish, his body became rigid with anger, and his eyes reflected revenge. His ensuing scream sounded something like a cross between a cave full of bats and a wounded grizzly bear. His mother didn't seem nearly as concerned as I was. Her yell shook the ceiling: *"Shut up!"*

The battle was on. The kid sandwiched demands for a candy bar between screams and yelps while his mother barraged him with ultimatums ("If you don't shut up, I'm gonna knock your head off!"). When this didn't work, she hit him with the "biggie": "If I tell Daddy, he'll beat you to within an inch of your life."

I don't think the kid really believed her because he kept on screaming and demanding a candy bar. Pretty soon the baby started screaming, and I knew the mother was in trouble when I saw sweat pouring from her armpits. I knew she'd lost the battle when she put a seven-pound rump roast in her cart without looking at the price.

The final triumph came as the weary trio approached the candy rack, which was adjacent to the toilet paper. While the mother soothed her frazzled nerves by squeezing the bun-wad, the little bandit dashed for the candy, ripped open a Three Musketeers bar, and jammed it into his mouth. His mother screamed, the baby screamed, the kid screamed, and I damn near ran into the rear end of a little old lady who was bent over, checking out the price of Ovaltine. I froze in my tracks with my mouth hanging open as the mother walked over to the kid, slapped him in the face, and yelled, "Don't you ever let me catch you doing that again."

The lady moved immediately back to the toilet paper, put two packages in her cart, and moved on. I stared in disbelief as the kid stuffed the rest of the Three Musketeers into his mouth and turned to me with a smug look of satisfaction beaming through the chocolate mess, as if to say, "The slap didn't hurt as much as the candy bar tasted good."

As I shook my head in painful concern and mused on the misfortune of the coming generation of thieves, the little crook stuffed two Milky Ways into his pocket and wiped the excess gooey chocolate on his shirt sleeve. As he walked past me, I heard him murmur, "She didn't catch me *that* time."

INTERPRETATION: Next to the spoon, the candy bar is man's worst invention. Not only does it destroy teeth and do strange things to the liver, but it also causes children to act like wild animals. This lady was a typical victim of the old candy-bar–supermarket-Ambush ploy.

She was under a great deal of pressure (the impossible dream of trying to buy fifty dollars worth of food with the twenty-five she had to spend) and was unable or unwilling to give her son the attention he needed. Her biggest mistake was yelling "No" so nonchalantly. Such an action is like touching a match to dynamite or slapping the face of a mean dog.

During this Ambush, the mother demonstrated how undermined her authority was. She couldn't expect her son to respect her when she yelled, made random threats, and then dared him to be more deviant ("Don't you ever let me catch you doing that again").

This kid needed to learn very quickly that his mother is in

charge. As of this transaction, it was clear that he was in charge. His family is headed for bigger trouble.

RECOMMENDATION: The kid's first reaction ("I wannaaa candeee barrr") should have been ignored. The mother should have gone about her business and allowed him to carry on all he liked. At the point of the candy-bar theft, the mother should have taken the candy from him, wrapped it up, put it in the cart, and told her son that he would pay a penalty for having swiped it. If she'd felt up to it, the mother might have taken her son to see the manager of the store, who could have given him a short lecture concerning respect for other people's property.

This all could have been avoided if the mother had been active with her son instead of being reactive. For example, she could have taken her son to the store and made it seem like a privilege. Asking him to help pick out the cheapest margarine, the best price on green beans, and a special dessert of his choice would have given her son the feeling that he was needed. He could have received attention for helping rather than hassling his mother.

LESSON: If more couples could see a five-year-old's reaction to the word "No" before they became parents, they would demand protection lessons.

SITUATION: During the discussion following a Protective Parenting lecture, a young mother asked me to comment on the seriousness of her son's stealing. According to her story, five-year-old Freddie took money from her wallet, from his older sister's piggy bank, and, recently, from Grandma's purse.

When asked how she knew that Freddie had sticky fingers, she said, "He always gets caught." She explained further that her son would attack the piggy bank so loudly that his sister several rooms away could hear the racket. Freddie had ripped his grandma off while she was cooking dinner and then gone to her and said, "Grandma, I didn't know you had a picture of me in your billfold."

As for stealing from his mother, Freddie invariably left his mother's purse opened and the contents strewn about. In all instances, Freddie took coins, not bills.

REACTION: The mother told me that she had spanked Freddie, made him return the money with apologies, kept him indoors, and taken away his bicycle for a week. She'd thought these methods were working until she discovered that his stealing hadn't changed, he was just getting caught less often.

INTERPRETATION: Freddie's behavior had to be taken seriously. Stealing is the lifeblood of disruptiveness and social deviance. Unchecked, it can multiply into innumerable variations of trouble. At five years of age, stealing is mostly a source of matchless excitement. However, without careful discipline, this excitement can lead to a general disrespect for another's property. In some cases this disrespect can grow to include disregard for human life.

Freddie wasn't a confirmed thief, nor was he anywhere near being dangerous. He was absorbed in a game of "cops-and-robbers," modeling various TV heroes and acting out much of the food for thought contained in cartoons, commercials, and the many times he had heard adults say, "Hell, I won't get caught!"

The increase in sneakiness represented Freddie's attempt to put more excitement into the game, in addition to trying to avoid some of the punishment. His theft of coins rather than bills confirmed my interpretation that Freddie wanted a chase, not a new toy.

It would not be long before Freddie began to receive feelings of self-worth from his ability to rip others off. Then he would concentrate more effort into not getting caught as he advanced to the next level of sophistication in the criminal game; that is, "Catch me—I bet you can't."

I have found that the best answer to the streak of crookedness within each of us is to turn our attention to the future. Those of us who have the courage to be honest would admit that we could find it exciting to steal something without being caught. However, the law is there to demonstrate the destructive influence of illegal behavior. Getting into trouble shows complete disrespect for our hopes for tomorrow. In this case, therefore, Freddie needed to learn that his stealing was an extremely unwise investment in the future.

RECOMMENDATION: To show Freddie that today's misbehavior will return disappointment tomorrow, I suggested his mother do the following. The next time Freddie stole something from Grandma, she was to refuse to take him to the ice cream store for three days, each time reminding him why she wasn't taking him. If he took something from his sister's piggy bank, she was to refuse to read him the Charlie Brown comic strip for three days; if from Mom, she was to refuse to play checkers with him for the same period of time. When he didn't steal and helped each person with their work, he received extra praise and his regular treats.

LESSON: The golden rule of Protective Parenting is: If you do unto me what hurts, I shall refuse to do unto you what feels good.

SITUATION: A young couple sought my help with their five-year-old son. Rex, their only child, was an habitual liar. They weren't able to control this behavior. His lying took place when Mom and Dad asked him questions about what he had done during the day. He told stories about almost everything he'd seen or done.

They gave the following examples of his lies. He told them he'd seen a robbery at the drugstore when in fact he hadn't left the yard. He "confessed" to beating up three kids in kindergarten, but a check with the teacher indicated no such fighting. Other fibs included his story that he'd eaten an ant that had stuck its head out of his sand pile, his belief that the neighbor's dog could roller-skate, and his dead-serious avowal that the Bakers, who were close personal friends, were his real parents.

REACTION: Although they occasionally found one of Rex's stories amusing, the parents weren't laughing when I talked to them. They viewed the situation as serious and responded accordingly. Their most frequent verbal responses were challenging: "You know it's not nice to lie" or "Now, Rex, you know that's just a fib."

When these tactics didn't seem to work, one parent assumed a heavy hand, saying, "Rex, you stop your lying or else I'll spank." When he'd lie again soon after such a threat, his father or mother would spank him. They even tried telling him, "If you

always lie to us, how do we know when you're telling the truth?''
Yet nothing they said or did made any difference.

INTERPRETATION: Rex had found a way to use his imagination (with a
little help from the anteating aardvark of Saturday morning fame)
to get his parents' attention. Their emotionalism and occasional
laughter more than outweighed their threats and infrequent spankings.

Rex found excitement in his lies. It was fun to make them up
and even more delightful to see the impact they had on his
parents. However, his parents were correct in seeking an end to
the lies.

It is possible that Rex could eventually find that switching from
one "truth" to another was as simple as plugging in another creative fantasy. The major problem with this is that Rex's creative
thoughts could gradually move away from reality. He could find
it increasingly difficult to distinguish truth from fiction.

If allowed to flourish in an undisciplined atmosphere, this trend
could lead Rex to the bizarre state in which his reality would
center on his thoughts, no matter what feedback he received from
the real world. The resulting conflict would generate much anxiety
and anger. If he sought revenge toward others, he'd land in jail; if
he took it out on himself, he'd go crazy. I've dealt with five such
rare cases in eight years of practice.

RECOMMENDATION: Rex needed prolonged exposure to reality. The
best way for him to distinguish between his creativity and reality
without being subjected to the damaging effects of guilt or harsh
punishment was to let nature take its course. Therefore, I made
the following recommendation: when Rex lied, his parents were
to explain the natural outcome of the lie and then make sure Rex
experienced the outcome.

The story about the robbery should have resulted in Rex's confinement to the house for several days, "until the police catch the
robbers because you might be in danger as a witness."

The lie about the beatings should have resulted in more chores
about the house because of Rex's superior strength and lack of
outlet for his energy.

The wild one about the roller-skating dog could have resulted in an extra hour of daily spelling lessons so that he could write up the story for national publication.

If Rex wanted to believe that the Bakers were his real parents, then it would be natural to assume that he would want to move out and live with them. (''Get your bags packed, but you'll have to leave the bunk beds here because we want a son real bad.'')

Finally, the anteater imitation could have been handled by telling Rex that such creatures usually cause stomach upset, so he'd have to swallow some castor oil, Maalox, or other stomach medicine.

With these alternatives available, threatening, yelling, and especially hitting were unnecessary and even harmful.

LESSON: Wise parents can help nature take its course.

Stealing and lying are two of the most common forms of social disruption. One is illegal, and the other one should be. The kids in the above cases were beginning to play with fire. Whether or not they would eventually get burned depended upon the effectiveness of their parents' intervention.

Three forms of thievery can be seen in these situations. The supermarket bandit stole for material gain and personal satisfaction. Freddie ripped off some silver tokens in order to receive a token of recognition. Rex was stealing his parents' trust, possibly the most precious commodity of all. All three were using dishonesty to get what they wanted. In the process, they exhibited disrespect and were flirting with detachment from the world of law and order.

When a five-year-old steals or lies, it doesn't mean that he or she will grow up to be a thief or a liar. However, any time parents see such clear-cut indicators of disrespect, it is time for protective measures to be implemented. Whatever technique is used, it must teach the child more efficient use of the choice process. Choosing disrespect toward another individual ultimately leads to disrespect for oneself since, in the final analysis, how a person treats others is really a reflection of how one treats oneself. Thus, without self-respect, a person has no reason to stay out of trouble.

Lack of respect for oneself and others is learned in many ways. Billy and Donny learned by watching their parents.

SITUATION: Billy's father complained that his five-year-old son constantly fought with his three-year-old sister, Marsha. When asked to outline a typical example, he spoke of going out to a quick-service restaurant for a Saturday-afternoon treat.

No sooner did the family get in the car than Billy started making fun of Marsha's thumb-sucking. Yanking her thumb from her mouth, he said, "Don't suck your thumb; you're dumb."

REACTION: Marsha immediately started crying, and Mother accused Billy of being mean to his little sister. Billy protested his innocence, rejected his mother's judgment, and resumed his accusation that his sister was stupid. Marsha then screamed louder, and mother began screaming at Billy. Finally, Dad screamed at all of them.

INTERPRETATION: I saw this as an all-too-typical family out for a pleasant lunch with everyone screaming amid the crunch for joy-burgers. This type of interaction lays the foundation for a lifetime of screaming as the principal method of dealing with problems.

I also determined that Mother often criticized Marsha for sucking her thumb by saying, "That's stupid and childish." While siblings calling each other stupid is not exactly desirable, Billy should not be punished for imitating his mother.

RECOMMENDATION: I suggested that the mother find another means of dealing with Marsha's thumb-sucking. Likewise, screaming at Billy to stop ridiculing his sister made no sense at all. Mother and Father, in a united effort, were to tell Billy and Marsha that if they couldn't get along, there would be no "joy" in their burgers.

LESSON: Parents' words sometimes come back to haunt them.

SITUATION: Donny's mother sought my advice about the reputation that her six-year-old son had acquired, that of being the neighborhood bully. It seemed that Donny would take toys from younger children, walk into any neighbor's house without asking, and be very quick to hit any child who "bothered" him.

The situation came to a head one day when a neighbor lady asked Donny's mother to do something about her son's assaultive behavior and arrogant attitude.

REACTION: Donny's father overheard the conversation, came to the door, and lectured the woman about the necessity of his son's being rough and tough in a hostile world.

When Donny came in from playing, his father grabbed him by the back of the neck, shoved him into a corner, and yelled at him for causing a disturbance in the neighborhood. Donny protested his innocence and then started crying. His father sent him to his room without supper.

INTERPRETATION: Many Ambushes that take place outside the home are actually misdirected. In such cases, the kid wants to reject the parental directive but is too scared to do so in front of the parent.

Donny's bullying and inconsiderate behavior seemed to be a perfect reflection of his father's actions. The father, in trying to show his son how to survive, was teaching him how to be mean and nasty. Donny's mother did not agree with her husband's tactics but was too afraid to approach him about it.

RECOMMENDATION: The mother had the best chance to remedy the problem. I suggested she try to talk with her husband about his own childhood, which was filled with physical abuse. If he were more able to resolve his own anger, he might quit dumping it on Donny.

I also recommended that Donny be enrolled in beginning tumbling at the YMCA so that he might learn more appropriate outlets for his physical energies. Finally, I suggested she invite one of the neighborhood boys over and supervise cooperative play, rewarding and punishing as was indicated in the case of Stella and Tracey.

LESSON: Some kids can turn a "touch-and-smile" neighborhood into a "shove-and-smirk" jungle.

It is a well-received theory in behavioral-science circles that children learn many of their social skills by imitating people or characters that they believe are important (in most cases, parents must compete with Saturday-morning cartoon characters for first place in this personality derby). This "monkey-see-monkey-do" viewpoint is usually called "social modeling." It is important for Protective Parents to understand that through social modeling, children learn an endless number of ways to reject the demands of authority figures.

Billy and Donny were kids who demonstrated how parental weaknesses can be turned into social disruption. I don't believe that the parents involved wanted to teach disrespect or disruption. But their intentions turned sour when their kids imitated parental aggressiveness while interacting with others. Billy's mom and dad could easily set a new example. However, Donny's mom faced a more difficult challenge. The best she could hope for was to get her husband to tone down his "get-tough" policy to the point where Donny would not be overwhelmed with a model of physical aggression.

Parents who find that they or their spouses are unable or unwilling to change a certain inappropriate action toward their child should try to avoid the situation altogether. Exhibiting no behavior is better than demonstrating one that will lead to deviance. While this recommendation may mean that some children won't have a complete father or mother figure in their lives, it nevertheless leaves the child the option of choosing to imitate someone whose behavior is more appropriate.

An Ambush can be complicated by such phenomena as modeling. However, at ages five and six, it is usually easy to evaluate. For instance, look at Wendy and Penny.

SITUATION: A college professor friend of mine encapsulated his problem this way: "My six-year-old daughter, Wendy, just doesn't know when to quit fooling around." When asked to clarify his complaint, he outlined a typical example of her disruption.

When his brother paid my friend a visit recently, he spent the first few minutes playing with Wendy. He chased her around the kitchen, tickled her, and stuck his tongue out at her in a playful manner. After ten or fifteen minutes, he stopped and began talking with his brother and sister-in-law. However, Wendy wouldn't leave her uncle alone. Her tickle became a scratch on his arm, her mouth turned into a spit factory, and she jumped around, distracting their conversation.

REACTION: Wendy's father told her to go out to play, admonished her for the disruption, and warned her to calm down "or else Uncle Steve won't like you." Even this guilt-provoking tactic didn't work as Wendy persisted in her playfulness. Finally, my friend lost his cool and screamed at his daughter. She reluctantly retreated.

INTERPRETATION: Wendy wanted more and more of playing. She didn't know when the adults in her world, particularly Uncle Steve, didn't want to play anymore. Children never stop being children, but most adults turn their playfulness on and off like a water faucet.

Wendy needed to learn how to identify when a grown-up didn't want to play anymore. Then she had to learn how to turn her attention elsewhere. If she didn't, her poor timing could lead to unintended trouble.

RECOMMENDATION: Since Wendy was bright and well-adjusted and my friend was a kind and sensitive man, I suggested that he use my favorite technique, the old "evil-eye" maneuver.

I explained that the next time Wendy didn't stop fooling around when asked to, my friend was to avoid the guilt and screaming and stare at her for about thirty seconds. No words, no reactions, nothing but a stare was to be directed at her. Once he had gotten Wendy's attention, he was to move on to the second half of the evil-eye tactic.

With his eye firmly fixed on Wendy, he was to slowly and calmly repeat his directive concerning the cessation of her uncontrolled playfulness. Wendy would quickly learn the importance of complying with a directive when uttered in a slow and deliberate manner.

I cautioned him that he might have to add a firm grasp of

Wendy's shoulders the first few times he gave her the evil eye. Eventually, a lower voice and a fixed look would tell Wendy when it was time to stop fooling around.

LESSON: Someone has to teach children that life is not a continuous merry-go-round; it's sad but true.

SITUATION: I was pushing my grocery cart to my car when I witnessed a simple but frustrating Ambush. A lady was trying to put eight bags of groceries, four cartons of milk, and twenty pounds of potatoes, and four small children into the back seat of a subcompact automobile.

Halfway through the job, I heard her screech, "Penny, get out of there!" I paused long enough to see a little girl, about five years old, tearing at one of the sacks and screaming, "I want my candy *right now!"*

REACTION: The situation went from bad to worse as the mother threatened reprisals and the girl kept digging into the bags. Finally, the woman dropped the potatoes, yanked the girl out of the car, and hit her solidly several times on the buttocks. The girl started crying, and the mother yelled, "Shut up or I'll spank you again!"

INTERPRETATION: This is the stuff that constitutes the fundamental Ambush. Penny wanted what she wanted *immediately,* and Mommy's "No" made no difference. The mother got herself into such a dither that anger and physical attack was her quickest solution.

Such scenes are all too familiar. I see them in department stores, on playgrounds, in movie theaters, not to mention in and around supermarkets. This Ambush is typical of situations in which gentle warriors turn harsh. Parents must find solutions to such defiance that are not warlike.

RECOMMENDATION: The best thing I could have done would have been to help the lady put the groceries into the car. She was in no mood for Protective Parenting suggestions after spending all her household money on food and realizing, once again, there was nothing left for the beauty parlor or a new dress.

However, she could have lightened her load by asking store personnel to give her a "carry-out." Also she might have asked her husband to accompany her. Two other options available included not buying the candy in the first place or simply letting the girl have the candy.

The best suggestion would be to let the girl be responsible and carry the candy out in a separate bag.

LESSON: Hitting kids because of a sweet tooth will turn them sour.

These cases illustrate a typical Ambush. Wendy and Penny wanted immediate satisfaction, and they lacked tolerance for the frustration that accompanies the delay of gratification. As a result, they worked hard to circumvent the parental "No." The parents were weakened by frustration and anger, and they ignored their inner tension until it exploded. The kids won the battle when their parents lost control of the situation. But the two girls were losing the war because they weren't learning how to comply with authoritative expectancies.

Parents can turn the tide in similar Ambushes by promoting peace instead of war. Three survival strategies—preparation, patience, and persistence—are the key to successful negotiations.

Parents must always be prepared to be attacked by gentle warriors. This anticipation facilitates the growth of patience for the child's warlike antics and the lessening of parental anger and frustration. Finally, even in the face of trouble, parents must persist in trying to reduce the number of successful Ambushes. Elimination of all Ambush attempts is an unrealistic goal. Parents would have cause to worry if their kids didn't raise a little hell once in a while.

The last two kids stuck the arrow in and then twisted it.

SITUATION: I was standing in line in a quick-serve seafood restaurant when a mother and her five-year-old son came in. They were accompanied by what appeared to be the kid's best buddy.

Within a few seconds, the son was jumping up and down, yelping at the top of his voice, and tugging at his buddy's hair. The mother told him to calm down, but he continued unabated.

Without further warning, his mother grabbed his arm, jerked him off the ground, smacked him on the rear, and threw him toward the tables, yelling, "Richard, *sit down! Now!"*

REACTION: Richard promptly sat down at one of the tables, hung his head, and stuck out his lower lip in defiance. As his mother turned to place her order, Richard started shaking the tartar sauce on the tabletop, knocked the salt and pepper off the table, and opened the napkin dispenser, scattering napkins all over the floor.

INTERPRETATION: While Richard obviously needed some controls, the mother's physical attack only gave him reason to seek revenge. This Ambush demonstrates how rejection of parental demands can spill over into more complicated behavior.

Particularly bothersome is the fact that kids in this or a similar position always seem to take revenge on the nearest object, whether it's related to the cause of their disgust or not. It would not be unlikely someday for this same kid to break a streetlight or slash a tire because his mother had grounded him for sassing her.

RECOMMENDATION: The mother should have given Richard a more definitive warning as soon as he began his disruption. The warning could have embodied a limited choice ("or-else") option. She could have said, "Calm down, or else we'll leave right now." She should not have used the "or else" unless she was prepared to carry through on the threat.

This kind of choice-situation demands that a child decide on priorities for his wishes. That is, he must decide whether food or wild excitement is more important. If he calms down and gets the goodies, his learning will transfer to other situations.

LESSON: Parents should hit their kids with an "or else," not their hand.

SITUATION: Five-year-old Scotty lived with his divorced mother. She was nervous, jumpy, and had many personal problems. Concerning her son, she complained that Scotty changed his clothes no fewer than four times a day.

REACTION: Scotty's mother was very embarrassed when I asked her the details. She was convinced that Scotty had a severe mental disturbance, probably related to his father's having left the family.

Investigation uncovered the facts that Scotty refused to eat most food, wouldn't go to bed on time, and refused to talk except when he wanted to. Whenever his mother confronted him about his obstinacy, he would rush to his room and change his clothes.

Further investigation showed that Scotty ate well and took his nap willingly at school, and didn't seemed worried about getting dirty on the playground.

INTERPRETATION: Scotty's major problem was that his nervous, guilt-ridden mother was an easy target for this rather creative Ambush. Scotty's house was so clean that his mother's compulsive orderliness made her a sitting duck.

Scotty's changing of clothes was simply a way of controlling his mother, making her do what he wanted. It was not too late to change the situation because Scotty was still following the rules at school.

RECOMMENDATION: The mother entered psychotherapy in order to iron out her own emotional problems. She was told to ignore Scotty's clothes-changing. She enforced her rules by the use of giving and withholding one of Scotty's favorite treats.

I helped her get Scotty a Big Brother, who involved the boy in assorted activities (judo, swimming, tumbling) in which changing clothes was necessary. Scotty also helped his mother at the laundromat, at which time she was able to discuss the importance and method of cleaning clothes.

LESSON: Worry about mental disturbance *after* a kid follows the rules.

Scotty and Richard employed two-fisted Ambushes. Not only did they succeed in rejecting parental directives, but they also punished their mothers for making the demands in the first place. They took the usual resistance one step further when they counterattacked with strategies designed to make their parents suffer. They sought and achieved revenge, acting not unlike dedicated warriors.

The end result was that these kids forced their mothers to assume a defensive stance. Their Ambushes proved the effectiveness of a commonly held belief; that is, the best defense is a good offense.

Their actions told their parents: "Don't expect me to do what I don't want to do, or you'll get more of the same."

Both mothers should have reacted to the revenge tactic with the Kiss strategy, which would say, "Get your revenge over with so that you can comply with my request."

Scotty's creative maneuver is particularly enlightening when one considers that his innovative Ambush is only child's play compared to what he could be doing ten years from now.

After parents have established limits of behavior, they should encourage their offspring to make choices *within those limits*. No one has a completely free will. Reality is always there to remind all people that what they want is not necessarily what they get. Parents must bring this reality to their children as early as possible. If five-year-old kids reach adolescence still thinking that they have no control over what happens to them, they have no logical reason to control themselves. And without the control that comes with choice, the hell they raise can burn a lot of people.

9

Seven and Eight: Everyone Belongs Somewhere

Ages seven and eight are important periods for the growth of personal identity. The seven-year-old experiences pressures to act grown-up from parents, siblings, preachers, and teachers. Friends and playmates are the only ones who don't say, "You're not a baby anymore. Act your age." In their struggle to deal with these expectancies, these children will often express disappointment, uneasiness, anger, joy, or sadness in ways that are difficult to understand.

"Exploration" is the best word to represent the personality development of this age. Seven-year-olds want to investigate every nook and cranny of their world. They seek to explore the boundaries. Their major interest is not so much in testing the limits of their world as it is in discovering what those limits are. As in all explorations, these kids find comfort in knowing that there is a line beyond which danger is clearly imminent (even though they often yell about it). At this early age, parents have a clear chance to show that enforcing limits is an act of love, not suppression.

Children at this age level may become shy, withdrawn, verbally or physically aggressive at a moment's notice. Such sudden occurrences aren't necessarily indicative of serious trouble. More often than not, these kids are simply upset because they don't know where they belong. Parents need not worry too much about these identity problems. A soft voice of reassurance and a firm hand on the shoulder will calm them down.

At this age level, things are never quite so bad as they may seem. What is viewed as a major problem one day will be replaced by a completely different crisis a few days later. When parents see this changeable behavior, they should understand that seven- and eight-year-old kids often bound from place to place in an attempt to discover where they belong.

A strange psychological concoction starts brewing sometime around the age of seven when children become much more aware of what other kids are doing. The brew becomes most active when heated by a strong faith that the grass is always greener in the neighbor's yard. This potion is impossible to analyze or contain because its composition is constantly changing. However, the label on its empty container would read: PEER PRESSURE ** The double asterisk would refer the researcher to the following warning: **Social scientists have determined that peer pressure is dangerous to law-abiding behavior.*

Peer pressure is impossible to define categorically because it has its origin within the personality of the child. It results from a lack of self-knowledge and self-confidence. Its emergence is inevitable as kids, knowing little about the world and even less about themselves, push each other's consciences around, looking for the limits of their ego strength. I consider peer pressure to be a potentially dangerous social dynamic because it sets individual choice against the group consensus. While I recognize that peer pressure can have socially appropriate functions, it nonetheless forces a child to choose between what he or she believes and what others say to believe. It follows, therefore, that I maintain that the child's individual free will should be shaped by his or her family, not by peers.

The first two cases representing this age level introduce the never-ending challenge of peer pressure.

SITUATION: During a counseling session, Steve's parents told me that their son was pressuring them for an allowance. Although Steve's father could be considered a "liberal" parent, he held firmly to the belief that an eight-year-old doesn't need an allowance.

REACTION: When Steve came on strong, demanding money "like all my friends have," his dad hedged, questioned, and tried to avoid the issue. After continually hearing about what Jimmy, Scott, and Joe were getting from *their* fathers, Steve's dad gave in and awarded him an allowance of two dollars a week.

However, he constantly harassed Steve about how the boy was managing his allowance. No matter what Steve bought, Dad made judgmental comments about irresponsibility and immaturity. Steve, in turn, made increased references to what his friends were doing with their allowances. It was turning into a full-scale war.

INTERPRETATION: This was an elementary peer-pressure maneuver on Steve's part. He bugged his father with "Everybody is doing it" until he forced his dad to silence him with the two dollars a week. This was another example of how bribery works between parent and child. In short, Steve bribed his father by saying, "Give me the money, or I'll keep reminding you how much better other fathers are."

Even though he wanted to say "No," Steve's father finally gave in and became part of the Ambush. Instead of telling Steve the honest facts, his father played the game with Steve. Steve obviously won.

Father's dishonesty weakened him to the point where Steve could be successful. In fact, by the end of the session, I was convinced that the father had never dealt with the real truth: he didn't want his son to grow up. He was afraid that Steve would no longer love him once he became mature. He thought that by controlling the money he could *make* Steve dependent upon him and, hence, ensure his continual love.

RECOMMENDATION: Using the Kiss approach, I avoided the complicated reasons for the father's reluctance and dealt with the key issue: responsibility. Neither the mother nor the father was ready to talk about their own problems, so the best way to help Steve was to concentrate on the issue at hand.

They both wanted Steve to learn responsibility, and I saw that Steve needed to *learn how to earn*. Therefore, we set up the *Responsibility Checklist*.

Responsibility Checklist

Daily Responsibilities Mon. Tues. Wed. Thurs. Fri. Sat. Sun.
1. Feed cat.
2. Take out garbage.
3. Clean up room.
4. Clean off table after evening meal.

GUIDELINES FOR USE:
1. A check mark ($\sqrt{\ }$) is to be placed in the appropriate column and row each time a responsibility is observed being performed.
2. The checklist is to be totaled and the earnings given on Sunday evening according to these percentages:
   a. 90 percent completion, or twenty-five check marks, earns two dollars.
   b. 80 percent completion, or twenty-two check marks, earns one dollar.
   c. 70 percent completion, or nineteen check marks, earns fifty cents.
   d. Less than nineteen check marks means a bad week and no money.
3. No reminding of responsibilities by either parent is to be allowed.

4. Parents are to praise all compliance, remind *after* failure, and ignore all complaints.
5. Steve's responsibilities include ensuring that one parent confirms the completion of his work and enters a check mark.
6. The list is to be posted on the refrigerator so that all can see it easily.
7. No changes, except a new checklist for Monday morning, are to be instituted unless all family members agree.

I suggested that the next time Steve said, "But my friends don't have to do this," his father reply, "That's okay. Your friends don't live in this house, either."

LESSON: Responsibility each day will keep the policeman away.

SITUATION: Seven-year-old Tony was doing poorly in school. His teacher recommended that his parents talk with me. During our conference, I learned that Tony was showing off in class, pinching and hitting some kids who sat next to him, and acting "stupid" instead of studying.

REACTION: Tony's parents kept Tony in after school, refusing to let him see his best friend for a week, and his father regularly spanked him for his school misbehavior. However, the disruptiveness continued and finally reached a point at which the teacher was about to recommend that Tony be placed in a special class for "problem kids."

INTERPRETATION: After a lengthy case review, I was able to determine that Tony's poor school adjustment was a combination of many factors, not the least of which was his father's insistence that he get A's and B's.

In addition, Tony received a lot of attention from his classmates, who thought his antics were funny. The teacher reported that Tony disrupted her classes nearly every day. The disruption had reached such proportions that the least disturbance in Tony's area of the room brought admonitions and warnings directed toward Tony, whether he was involved or not.

Also, the teacher and both parents had come to expect poor

performance from Tony and paid attention to bad grades and disciplinary reports while they ignored any signs of achievement or compliance.

I concluded that Tony was fast adapting himself to the role of troublemaker. His identity was reinforced by authority figures and fellow students. It was only a matter of time before Tony solidified his internal thoughts into a deviant attitude; for example, he might say to himself, "I am one of the 'bad' people in life, so I might as well learn to live with it. Therefore, I'll do my best to be at the top of the class in troublemaking."

RECOMMENDATION: The major goal was to give Tony ample opportunity to excel in a positive direction. Initially, he would have to be led by the hand in doing socially appropriate things. Small steps of progress would have to be rewarded, and failure ignored. I suggested the following:

Tony's father was to take him roller-skating with a friend. The father was to verbally praise Tony's good skating and pay special attention to him when he helped his friend learn how to skate. Afterward, Tony was to buy treats for the group and then be praised for being kind to people.

Tony's mother was directed to purchase materials so that Tony and some neighborhood kids could stage a play, with Tony as the star. Tony was to be praised for cooperative costume-making, helping other kids learn their lines, and for a good performance. Disruptions and showing off were to be ignored. Each time the group worked cooperatively, they were rewarded with Kool-Aid and cookies.

I also talked with the teacher about giving Tony a second chance.

FOLLOW-UP: Tony enjoyed the play so much that he pressured the teacher into allowing a rerun during class. The teacher recognized Tony's creativity and found ways to put his energies to work positively. His school disruptions dropped off dramatically, and his grades slowly improved.

LESSON: One small step for a child can be a giant leap for society.

In order for the family to shape a child's moral code, the parents must not forget that they, too, have a choice when reacting to pressure from others. For example, Steven's father could have Kissed off his son's pressure for an allowance and said "No" to the request. But he lacked self-confidence and started comparing himself to other fathers. His moral code took a back seat to the group consensus, which was saying, "Everyone knows that kids *have to have* an allowance." Even though his moral standards were somewhat rigid and misguided, he threw away his values when faced with the "everybody-is-doing-it" hysteria. While he should have considered taking a second look at his moral code, he never should have abandoned it altogether. Thus, he, not Steve, was responsible for the pressure he felt. He demonstrated that, like children, parents are also subject to peer pressure.

Tony and Steve were exploring new ways of getting what they wanted. In their search, they stumbled upon magnificent power. They successfully convinced their parents that they were the helpless victims of overwhelming public sentiment. They reasoned that mysterious forces were responsible for their saying, in effect, "They *made* me ask for money" and "They *make* me act funny and disrupt the class."

Their parents tried to protect them from the "make-me" syndrome. However, instead of being protective, such intervention only reaffirmed their irresponsibility by giving substance to the irrational notion that somebody can *make* somebody else do something against his or her will. Such brainwashing might occur in a prison camp but not where most kids hang out.

The main ingredient in a survival formula for both parents and kids is self-love. Despite the claims that self-love is the same as selfishness (when, in fact, they're opposites), self-love breeds self-confidence and a thirst for self-knowledge. Self-knowledge permits expansion of one's freedom of choice. Thus, loving oneself is the key to personal freedom. And if kids can be free of ignorance and self-doubt, pressures from peers will fall on deaf ears.

The struggle between personal freedom and group pressures lasts a lifetime. Peer pressure plays a major role in most adolescent Ambushes, not to mention the proliferation of the corporate-success image and the composition of the guest list at a garden party. Peer pressure can even follow a person to the grave. I've seen the need for peer recognition distort the death of a loved one as families became more sensitive to words of approval about how they had laid the loved one to rest than to feeling the completeness of their loss. Thus, for the Protective Parent, ages seven and eight signal the beginning of a never-ending battle.

The next two kids, Elaine and Paul, demonstrated that sometimes parents misread signs of serious danger.

SITUATION: Eight-year-old Elaine lived with her mother, father, and four-year-old brother. Her mother explained that no matter how many times Elaine was warned, she regularly invited older boys into her bedroom while her mother was at the grocery store.

REACTION: When asked why, Elaine usually shrugged off her mother's concerns by saying, "They're my friends, and you said I could have my friends over to the house." The mother would then ask the boys to leave and warn her daughter never to do it again.

In the evening, the mother would dump her emotional tension on her husband, expressing fears about the terrible dangers of Elaine's behavior. The husband would talk to Elaine about minding her mother, and everything would be all right for a week. Then the entire scene would be replayed.

INTERPRETATION: After talking at length with Elaine's mother and father, it was apparent that the mother was a nervous wreck. She was so worried about possible sexual dangers that she couldn't eat, sleep, or be civil around her husband. She went so far as to say, "Elaine will surely become a loose woman."

Elaine was unknowingly crossing into dangerous territory by inviting thirteen- and fourteen-year-old boys into her bedroom. It was obvious that she was Ambushing her mother by doing something that caused her mother to get so upset.

Her mother further showed her overreaction by asking me such questions as, "Is she *starting* already? Can a doctor give her shots? Should I put her on the Pill?" She was a perfect target for Elaine's Ambush.

RECOMMENDATION: The mother received extensive help with her own hang-ups. Once she understood and accepted her own sexuality, it was easier for her to deal with the simple problem of Elaine's misuse of the privilege of inviting guests to her house.

Elaine's mother started taking her daughter with her to help with the shopping. Also, she issued simple penalties each time the privilege was violated (for example, grounded for two or three days, loss of TV privileges, and no skateboarding).

I cautioned the mother and father against talking too extensively about possible sexual problems, assuring them that if they stayed close to Elaine she would bring plenty of problems to them soon enough.

LESSON: Kids' sexual problems often get started when they listen to their parents.

SITUATION: Eight-year-old Paul loved to play cops-and-robbers. Paul's father, an avid hunter, bought his son a BB pistol for use during target practice. However, whenever Paul asked for his father's help, he'd give some excuse about "not enough time." And when Paul asked to accompany his father on hunting trips, he was told, "No, you're too young."

According to the father, the gun was Paul's favorite toy. However, Paul had to be constantly reminded not to point the gun at people and to play with it only when outdoors. One day, the situation was brought to a head when Paul accidentally shot a friend at close range, causing a nasty welt above one eye.

REACTION: Paul's father was shocked to hear the news from the friend's mother. He immediately grounded Paul and took his BB pistol away from him for one month.

INTERPRETATION: This was a serious situation, not so much because of the accident but because Paul was allowed to "play" with a gun without adequate supervision. Although he was given constant reminders about proper usage, Paul ignored his father's warnings.

I seriously question the easy access children have to guns, arrows, knives, swords, and other toys that are really miniature weapons. However, kids will be exposed to such influences and must be taught respect and a rational fear of such weapons, even if they take the form of toys.

I think such situations call for serious and prolonged parental intervention and monitoring, not overreacting. Paul's grounding and loss of a favorite toy was too much, too late. Some accidents can be prevented long before they happen.

RECOMMENDATION: I told Paul's father to take his son on practice hunting trips so that he could learn the proper use of and respect for weapons. If Paul's father modeled careful and thoughtful use of guns, knives, and so on, Paul would do the same.

I also suggested that Paul receive some other types of gifts for Christmas and his next birthday. I told the parents that grounding Paul wasn't nearly so effective as spending time with him and teaching him the proper use of dangerous weapons. The best thing they could have done was take away the arsenal of "toys" Paul had in his room.

LESSON: It takes two to kill—guns *and* people.

Elaine and Paul were playing with fire. Whether or not they got burned would depend upon parental wisdom and timely intervention. Neither child knew the meaning of molestation or manslaughter, yet both were flirting with such dangers. Inviting strangers into a bedroom or playfully pointing a gun at a friend can all too easily end in tragedy. Such situations call for the rigorous application of Protective Parenting.

When faced with the volatile issues of sex and violence, many parents react to their own fantasies of the disaster that could have been rather than the problem at hand. Still others are so busy with their own lives that they don't see the danger ahead of time. Elaine's mom overreacted to her daughter's behavior, and her own hang-ups distorted the problem, adding more confusion than was actually present. Paul's father ignored a potentially dangerous situation, more intent on his own pleasure than on protecting his child. Although different in nature, both cases support the conclusion that there is no substitute for parents taking time to concentrate on what the child is doing, not on what they, the parents, are thinking.

The Kiss would have helped both parents immensely. All extraneous thoughts and worries could have been eliminated if the parents had dealt with the two fundamental issues involved: the abuse of visiting privileges and the improper use of a gun. The simplified approach would have given both kids a fundamental message about the difference between right and wrong (something like, "If you use the privilege this way, you will receive praise and more privileges. However, if you do the opposite, you will receive punishment"). Such a message embodies the functional meaning of discipline; that is, to teach. Kids playing with sex and guns need all the guidance they can get.

We shall now move from two kids who played with danger to three who played with their impulses. The bodily dangers were lessened, but the carelessness remained all the same.

SITUATION: A young mother explained that her two daughters, aged seven and eight, quite often invited a neighborhood friend over for afternoon visits. Their favorite pastime was to reenact the schlocky comedy of the Three Stooges, complete with face-slapping, head-bopping, and other antics.

REACTION: The mother admitted to "losing her cool" regularly. She typically screamed and demanded that they stop. The children would retreat into a private area and continue their game. Eventually, the mother would discover their secret and yell at them. Then she would send the friend home.

INTERPRETATION: Although not easy to spot, this mother was the victim of an Ambush. Although she didn't realize it, her authority was being eroded by her daughters' hiding behavior. She branded their game as "foolish," and they were rejecting her judgment.

I didn't observe their antics, but I don't imagine that three eight-year-olds could do much damage by slapping each other. However, they might hurt one another unintentionally. This could be avoided if Mom monitored their antics.

The biggest problem was that the mother's belittling could easily result in a situation in which her daughters, when fifteen and sixteen years old, respectively, would hide other antics from her.

RECOMMENDATION: I suggested that once she determined that no one was getting hurt, the mother should probably ignore the entire situation. She might, however, join the girls in order to monitor their actions.

I told the mother to interrupt her daughters' activity after ten or fifteen minutes, just long enough to suggest that they all use body lotion in order to keep their hands and face "young-looking."

LESSON: Parents should not forget that they did dumb things when they were young.

SITUATION: At a party one evening, the father of seven-year-old Chuck cornered me, seeking some quickie advice. It seemed that Chuck liked to jump off tall things—fences, porches, cars, garage roofs, and anything else higher than four or five feet. Unfortunately, Chuck was teaching his two-year-old brother the same behavior.

REACTION: The father, worried about an accidental injury either to Chuck or his younger son, confided that he had spanked Chuck several times and tried to keep him from going outside. Chuck agreed to be more careful but continued to do the same thing as soon as he could get out of his parents' sight.

INTERPRETATION: After asking a few questions, I was able to determine that Chuck genuinely enjoyed jumping from high places and wanted to teach his brother the same fun. The father's action, coupled with the mother's worried screaming, had dampened Chuck's spontaneity, but not his thirst for excitement.

Parental intervention was needed, not because Chuck was playing inappropriately but because his carelessness could result in injury. Jumping isn't necessarily bad, but jumping without forethought can result in unintentional trouble.

RECOMMENDATION: I suggested two courses of action. First, Chuck was to be involved in tumbling classes where he could learn to fall without hurting himself. Furthermore, he could learn the best method of jumping.

Second, Chuck was to learn the potential dangers of jumping (probably through a demonstration) and be encouraged to act as a protective big brother for his little brother.

LESSON: Every Ambush has a key behavior; think of a constructive manner in which the child can engage in the behavior (in this case, jumping is the key behavior).

SITUATION: Hank's mother complained that her seven-year-old spent too much time in the bathroom. She explained that her son went to the john ten or fifteen times a day. It was not clear what he did there, and inquiries were always met with the same answer: "Oh, nothin'."

This behavior usually occurred in the evening and on weekends, but never at school. While he was in the bathroom, water could be heard, and occasionally the toilet would flush.

REACTION: Hank's mother was so upset about her son's behavior that she asked her physician whether anything could be physically wrong. After discovering that Hank had no physical problems, his mother began to prohibit him from entering the bathroom except when he could prove beyond a doubt that he really needed to use the facility.

If Hank stayed in the john too long, his mother would start yelling at him to "get out of there." Hank seemed to pay no attention to his mother and dilly-dallied in the bathroom for up to thirty minutes at a time.

INTERPRETATION: Hank's mother was overreacting to Hank's bathroom activity. From what I could determine, Hank simply liked to play with the water. He didn't pay much attention to his mother's warnings because she was obviously "blowing hot air."

The only problem here was that Hank was wasting water, and his wastefulness should be dealt with simply and unemotionally. The proposition that Hank was disturbed was without merit.

RECOMMENDATION: I suggested that Hank's parents use this situation to teach their son a lesson in economy. If this were done correctly, Hank would have more respect for his share of the living costs in the home.

I recommended that Hank have to pay for his play. In order to earn his fun, I proposed that Hank pay five cents each time he played in the sink. There was to be no charge for using the john or taking a shower. In addition, Hank was to sit down with his father the next time Dad paid the water bill, to emphasize the cost of the utility.

LESSON: If kids are gonna play, then they gotta pay.

The key feature of these cases is how impulsiveness can lead to carelessness, which, in turn, can promote the growth of trouble. While parents are well-advised not to look for trouble in everything their children say or do, they still must be careful not to let wastefulness or carelessness become habitual.

A less noticeable characteristic of these cases is how the growing complexity of childrens' antics, especially their impulsive actions, can hide the rebelliousness contained in an Ambush. All the children involved in the foregoing situations rejected parental admonitions. However, the rejection was sophisticated and clouded by other issues. This sophistication signals the beginning of a trend in which the Ambush becomes harder to detect and more difficult to cope with.

In one way, these cases are the most challenging thus far; that is, one could argue that the kids might have been better off if left alone. Leaving a child to his or her own silliness (which often eliminates itself) is better than intervening and messing things up for sure.

The best barometer for parents to use in deciding whether or not to step in and take some disciplinary action is contained in their own personal level of tolerance for disruption. If the tolerance level remains fairly constant from one day to the next, and then abruptly drops, the child will quickly get the message that Mom or Dad has had it with foolishness.

Of course, some parents have more patience than others. Since there is no clear-cut formula for deciding how much tolerance of foolishness is good, parents might as well stick with their own gut-level reaction that says, "It makes no difference *why,* I've just *had it* with your foolishness." This suggestion is a license for tyranny unless tempered by love and respect. However, it is especially effective when one considers the fact that, in order to promote the sanctity of the family, every child must learn to live within the guidelines set by his or her parents.

From Hank, Chuck, and the Three Stooges, we now move to Stuart and Ed, two kids who wanted to assert themselves but needed some help in learning how to do it.

SITUATION: Seven-year-old Stuart lived with his mother, father, and three older sisters. His parents weren't rich, but they paid their bills, had a nice home, and were saving for their children's college education. The mother's complaint was that Stuart constantly disrupted the family by bothering his sisters. He hid their makeup, interrupted phone calls from their boyfriends, and did his level best to make their lives miserable.

REACTION: The mother, realizing that ignoring such actions could have a beneficial effect, encouraged her daughters to ignore Stuart's disruptions, assuring them that he "would soon grow out of it." However, the girls' patience was not as sturdy as their mother's words. The sisters were becoming more and more agitated because Stuart didn't seem to take the hint.

INTERPRETATION: It seemed obvious to me that Stuart saw his sisters' lives as more exciting than his own. Besides, despite his mother's good try, Stuart was receiving a lot of attention from his disruption. His mother could ignore him because he didn't bug her that much; his sisters, however, had too many problems themselves to put up with Stuart's nonsense.

Ignoring seven-year-olds takes a great deal of patience and more than just a few minutes in order to be effective. Stuart was bright enough to know that he was bothering his sisters, even when they tried to ignore him.

In this case, ignoring wasn't enough; some positive action was necessary. Stuart needed specific activities that would provide excitement, interest, and physical involvement. Punishment should be the last thing on the parents' list of alternatives.

RECOMMENDATION: Upon my insistence, Stuart's father took the initiative, getting Stuart involved in sawing firewood and working in the basement. Such "manly" activities fit nicely into the values operating in this particular family.

I also suggested that Stuart be given the opportunity to learn how to cook and sew buttons on pants, both of which are becoming necessary survival techniques for girls *and* boys during college days.

In conjunction with these activities, I encouraged the family to continue ignoring Stuart's disruptive behavior. If it didn't subside, I recommended that they employ two other tactics. First, they could point out to Stuart that his antics only proved he was still a baby (negative attention, so to speak). Second, I suggested that Dad deduct fifty cents from Stuart's two-dollar-a-week allowance each time he interrupted a phone call (which was the most aggravating of his actions).

LESSON: Parents must have a kid's attention before ignoring will work.

SITUATION: Seven-year-old Ed never talked much. His well-meaning parents were worried to death about his backward nature. They regularly hassled him about his reluctance to speak. They pressured him with questions about how he was feeling, what was wrong, and why he didn't talk more. Ed usually shrugged his shoulders in a gesture that seemed to say, "I don't know."

Ed's mother often approached her son carefully, believing that he had "something on his mind." The father lectured Ed about the need for "a man to be a man," warning him that he'd never grow up if he didn't become tougher and more responsive.

The situation came to a head one afternoon when Ed was playing with his best buddy. When his friend unintentionally spilled dirt on Ed's dump truck, Ed slugged his pal square in the eye.

REACTION: After talking with the friend and his parents, Ed's father took charge. He yelled at Ed about his "meanness" and demanded to know why Ed had hit his best friend for "no reason at all." Ed's mother spent most of her time worrying about how "terrible" the injury to the little boy might be, not waiting to hear Ed's explanation.

In fact, Ed didn't give much of an explanation. He shrugged his shoulders, started crying, and said, "I don't know." His father suspended his allowance for two weeks and confined him to the yard for one week. In an effort to discover the underlying cause of Ed's unresponsiveness, the father asked me to make a house call.

INTERPRETATION: After playing with Ed for fifteen or twenty minutes, I asked him a few questions about his friend, his dump truck, and the dirt. He didn't have much to say to me, either, so I concentrated on his parents.

It became clearer the more we talked that Ed was slowly but surely adopting an unhealthy attitude toward authority, especially his father. He was getting the idea that authority figures could be manipulated easily by the simple act of silence.

Ed's parents were misjudging their son's silence. What they thought was some type of inner turmoil was actually Ed's way of getting all sorts of attention. Ed realized that the more he shut up, the more special consideration he would receive.

The sudden and unpredictable aggressiveness was simply Ed's way of experimenting with being tough. His father, acting out of frustration, had given Ed too general a directive, and Ed was attempting to comply.

Ed felt no inner turmoil; there were no hidden passions or strange illusions or psychological demons roaming around his mind. However, his parents, acting as if there were such mysterious forces, were creating an atmosphere in which some of the things they feared might come true.

RECOMMENDATION: The entire situation was much more complicated than it needed to be. Since Ed could talk quite well when he wanted to, and since a child's silence can be golden, I once again recommended the Kiss approach.

First, I told the father to spend more time with Ed, explaining self-defense and how to use his mouth instead of his fist.

Second, I suggested to both parents that they simply ignore Ed when he wouldn't talk to them, and let nature take its course. For example, if Ed refused to speak his mind about what he wanted for dinner, then he should eat whatever was set before him.

Third, I recommended that they lift the yard restriction as soon as Ed explained to them how he planned to handle future confrontations with other children without hitting them.

Finally, I suggested to the mother that she stop worrying about the neighbor boy's black eye. Ed had made a mistake, but no one was badly hurt. Anyhow, she should save her concerns until Ed was on the receiving end of some other kid's mistake.

LESSON: A "right" is a privilege to be spoken for, not something to be used to hit another person with.

Self-assertion is an essential element in a healthy adult personality. However, the components that make self-assertion productive can become entangled in a web of suppressed anger and hatred and form the foundation for deviant and/or antisocial behavior. For children growing into adolescence, a little self-assertion goes a long way.

Stuart and Ed got carried away in their search for the glory of self-assertion. Both found power in letting people know that they were present and must be counted. Stuart did it by talking at an inappropriate time; Ed did it by not talking at all.

Ed's burst of self-assertion in hitting a friend is the type of thing that occasionally gets a kid into deep trouble in a matter of seconds. His act was a miniature version of the all-too-frequent "crime of passion." This type of offense is poorly contrived and committed in a moment of emotional blindness, but it is a crime nonetheless.

Whether premeditated or occurring on impulse, misuse of self-assertion calls for prudent parental intervention. What it does *not* call for, but what many parents react with, is extreme emotionalism. If a kid loses his or her head in exploring the limits of self-assertion, it is crucial that Mom and Dad do not. If parents don't keep their wits about them, they can add to the problem by demonstrating that the restrictions set by authority figures can be blown away with a puff of emotionalism.

The cases of Stuart and Ed pointed out that as Ambushes lose their simplicity, the resultant uproar can be exceptionally draining for parents' emotional lives. The next two cases, those of Barbara and Ellen, tell the story of two darlings who used their delicate little brains to pull sophisticated Ambushes and came out looking like absolute tyrants.

SITUATION: After one of my parent-training conferences, a mother approached me, obviously upset. The antics of her seven-year-old daughter had her in a dither. Each time Barbara got into conflict with her mom (which usually happened when she wouldn't stop fooling with an appliance, such as the blender), she ran to her dad, crawled into his lap, and said, "I love you, Daddy."

REACTION: Barbara's mom felt deeply frustrated by her inability to discipline her daughter. She knew that Barbara shouldn't be getting away with this behavior, but she also realized that her daughter needed her daddy's love and attention.

The mother tried to solve her dilemma by saying to her husband, "Honey, you know Barbara shouldn't be allowed to do what she's doing." He typically said, "Yes, dear," but continued stroking his daughter.

INTERPRETATION: Barbara was learning at a young age how to employ the technique of "Let's you and him fight." She knew that telling Daddy how much she loved him was a slick way out of trouble with Mom.

With her "I-love-you" routine, she had found a nifty way of playing Mom and Dad against each other. (Ten years from now, she will say "I love you" to a young man and be very distraught and disgusted when he is unable to protect her from the hassles of life.)

Barbara's mother needed to take simple but immediate action.

RECOMMENDATION: I told the mother to have a long talk with her husband. I suggested that she tell him, in a loving way, to "get his act together" and quit playing the chump to his daughter's games. I recommended that she explain the long-term effects of his phony protection scheme the way I had. The next time Barbara jumped into Daddy's lap, he was first to deal with her con game and then willingly accept her love.

LESSON: There once was a girl, oh so sweet,
    Dad's lap was her fav'rit retreat.
    When Mom got mad,
    She ran to Dad.
    But now she's pursued by the heat.

SITUATION: During a break in a duplicate bridge game, Ellen's mother told me how her seven-year-old daughter regularly sent her into a tailspin. It happened each time she invited guests to dinner.

The most recent incident had occurred the previous Sunday, when Grandma had come for a visit. Mom had prepared ham, turkey, sweet potatoes, corn, peas, and homemade biscuits. True to form, Ellen hadn't eaten a thing. When her plate had been filled with the goodies, the gentle warrior had sat there and made all sorts of faces, acting as if she were about to die.

REACTION: Ellen's mother admitted that she had yelled at her daughter for acting like a baby. Characteristically, Grandma had admonished Mom with her usual comment: "Now, Helen, you know that you were fussy when you were young. Leave my granddaughter alone. She'll eat when she wants to."

Feeling guilty, Ellen's mom, not wanting to appear a failure, had jumped from the table and fixed Ellen the only thing she would eat, a hamburger.

INTERPRETATION: It was only a matter of time before Ellen would graduate to bigger and better forms of deviance. She was four steps ahead of the usual disruptive pace, leading the way for kids like Butch McDowell (see Chapter 2).

I hated to be so blunt, but I was losing at cards, so I told it exactly as I saw it. Ellen was spoiled rotten. She was fast learning that the world could be shaped into any form she wanted.

First would come rejection of the food set in front of her, and then rebellion against other realities. Ellen needed to learn about the harshness of give-and-take, and she needed to do it *immediately!*

RECOMMENDATION: Since I had met Ellen before and didn't have unlimited time to listen to Ellen's mother, I employed the Kiss approach. I told her to trust biology and let Ellen go hungry a few times if she didn't eat what was prepared. I assured her that Ellen's desire for food would eventually overcome her fussiness.

Most of all, I cautioned her not to be intimidated by Grandma's overprotectiveness. After all, grandmothers will always spoil their grandchildren, and mothers will always have to counteract the effects.

LESSON: Feed compliance, starve a tantrum.

Both Barbara and Ellen needed lessons in the Three R's. They were disrespectful and disruptive, acting as if the rules of life didn't apply to them. What's worse, their parents were letting them get away with it. When they acted as if they were saying "I'm not going to follow those rules," their detachment was apparent. The parents involved had an opportunity to reply, loud and clear, "Oh, yes, you are!" However, they became sidetracked by reacting to the other authority figure involved (the father and grandmother) instead of dealing with the problem at hand.

The girls' beauty and personality didn't make things any easier, either. Barbara was an absolute gem. Her dark brown curls usually covered a part of her soft, pink face. Her brown eyes flashed like two bright candles in a darkened room. She bounced untiringly around the house exhibiting a bubbling personality that a politician would envy. She was quite advanced for her age. She belonged to that crowd of children who cause parents and nonparents alike to say, "I don't know what this generation is coming to. These kids nowadays are too smart for their own good."

Ellen had the sparkle of deviance born into her eyes. She was just as blond as Butch McDowell but much more of a master at playing one adult against the other. Her crystal-blue eyes spoke a gentle love song as they looked for mischief to be made. She was stubborn, conniving, possessed an endless inquisitiveness, and would never say die. She was the prototype of the gentle warrior. If handled well, there was little doubt that she could help change the course of the world for good or evil, depending upon whether she selected creative conformity or destructive deviance as a way of life.

It is in handling these types of cases that the Kiss approach is most useful. Since kids like Ellen and Barbara throw everything they can think of at their parents during an Ambush, parents must be adept at throwing most of the issues away. The smoke screen created by these kids can be cleared if issues are eliminated until only one or two main problems are left. If applied uniformly, this approach can set the Three D's of deviance in their proper place—in the closet of childhood memories.

The eleven cases reviewed in this chapter demonstrate how the Ambush becomes more complicated as the child grows older. Testing limits sets the stage for exploration of those limits. Exploration stimulates retesting of the limits, which necessitates more exploration. This circular pursuit is not unlike the activities of the fictional mad scientist who sits tirelessly in his lab searching for the magic potion that will solve all life's problems. As was suggested, these seven- and eight-year-old junior researchers don't know where they're going, but, by golly, they're going to go, even if it means trial-and-error (with an emphasis on ''error'') all the way. Although the junior scientists aren't mad, their antics can drive their parents to figuratively develop fangs, drink all sorts of bloody concoctions, and stagger around like Frankenstein's monster.

Exploration is necessary for an eight-year-old if he or she is to have a satisfactory adolescent adjustment and a contented adulthood. As children examine the limits of reality, parents must also expand the horizons of their own knowledge. If a child constantly searches for new answers to old questions while the parents remain convinced they already have all the answers, then the mother and father will become close-minded and their attitudes will solidify as if cast in stone. When this happens, parental rigidity and the child's need to explore will meet head-on. The crash can easily result in the child's active rebellion. Associated with rebelliousness is the development of sneakiness and deviance, which the child will employ as methods of coping with what is perceived as tyranny.

The worst outcome, and one that occurs more frequently than imagined, is the situation in which the child learns to ignore the boundaries of life altogether. And, by definition, that's big trouble.

10

Nine and Ten: Try Listening

There's only one thing more important than talking to a ten-year-old, and that's listening to one. Being able to really *hear* what children say is much more complicated than simply adding up the collective meaning of a bunch of words; that is, there's more to their messages than meets the ear.

Decoding their language and enhancing communication is made difficult by several confusing features of their messages. The two most notable features are the following:

1. Questions are often camouflaged by simple statements. (For example, "My teacher says I'm smart" could mean "Do you think I'm smart?")
2. Declarative statements can take the form of questions. (For example, "Does God really know what you're thinking *all* the time?" could mean "I'm worried about something.")

These enigmatic flip-flops are sometimes the result of attention-getting strategies or games intended to confuse Mommy or Daddy. Often, however, the messages are hidden as a result of the child's inability to understand what he or she is really trying to say. These hidden meanings are a challenge to anyone who wishes to understand what the child wants to convey. Also difficult to comprehend is the frustration children experience as they realize they're not getting their message across. The entire scene can become totally incomprehensible when this frustration turns into revenge.

Overall, parents are well advised to play the role of follower as children explore the deep recesses and caverns of the mind. When exploration of the child's world turns inward, parents must walk a thin line between understanding and control, doing their best to stay out of the child's way without yielding the reins of authority. This is best achieved by taking a few steps backward.

If parents follow closely behind their children, they'll soon discover that the key that unlocks the mystery of hidden meanings is the right question asked at the right moment. "Are you feeling . . . ?" "Do you think that . . . ?" "What do you think will happen if . . . ?" are initial probes that can help free the child as well as the parent from the perplexity of hidden meanings. Thus, when a parent is in doubt as to the meaning of a child's message, listening *and* hearing are best accomplished through the art and science of questioning. Such probing is always appropriate, except, of course, when it is overdone. (For example, when a child with a bloody scrape is asked, "Does it hurt?," it would be logical to answer, "Of course it hurts, can't you see?")

At this age level, the parental posture of director, which dominated the first eight years, should slowly shift to the stance of guide. Depending on intelligence, family composition, and other special considerations, parents should begin to employ a low profile when dealing with children. While the policy of backing off should not be construed as a license to ignore a child, it does suggest that a parent should *guide* the older child through challenging waters instead of *demanding* that certain things be done. Listening becomes the key to this guiding light since nobody—least of all, parents—can guide a child without knowing what the kid is thinking.

If parents succeed in this guidance approach, they'll go far in avoiding the portrait that a lot of ten-year-olds draw after listening to their parents: "Grown-ups are fakes. You can't trust them. I don't think I wanna grow up!"

Let's take a look at a few kids whose antics made it difficult to hear what they were trying to say.

SITUATION: Ten-year-old Charles, a fourth-grader, brought home his report card, which contained three D's, two C's, and two check marks, one for "poor motivation" and one for "fair cooperation."

REACTION: Charles approached his mother with the card and, with the grades concealed, said, "Sign this for the teacher." Mother, hurriedly getting ready for her volunteer work with the Ladies' Aid Society, signed the card without looking at it.

Charles's father overheard the transaction and asked to see what had been signed. When he discovered the situation, he promptly blew his top. Without any discussion and in a heated voice, he grounded Charles until the next reporting period. When Charles began to protest, his father said, "That's that. There's nothing more to talk about."

INTERPRETATION: In short, Charles was playing around in school when he should have been studying and paying attention to business. It was possible that Charles would not only fail in school next term but also that he might slowly turn to social deviance.

The father's dictatorial method of handling the poor grades and his complete avoidance of the lie convinced me that he had little communication with or understanding of his son. In fact, given the level of disrespect, I wondered whether the father even liked his son.

While the father was harsh, the mother was disappointing. She was too busy "helping" others to take time to listen to her son. Charles will possibly turn his playfulness into hatred for his parents, and as it builds within him, he will find more and more effective revenge tactics for getting even. Charles is a candidate for Level 5 trouble.

RECOMMENDATION: I have no fail-safe recommendations for parents who don't take time to respect their children. The best shot I can give to those who are honest enough to admit that they don't know how to work with children's deviance is to seek professional help.

As for Charles's situation (brought to my attention by his teacher), I can only give suggestions to the thin air. In a relaxed manner—possibly at the kitchen table after dinner—mother, father, and Charles should talk about his poor grades and low level of motivation and cooperation as well as his rather ingenious sneakiness. Strategies should be devised for remedial work in all areas, work to be shared by the parents as well as Charles.

A follow-up conference with the teacher would be in order. Instead of punishing Charles for laziness, his parents would do well to set up a program of rewarding him for doing extra makeup work. However, he should not be rewarded for doing his regular schoolwork.

LESSON: There are some parents who shouldn't be.

SITUATION: While I was visiting a professional colleague, he told me of a distressing habit that his nine-year-old son, Pete, had developed. I knew Pete personally and had always found him to be intellectually advanced for his age, enjoying such things as stamp-collecting, reading, and mathematics.

His parents set high standards for him, and he seemed to work well within the family's need for achievement. However, without warning and often at solemn moments, Pete would switch languages.

While plain, simple English was the only language spoken in the home, Pete occasionally conversed in Animal English. (This is the language spoken by Scoobey-doo, of Saturday-morning cartoon fame.) Pete's father told me of a time during a wedding banquet, when, asked what he wanted for dinner, Pete responded, "Rrruffee rrrants rrots wwof rrrake."

REACTION: Pete's father admitted to being boiling mad. He believed that his son was much too mature to act so foolishly. He would castigate Pete by saying, "Peter, talk like a young man and not some stupid animal." Pete, in turn, would say, "Rrrall rrrrite." The battle would continue in this vein until his dad threatened grave reprisals if Pete did not stop growling immediately.

INTERPRETATION: Pete had found an excellent way to unnerve his father. Obviously, Pete had a lot of fun and excitement with the language. The adventures of Scoobey-doo are designed for children (I should know—I never miss him), and kids frequently imitate his antics, including his speech.

Also, Pete knew how angry his imitation made his father and was using it to push out the limits of his father's strict expectancies. The father needed to loosen up and spend more time listening to his son's playfulness.

RECOMMENDATION: I suggested to my friend that he relax his standards a little bit so that Pete would have a chance to have some fun with his father. I also recommended that he look at the positive side of Pete's Ambush—his son was using a very creative and imaginative technique of defiance, something Dad could be proud of.

Pete's father wasn't too thrilled when I suggested that he watch Scoobey-doo with his son some Saturday morning. I assured him that he would be more tolerant of his son's antics if he did. I don't think he believed me.

LESSON: If a gentle warrior is smarter than a parent, the parent should dull the tip of his arrow.

Pete and Charles weren't bad kids. In fact, their parents should have considered themselves lucky. Their children's larceny was clearly visible and indicated that they had the courage to try to manipulate the world. I tell parents who are faced with such ingenious Ambushes to be thankful that their children are normal and to concentrate their time and efforts on redirecting their energies toward constructive ends.

The attempts by Pete and Charles to get around their parents' authority are the type of flimflam maneuvers that should stimulate a spark of understanding, not anger, in parents' hearts. These two warriors were saying, "I don't think you're as smart as you look. I'm gonna see just how good you really are." Instead of hearing the challenge and teaching them a lifelong lesson, one parent took it too seriously while the others didn't listen at all.

Pete and Charles had a similar goal in mind. They wanted to make themselves happy. It was the means to their end that caused the problem, not the end itself. If the parents had Kissed off their preoccupations and stuck to the issues at hand, they could have taught their children how to get what they wanted without interfering with the rights and freedoms of others. Such a lesson is one stone in the foundation of creative conformity.

Another critical stone in the foundation is school adjustment.

SITUATION: On the par-five 565-yard water hole, my golfing buddy told me of a problem with his nine-year-old son, Terry. He said that his son's teacher had complained about Terry's failure to follow directions at school.

The third-grader wouldn't finish his arithmetic, even though he excelled in numbers. He wouldn't get in line after recess, and he usually ignored the teacher's warnings about sitting down, being quiet, and paying attention.

REACTION: When confronted by his father, Terry denied any wrongdoing, saying, "I always do what Mrs. Wilson says." When specific examples were outlined, Terry professed ignorance regarding the entire problem. After being told that he'd better start complying with the teacher's rules or else face the loss of his bicycle, Terry walked away.

Ten minutes later, he returned and said, "Dad, I think I might need a test at school tomorrow." When asked to elaborate, he said, "I think my ears need checking. I might have bad hearing."

This was said in such a serious tone that Terry's father called the school the following day and arranged an audiometric examination for his son. (When I heard this, I drove a fairway wood into a sand trap.)

INTERPRETATION: Terry's strategy of pretending ignorance was supposed to make his father believe *him,* not the teacher. When it backfired, he implemented a second Ambush in order to cover for the failure of the first. Dad put the pressure on Terry, and he countered by redoubling his efforts with an ingenious use of the school nurse's pride in her testing equipment.

The father had been on the right track until he was sidelined with this old wild-goose-chase scheme. Terry's disruption in school was serious and could easily be handled once the parents, teacher, and nurse got their heads together. Dad needed to worry less and listen more.

RECOMMENDATION: On the day he told me the story, Terry's father knew how he had been Ambushed. He didn't mind his son's winning one battle, but he didn't want him to win the war.

I told him bluntly that before he could begin to win some of the battles, he had to quit trying to be so damn perfect. That way he would give Terry less opportunity to take advantage of him. For example, he would do well to ask more questions, testing the validity of Terry's complaints or pretended ignorance of the problem.

Terry would probably be a masterful manipulater for many years to come. His inventiveness suggested that he would easily adapt to new situations with more appropriate behavior.

The threat of losing the bicycle was excellent, except it lacked implementation.

LESSON: Investing too much worry will result in overdone interest that can yield problems that are compounded daily.

SITUATION: Ten-year-old Larry's parents were referred to me because of a school-adjustment problem. Several days prior to our meeting, Larry had been sent to the principal for the sixth time in a month for mouthing off to the teacher.

When asked to sit down or be quiet, Larry would say, "You're not my mother; I don't have to mind you." He also talked to other kids during study time, took things from fellow students, and habitually was tardy in returning from the bathroom.

REACTION: The principal had spoken with Larry's father over the phone on several occasions. He now wanted to have a conference with both parents, Larry's teacher, and the school guidance counselor.

The father was worried about his son's disruptiveness. He could offer little or no insight into the reason behind it. He did admit to being very sensitive to friends' and neighbors' criticism of Larry's budding "delinquency." He remembered commenting to Larry more than once, "Don't get into trouble, son, you know how the neighbors would love to talk about your mother and me." When Larry was pressured to explain why he was disruptive, he responded, "I don't know."

INTERPRETATION: With his entry into the social circles of school, Larry had found a parental weakness and was attacking it in order to discredit authority figures. The weakness was embodied in the parents' worry about what others would say concerning Larry's behavior. This was a good example of parental peer pressure; that is, parents' paying more attention to what their neighbors say than to their child's actions.

At this age, such disruptiveness is fairly easy to deal with. However, if allowed to continue unchecked, Larry's disruption could result in academic underachievement and anger at his parents for being more worried about what their friends would say than about him. These two things could lead to worse trouble, which could take a variety of forms, all of which would be Larry's way of getting his parents' undivided attention as well as reaping revenge for past parental mistakes.

RECOMMENDATION: In Larry's presence, I told his parents firmly to stop worrying about the reaction of their country-club friends and start concentrating their efforts on solid disciplinary measures with Larry.

In a similar castigating tone, I warned Larry that now that his "game was busted" he'd better get his act together or he'd end up in big trouble. Sober silence suggested that I had achieved my goal—getting their attention.

LESSON: Parents should covet their kid's respect more than a neighbor's praise.

SITUATION: Nine-year-old Todd's father cornered me in a bar one night and explained his difficult problem. Todd was in fourth grade and failing most subjects. He was bringing home highly negative school-adjustment reports and was practically uncontrollable in the classroom. Just prior to our meeting, Todd had been sent home after intimidating his teacher with a yardstick and threatening to hurt the principal.

REACTION: According to the father, Todd's behavior had prompted the principal to demand his presence at conferences on more than one occasion. In front of Todd's teacher and the principal, the father had spanked his son quite hard. He had then encouraged the school authorities to do the same whenever Todd misbehaved. Todd refused to cry but supposedly was learning a lesson.

INTERPRETATION: With detailed questioning, I learned that Todd was not only acting out in school, but he was also troublesome in the neighborhood. He had recently thrown a brick at a fellow student who had called him a "nigger."

His father admitted that he had carefully taught his son to avoid fights at all costs. Being black in a predominantly white community had necessitated this nonviolent stance. However, being the brunt of many degrading remarks, Todd had overreacted to his father's advice and become a doormat—something that others could wipe their hate on.

Finally, Todd could stand it no longer. Not only did he begin to express his anger at kids' hatefulness, but he also dumped some of his pent-up resentment. Since Todd had learned to survive under fear and punishing life circumstances, spanking would only lead to more anger and revenge. It was way past time for Todd to start finding praise and rewards for decency and socially appropriate behavior.

RECOMMENDATION: I told Todd's father to search out new experiences for his son. I recommended enrollment in Little League baseball and scouting. Since Todd was a bright kid but hooked by poor achievement, I suggested that he be taken to the library and involved in the junior readers' club.

As for the current school problem, it was important that Todd be allowed and even prompted to talk about his anger and resentment. He really needed to learn how to talk about his pain, and his father's willingness to listen was the key to unlocking his mouth.

I tried to eliminate the possibility of future spankings by warning Todd's father that his son's anger could accidentally lead to serious bodily injury. He needed to get words and concepts straight in his head without further physical attacks, from his father or anyone else.

LESSON: Believe it or not, a nine-year-old can talk it all out.

When kids go to school, they enter the first formal testing ground of parental training. Parents who worry about whether or not their children will have problems in school are wasting their time. They must realize that *all* kids have problems when they venture outside the home and try to adjust to a classroom situation. Lucky parents are faced with a missed bus, a torn skirt, or a child who threw up during recess. Less fortunate moms and dads must deal with classroom disruption, lack of attentiveness, poor achievement, and damaged property.

When Terry, Larry, and Todd went to school, they exhibited three different problems. Their difficulties represented divergent degrees of trouble but only a small sample of the countless tribulations associated with school. They were lucky because they had parents who cared enough to seek help with their problems. If the recommendations were implemented, these three kids had a good chance to learn from their mistakes and realize that the classroom can be a place to pursue academic excellence rather than struggle for interpersonal supremacy.

These cases demonstrate how, after a year or two of compliance, kids may begin to apply their Ambush tactics to authority figures other than Mom and Dad. During kindergarten, first and second grade, the "Yes, Miss Pruitt" syndrome dominates most kids' reaction to their teachers. Sooner or later kids will see that teachers are just as vulnerable as their parents. That's when the teacher becomes a target.

When kids begin to experiment with disruptions associated

with school, the movement away from the simple Ambush is evident. School and similar situations outside the home give children a broader opportunity to view authority figures. The result is a situation in which parents and teachers no longer have to say "No" to be the victim of an Ambush. Their *very being* says "No"; they don't have to utter a sound.

The following Ambushes, pulled off by Jill and Rita, involved simple listening issues.

SITUATION: When a potential client asked me to have breakfast with him to discuss a problem, I didn't think he would bring the problem with him. But there, bouncing up and down in the booth, was a dark-haired, wide-eyed, nine-year-old piece of human dynamite named Jill.

The father began his story about Jill's persistent disruption of his wife's household routine. He talked at length about his wife's oversensitivity to the typical antics of a nine-year-old.

Throughout our conversation, Jill kept tugging at her father's sleeve and saying, "Daddy. Daddy. *Daddy!*"

REACTION: Jill's tugging and whining were quite disruptive to our conversation. Her father said, "Shut up!" at least ten times in ten minutes. However, he didn't seem to be aware of what was going on. He pushed her hand away a dozen times without breaking his train of thought. After Jill spilled some of his coffee, her father growled, "What is it?"

Jill answered, "Did you see that little baby over there?"

Dad blurted, *"No!"* and resumed his remarks about how his wife couldn't deal with Jill's disruptiveness.

INTERPRETATION: Jill's father was so blind I couldn't believe it. There he sat talking about his wife's problems as he ignored a child who was raising hell right next to him. It might have been true that Jill's mother was having problems with her daughter, but at least she was aware of Jill's presence.

Jill's desire to make an observation was quite legitimate. However, her tugging and whining were inappropriate. She needed to learn respect for another's right to speak uninterruptedly. But she'd never do it unless her father opened his eyes and ears and saw and heard what she was doing.

RECOMMENDATION: I put my recommendation into action. When the father paused to munch on his toast, I questioned, "Is Jill's disruption around her mom anything like what she did a few minutes ago?"

Not giving the father any chance to answer, I continued. "She squirmed in her seat, tugged at your coat, interrupted our conversation beyond belief, and asked unsuccessfully for your attention at least fifteen times." I then suggested that he was contributing to Jill's continual disruption.

When he said, "Yeah, but I ignore her," I took time to explain how ignoring without teaching the proper alternative only serves to promote the same old disruption. He should have found time to say, "Jill, as soon as you sit still and let Daddy finish with his thought, you can talk." Obviously, he should follow through with this expectancy.

LESSON: A child's need for attention is often difficult to hear.

SITUATION: After a long day at work, I was sitting in my favorite bar drinking a beer. The couple next to me had their ten-year-old daughter with them. Within five or ten minutes, they had started unsolicited bragging about her maturity. "Rita is so smart. She's more grown-up than most adults I know," said her mother.

Rita sat quietly at the bar sipping a kiddie cocktail as both parents continued to babble about how fantastic she was. I looked at her several times and saw an ominous look of self-satisfaction on her face.

Rita ordered another red-colored cola as her parents soaked up the happy-hour booze. Then she moved with her Ambush. She asked her mother for money to play some music, went to the jukebox, and returned to the sounds of "Bad, bad Leroy Brown." Her mother gave her a passing hug and said (so that everyone in the bar could hear), "Boy, you sure do know how to play good music."

REACTION: In a voice like a siren, Rita responded, "You like that kind of music? I thought you were too old to enjoy rock 'n' roll."

Mom looked at Dad as if to say, "Whose idea was it to bring her?" Dad shrugged his shoulders and said, "Honey, she's your daughter all the way."

INTERPRETATION: Rita was being used by her parents as bait to attract praise from other people. Rita, in turn, had found an excellent place to demonstrate the folly of her parents' pride. She could use this situation to get a lot of goodies later on. She had sweetly set them up for an Ambush and then—*pow!* right in the schooner.

RECOMMENDATION: I was too busy chuckling in my beer to make more than a silent suggestion. A bar is no place for a kid. They should have left Rita at home with a sitter and enjoyed each other's company.

LESSON: There are some places where children should be neither seen nor heard.

The parents in the above cases set themselves up for the Ambush. Jill's father thought his parental armor impenetrable to his daughter's disrespect. Therefore, he simply didn't hear what was happening. Rita caught her parents acting cocky and chipped away at their authority by showing their pride to be foolish. Both kids walked away from the situations with a tarnished image of an authority figure resting in their mind's eye.

The parents were strutting around like proud peacocks showing off their brilliant plumage. They were so busy polishing their own perfectionism, they didn't see how vulnerable they had become. These cases amply demonstrate how the perfectionistic attitude of parents can set them up for an Ambush.

The best alternative to self-indulgence is good, old-fashioned humility. Parents who are willing to admit that they are less than perfect, especially in front of their children, will go far in disarming their gentle warriors.

Jill and Rita really stuck it to their parents. Helen and Donna did likewise, but they were helped by an all-too-frequent social malady, divorce.

SITUATION: The mother of one of my wards (kids in jail) asked my advice about her ten-year-old stepdaughter. The girl, Donna, was her second husband's only child from his first marriage, which had ended with his wife's death.

According to the lady, Donna was a "terror." She noted, "She makes Scotty [the woman's son in my custody] look like an angel." A typical "terroristic" activity had occurred the previous Sunday. Five minutes before they were to leave for church, Donna had emerged from her bedroom wearing a miniskirt, the hem of which was six or seven inches above her knees.

REACTION: Her stepmother had exploded, saying something like, "Why do you do these things to me? You know I can't let you go to church looking like that. What would people think of me if I let my daughter go to church looking like a tramp? You don't have time to change, so you'll have to stay home."

INTERPRETATION: There were several things going on in this situation. Investigation uncovered that Donna carefully preplanned such noncompliance. She was very well acquainted with her stepmother's standards of decent attire and regular churchgoing. It was equally apparent that Donna didn't want to go to church and that she wanted to undermine her stepmother's authority in the process.

This woman had opened herself to part of the Ambush by being so obvious in her concern about what other people thought of her. She should have concentrated more on Donna's improper attire and less on what other people thought.

Another complicating factor was that Donna appeared unable or unwilling to talk about her feelings of anger with God for "taking away her real mother." Her anger was taking the form of revenge against her stepmother, a confusing situation, to say the least.

RECOMMENDATION: I suggested to the stepmother that she ease up on pressuring Donna to attend church and play down her feelings of worry about other people's evaluation of her.

Recognizing that her moral code would not tolerate very short skirts, I recommended that she make it *very* clear to Donna that she would not allow her to leave the house (for *any* reason) if her skirt was too short. I cautioned her not to argue about inches, but to set a standard. (Many parents are content with the following definition of "short": when you kneel on the floor, the hem of the dress is four inches above the floor.)

I further suggested that she could eliminate much of Donna's need to fight by occasionally speaking of Donna's natural mother. She could tell Donna she knew how special her real mother must have been and assure her that such people are sorely missed by those who loved them. Most of all, she must not try to compete with a painful memory.

LESSON: Hearing the wrong thing can be worse than not listening at all.

SITUATION: Ten-year-old Helen's mother had recently remarried. She continued to have considerable difficulty with her ex-husband, who had been physically abusive to her prior to their divorce. He remained verbally abusive. The mother carried a great deal of unexpressed pain in the form of anger, frustration, and hatred.

Helen's stepfather was very gentle and concerned about the welfare of his new family. One evening, after a very heated argument with her ex-husband, Helen's mother started a fight with her present husband, complaining about the way he disciplined her daughter.

The yelling was very loud, easily overheard in the child's bedroom. The next day, when Helen was reprimanded by her mother for not eating properly, Helen countered, "You yell at everybody, don't you? Why are you always screaming?"

REACTION: Helen's mother damn near hit the ceiling. She reacted to her daughter's Ambush by screaming, "You have no right to talk like that to your mother. You don't know the hell I go through for you. Now, you apologize to Mommy—*now!*" Helen hung her head and cried.

INTERPRETATION: Helen hadn't realized how her Ambush would backfire. What had started out as a good-natured attempt to avoid eating had suddenly turned into an ugly scene filled with feelings of anger, hatred, and guilt.

There's a good chance that Helen will eventually seek revenge on her mother for dealing so harshly with her. Helen was a punching bag in this situation. Her mother dumped her pent-up emotions on her daughter, believing that Helen could take them and bounce back unhurt.

If this type of thing continued, Helen would have pent-up emotions of her own to deal with. She might dump them on her mother in a very troublesome manner. Then the mother would have still another source of pain to add to her general misery.

This was one of those situations in which a parent's problems and a kid's Ambush become so entangled that separating one from the other is almost impossible.

RECOMMENDATION: Since the mother was still fearful of physical abuse, she didn't feel safe in dumping her pain on her ex-husband (where it belonged). The minister at her church was well trained in pastoral counseling, so I suggested she schedule some sessions with him so that she could air out her pain. She could also eventually turn to her new husband to share her pain.

The result of this work was that she could approach Helen with a clear head and more objectively deal with the child's attempts to circumvent her authority.

I recommended that she use my formula for compensating for "verbal spankings" by giving Helen three kind words or phrases for each harsh outburst.

LESSON: Compensate for verbal spankings before kids decide to strike back.

Unresolved emotional pain is often carried into second marriages. If not expressed and worked through, it can become an ugly breeding ground for countless disruptive situations, not the least of which are elaborate forms of Ambush.

This pain is hard to hear because it's usually buried beneath a desire to forget bad memories and find hope in renewed dreams. In Donna's case, the child was not prepared to verbalize her feelings. Her stepmother's words of reassurance and respect for a lost love would help Donna uncover some of the pain, feel it, and forget it.

Helen's situation was reversed. She sensed a tender spot in her mother's makeup and poked at it in order to weaken parental authority. However, she didn't understand the nature or degree of the pain her mom was actually covering. Her mother had the responsibility of listening to the nonlethal nature of Helen's Ambush without letting it burn so deeply into her heart.

Parents who enter second marriages must stay alert for at least a year, listening for hidden pain, both in their children and in themselves. As we shall see later, they must also be sensitive to any projection that might occur; that is, seeing pain in their child when it actually is within themselves. Thus, when divorce plays a part in children's disruption, fathers and mothers, step or natural, must listen extra carefully to their kids. In fact, parents who embark on the "second time around" are ahead of the game if they listen twice and speak once, instead of the reverse.

Listening to what children say covers many areas. As is pointed out below, it also includes hearing whether or not children heard what was said to them.

SITUATION: Nine-year-old Steve became frightened of his father rather quickly. It happened over a period of two or three weeks. Finally Steve refused to participate in any activities with his dad, preferring instead to play alone in his room.

REACTION: Steve's father was very concerned and had many long discussions with his wife and friends. His attempts to communicate with Steve were thwarted by Steve's silence. When pushed to say why he wouldn't play with his father, Steve would say, "I don't know."

The usually happy, playful mood of the home turned morose, somber, and deathly silent. The father tried even harder to engage his son in meaningful activity with him. He bought him a new bicycle and several new toys, but nothing worked. After several months, Steve's father pulled me aside after a handball game, asking my advice.

INTERPRETATION: I investigated the situation by sitting with the family and asking questions. It seemed to me that Steve was involved in two different but overlapping problems.

First, Steve felt intimidated by his father's superior physical capabilities, realizing that he couldn't keep up with the man he admired so much. Therefore, rather than suffer from feelings of inferiority, he simply avoided his father.

In tandem with this problem was Steve's awareness that he could get even with his father for being superior by "icing" him; that is, he magnified his discouragement by using coldness and aloofness to try to *make* his father feel bad. In so doing, he reaped special goodies. In a nutshell, Steve took his masculine identity crisis and converted it into an Ambush.

After an in-depth interview, I was able to pinpoint why Steve thought he was inferior. During their workouts, Steve's father would often groan, grimace, and gripe about the entire activity. Steve thought that he was the cause; however, the real cause was that an overweight, out-of-shape, middle-aged man was expecting his body to perform like that of an eighteen-year-old.

RECOMMENDATION: I prescribed a long talk with Steve in which Dad was to point out several things. First, he loved his son and wanted to play with him. Second, groans and grimaces are the result of fat and fatigue, not displeasure. Finally, if Steve continued to have a "problem," no further special privileges would be forthcoming.

FOLLOW-UP: The next week, I saw Steve and his father playing racketball together.

LESSON: A child has a right to his or her own problems. If parents try to make their child's problem their problem, they're going to have even more problems than they already have; and that's a problem!

SITUATION: Ten-year-old Lori and her brother seemed to be fighting constantly. According to Lori's mother, Lori usually said something to her brother about being younger, he protested, she made fun of him, and he shoved her. Every time her brother shoved, she would sock him.

REACTION: Lori usually got punished after her brother ran screaming to Mom or Dad. When asked by her father why she always hit her brother, Lori would say, "Well, you told me not to let boys bully me just because I'm a girl. And my brother is a boy, isn't he?"

Lori's mother admitted that her husband didn't know what to do with this double-bind situation. He had tried to say, "But this is different." But this only got him into more trouble because Lori would say, "How?"

INTERPRETATION: Although Lori was raising hell with her family, she did have a good point. However, she was taking the ambiguity contained in the situation and using it as a justification for her actions.

If the father wanted to give her advice about fighting back, he had to take the time to talk about the conditions under which alternatives other than hitting might be effective. He probably should role-play other behaviors Lori could use to avoid bullying.

Giving a child unrestricted license to hit another is asking for serious trouble. There's too much hitting going on as it is.

RECOMMENDATION: I suggested that Lori's father counsel his daughter about ways to avoid being bullied. She was to learn the beneficial effects of ignoring, talking, changing the subject, asking authority figures to step in, and even threatening. Moreover, she herself was not to tease younger kids.

LESSON: Use extreme caution before advising a child to hit someone.

"What we have here is a failure to communicate." This often-quoted explanation for interpersonal difficulties is applicable to the foregoing cases. The parents' good intentions and expectations were supposed to be transmitted to their children. However, the parents said one thing, and their children heard another. It takes more than a generation gap to account for the loss of such messages. Usually they're lost because a child is too busy thinking to listen.

In such cases, there is no substitute for checking to see if a message has been received in the same form it was sent. It is relatively easy for a parent to say to a child, "Tell me what you heard me say." This simple request can be used to measure a child's listening skills and help parents cope with Ambushes. Steve and Lori's fathers could have saved everyone a lot of grief by employing this technique. It could have uncovered Steve's disappointment in himself and Lori's belief that she had a license to hit indiscriminately.

While this technique can be effective, it can be overdone. Although parents should take time to help a child understand their inner wishes, they should not waste time worrying about whether the child *completely* understands their intentions. Once a child hears instructions, discussions about intentions must not interfere with compliance with those instructions.

Compare Randy's Ambush.

SITUATION: Ten-year-old Randy's father told me this story in hopes of finding an innovative solution to a challenging situation.

One evening Randy was told that he had twenty minutes to put his toys away, finish his chores (feeding the dog), and get ready for bed. Ten minutes passed, and he hadn't moved a muscle. His father then warned him, "Do what your mother said, *or else!"* Still nothing.

Two or three minutes later, Randy was still not moving, so his father grabbed him firmly by his collar and began to move him bodily. Startled, Randy calmly said to his dad, "What are you doing? You know you shouldn't grab me like that. Do you realize that you're hurting me? Maybe you'd better calm down."

REACTION: Randy's father damn near had a heart attack. He grabbed Randy more firmly, gave him a swat on the butt, and shoved him on the bed. Then he bellowed, "Don't you ever talk to me that way again, or you'll have red marks from your toes to your nose. *Understand?"*

Randy muttered, "Yeah." After Randy went to bed, his

mother and father had a long discussion about Randy's insolence and lack of respect. Randy's mother was so concerned that she wondered whether their son was disturbed. Randy's father was just plain mad.

INTERPRETATION: Without being offensive, I told Randy's father that what he had on his hands was basically a smart-ass. Several errors were made on all sides and compounded through lack of parental follow-through.

Randy didn't want to stop playing and thereby conform to his parents' instructions. He played a waiting game. Meanwhile, his parents failed to take any action on their original request until the situation was red hot. The "or-else" threat just wasn't potent with Randy—obviously, he had heard it many times without any negative consequences.

Randy played the role of "junior shrink" to the hilt. He remained calm and clinical while his father became dominated by emotions. It was surprising that Randy had used such a sophisticated Ambush at such an early age. The situation called for super parenting.

RECOMMENDATION: I told Randy's father not to wait so long next time he made a request of his son. He was to make the request *once,* and if Randy did not comply he was to institute a penalty immediately (take a toy away for two weeks, for example).

The next time Randy tried the "junior-shrink" routine, the father was to avoid any physical contact, saying, "I choose to come over here because you choose not to move. If you moved when I asked you to, there would be no problem. So if you want to avoid a hassle, *move!"*

LESSON: An "or else" without follow-through gives a child live ammunition.

To put Randy in a category with others would be an injustice. He was in a class all by himself. Such a combination of ingenuity, sensitivity, verbal skills, and coolness under fire seldom occurs. While his parents had a skilled Ambusher in their home, they could take heart in the realization that Randy would be receptive to family discussions. In some ways, he was ten going on thirty.

There are four general survival strategies that parents should keep in mind when dealing with the verbal acrobatics of nine- and ten-year-old children. First, they should never stick their necks out by assuming automatically that they know what a kid is trying to say. Second, when a question or statement causes doubt, parents should never hesitate to ask questions or make inferences. For example, good things to say would be: "Do you like your teacher?" "You feel bad, huh?" "Sounds like you don't know for sure." "You act as if you're angry with me." Third, if a child asks for a parent's reaction, the answer should be kept as simple as possible. (The Kiss approach helps eliminate unnecessary issues.) Finally, a parent should never be afraid to say, "I don't know."

Sometimes, "not knowing" is the best way to get a child's attention. And after all is said and done, paying attention is the key to listening.

Words of Caution

I am about to review the most difficult time period of Protective Parenting, adolescence. Somewhere between the ages of eleven and nineteen, 99 percent of all parents are confronted with some type of trouble. It usually occurs amid heart-stopping and hair-raising circumstances. During this time, the protective role is severely tested. The ABC Assessment can be a lifesaver. Making a movie of teenage behavior can help the family survive.

Identifying the elusive adolescent Ambush is an accomplishment in itself. Once it has been pinpointed, parents can use the coping comebacks detailed in Chapter 13 to get out of many sticky situations. The comebacks can be applied throughout all age levels to help parents get out of blind alleys while retaining the integrity of their authority.

Even when faced with failure, parents can still take heart in one piece of awareness: parental mistakes provide a reference point for their children, who, upon becoming parents, will say, "I won't make the same mistakes my parents did." (What the children don't realize is that while avoiding old mistakes, they'll make new ones. Then, when the grandchildren become parents, they, in turn, will say, "I won't make the same mistakes *my* parents did.")

11

Eleven and Twelve:
The Beginning—Again

After a decade of enduring secretive manipulations, withstanding onslaughts of uncivilized behavior, sorting out truth from fiction, and protecting children from their innate carelessness, Mom and Dad are only about halfway through the job of Protective Parenting. As children approach eleven or twelve years of age, many of life's problems are just beginning. In many respects, parents are also just beginning—all over again.

If the parents were successful in teaching the rudiments of self-control during the first ten years, the second ten won't be much worse. However, if the child failed to learn the fundamentals of compliance, discussion, compromise, self-confidence, and individual choice, the time between ten and twenty can be hell.

At twelve years of age a kid has faced, is facing, or soon will face problems of personal identity, sex, friends, drugs, alcohol, school achievement, and parental authority. He or she will have to form some initial values regarding popularity, self-esteem, personal appearance, individuality, trust among friends, and other social issues. Each kid moves at his or her own pace, so it's impossible to state categorically in what sequence or time span all of this will happen. All I know for sure is that it *will* happen.

At eleven or twelve, kids stand at the entrance to a time of life when fads mean excitement, friends are forever, discomfort is unbearable, and being "cool" is the only way to go. They have monumental questions without an answer to their name; they don't realize what's happening but are convinced they're right; they travel in every direction without the foggiest notion of where they're going; and their heads are full of dizziness from trying to do everything at once. They search for "heavy" or "bad" experiences to make the dizzies dissipate, and they complain to authority figures when things don't go their way.

This time of life could be called many things, most of which would be derogatory. However, the general term for this time span is "adolescence." To paraphrase Dickens, "It is the best of times; it is the worst of times." It is the best because parents are able to see a total person begin to function. It is the worst because children often behave as if they hadn't learned a thing about civilized manners during their first ten years on earth.

Many parents have asked me how they can recognize the beginning of this era of errors. I usually tell them, "Your child has reached adolescence when he or she stands in a room full of new toys and says, 'There's nothing to do.' "

One of the more confusing aspects of this preteen period is the reactivation of impulses that have seemingly been under control for several years. The most troublesome of these drives is the wish to receive immediate satisfaction of all desires. Even if a parent has been successful in teaching a child prudence in self-gratification, an all-too-familiar battle cry returns: "I want *more!*" It can take many forms, here are just three.

SITUATION: The mother of twelve-year-old Jerry complained that her son watched too much TV. "He just won't stay away from the darn TV set," she wailed. "No matter what time of the day or night, if he's awake, the TV is on."

REACTION: The mother said that she had tried to explain to Jerry that too much TV was bad for him. "I tell him that it will hurt his eyes and he should be outdoors playing with other kids." She went on to explain that Jerry would answer her by mumbling, "Yeah, Mom," and keep on watching the tube.

His mother tried to turn off the TV once, but Jerry raised such a fuss that she decided to leave him alone, thinking he would grow out of it. She admitted that Jerry socialized very little and that his grades were slipping. Jerry's father and mother were divorced, so there was no other authority figure around the house to take any action.

INTERPRETATION: As I listened to the lady, I had to wonder who the boss really was in that household. It seemed pretty obvious that Jerry was running things. The lady needed to get him under control quickly, or else Jerry would soon become an inconsiderate, uncontrollable teenager.

Television has many fine qualities and teaches children many things. It was understandable that Jerry liked to watch it. However, when TV-watching excludes other, essential activities, it's time for a change. Jerry's addiction to TV could cause two harmful side effects. First, he might fall far behind in school because of little study. Second, he might become more susceptible to going along with the crowd due to his habit of being passively entertained.

Also of major concern was the noncompliance demonstrated by Jerry when asked to turn off the TV. Since Jerry didn't respond to such simple requests, I was afraid to ask what other things he wasn't doing. Anyhow, I imagined that his mother didn't even notice anymore.

RECOMMENDATION: I told the lady to do two things. First, she was to enforce her requests by turning the TV off, and if Jerry fussed, she was to say, "The longer you yell, the longer the TV will stay off." If he didn't shut up and do something more active, she was to tell him he couldn't watch his favorite show for one week. For every subsequent yell he would lose another show for one week.

I also suggested that Jerry be helped to develop his own personal interests. Since her husband didn't come around very much, I recommended that Jerry become involved in Junior Achievement. Also, a friend's husband had volunteered to take Jerry and his own son swimming once in a while.

Jerry definitely needed more time for reading and studying. I recommended a study period of one hour each night.

LESSON: The more a kid watches the tube, the more likely he'll be a boob.

SITUATION: Chad's dad laughed about his eleven-year-old son's insatiable desire for carbonated drinks. Chad would drink any refreshment that could even loosely be called a soda. There were no physical problems; Chad just loved soft drinks.

Even if some member of the family had a cola in his or her hand, Chad would attempt to get it away. He was a real pest. His father warned him repeatedly about his disrespectful actions. Chad seemed to pay attention but failed to take heed of any admonition.

One evening at dinner, Chad gulped down his sister's soda while she was gone from the table.

REACTION: His father calmly rose from his seat, took his own cola in hand, and walked over to Chad. In a soft, affirmative voice, he said, "You want more to drink? Here is more to drink." Then he poured the cola on his son's head.

INTERPRETATION: While I had to admit that his actions were innovative and somewhat successful (after that, Chad didn't take anyone's cola in his father's presence), I had to wonder whether Chad had learned the lesson he really needed. Punishment alone was not sufficient.

Chad was exhibiting the grown-up version of the ketchup Ambush detailed in Chapter 6. He needed to learn the definition of "enough" much more than Brian, Billy, or Pete. If self-control doesn't start with simple things like drinking soda, there's no reason to assume that it will operate during a drug or booze party.

It was logical to assume that Chad had learned not to steal

drinks when his father was around. However, there was no indication he would internalize the temperance lesson in his father's absence.

RECOMMENDATION: First of all, I recommended that the father bring more milk and less soda home from the store. Then I tried to convince him of the potential seriousness of the situation by outlining what a drug overdose looks and sounds like. He appeared quite concerned at this.

We discussed alternatives he could use to discourage Chad's poor self-control. We decided to start using soda as a special treat rather than something constantly available. Therefore, Chad was to receive some type of soft drink whenever he completed his chores properly, played cooperatively with friends, or successfully completed some special assignment.

Any misuse of sodas (for example, drinking without permission or taking another's drink) was to result in three days of no soft drinks whatsoever.

LESSON: Overindulgence can be addictive.

SITUATION: While visiting a friend one evening, I witnessed a superslick Ambush. At 9:00 P.M., Wendy's father told his eleven-year-old daughter to "say goodnight and go to bed." Wendy followed directions perfectly—at least to a point.

She reappeared after being gone about ten minutes, dressed in a cute nightie with her hair in pigtails. She looked darling. She said "goodnight" to me, crawled onto her dad's lap, and whispered something in his ear. He shrugged his shoulders, shook his head "Yes," and hugged her.

As if she had been awaiting the chance for years, she began to tell about how her father had fixed her a playroom in the basement. Her story left out no details. She giggled and he blushed. She said that he was the greatest daddy in the whole wide world, and he grinned approvingly.

After twenty minutes, he again repeated his bedtime message. She kissed him again, said goodnight to me once more, and, as she reached the doorway, paused and asked if she could have a glass of milk. "Okay, then straight to bed," replied her father.

REACTION: To make a long, long story quite short, Wendy was wide-eyed and bouncy as she said goodnight to me when I left their home. It was 10:30 P.M. As I moved down the hall of the apartment and out the door, I saw Wendy's father grab her gently and heard him growl lovingly, *"Now,* young lady, you go to bed."

INTERPRETATION: I guess every girl should be allowed to manipulate her father once or twice during preadolescence. The only trouble with this situation is that it can easily lead to bigger and more disruptive manipulations.

Wendy wanted to enjoy "grown-up talk," which is absolutely fine. However, she used physical affection and apple-polishing to get what she wanted. I don't think her flattery was necessarily false, but she shouldn't learn to use it as a way of getting around an authority's request.

I don't know whether or not her dad knew what she was doing. Either way, there were a couple of things he could have done to make sure she wasn't learning a bad habit.

RECOMMENDATION: Although he never asked me, I would have suggested to Wendy's father that he either make his original request stick, making sure she went to bed, or allow her the special privilege of staying up for an extra time period (thirty minutes, perhaps) to enjoy grown-ups.

Also, I would have asked him to make sure that Wendy's hugs, kisses, and praise were spontaneous, not just part of an Ambush.

LESSON: Some parents get kissed one minute and Ambushed the next.

I've heard many parents lament, " 'Gimme, gimme, gimme'—from a twelve-year-old? I thought I was finished with that nonsense!"

Sometimes this answer helps: "Relax, ma'am, your child isn't becoming a wild, senseless, uncontrollable renegade, he's just practicing to be an adolescent."

Jerry, Chad, and Wendy were three kids who wanted more—more TV, more soda pop, and more time before bed. They pushed their demands beyond the limits imposed by their parents, and the consequences they suffered were not strong enough to deter them from their persistence. Jerry heard his mother yell, while Wendy paid no attention to her father's gentle reminders. Chad, on the other hand, suffered an immediate consequence but learned little in the long run. After all, what can a kid learn from one bout with the "wet head"?

All three kids showed some spunk. Their budding self-confidence gave them the courage to test once again the limits imposed by authority figures. For all parents, this second time around proves more challenging than the first. When a child is four years old, parents can set and enforce limits rather subjectively. When the kid is twelve, parents must *help* set the limits. This is when the objective of Protective Parenting (turning to one's "self" in troubled times) begins to take shape.

The toughest hurdle in this struggle is the obstinacy contained in the child's "you-can't-*make*-me" challenge. Parents must meet this barrier head-on by saying, "You're right, I can't *make* you do it, but you'll suffer some stiff consequences if you don't make *yourself* do it!"

Parents involved in this kind of situation need to reemphasize the importance of delaying self-gratification—or, as my mom might say, "doing without." The use of negative consequences to back up a "No" can teach kids the self-protective skill of saying, "No, I've had enough," even when under pressure to be like the rest of the kids.

Jerry, Chad, and Wendy could avoid serious trouble by thinking ahead to possible negative consequences and saying, "Enough!" The next two kids were already in trouble and needed more than simple preventive intervention.

SITUATION: During one of my many afternoons spent studying Ambushes, I saw an eleven- or twelve-year-old kid excitedly lighting matches in the doorway of a bustling downtown store. An older woman, who appeared to be his grandmother, was window-shopping, paying no attention to him and another boy standing nearby.

When he noticed I was watching him, the boy turned quickly

away, shouted to his buddy, and moved down the street. I followed him into another store, where he attempted to order some food but tired of waiting and spent a lot of money on trinkets before leaving.

He moved back down the street, lighting matches and tossing them carelessly aside. He paused to admire the way three older kids were "hanging around."

REACTION: The boy and his friend returned to the store and started dashing up and down the aisles. I slipped quietly into the store, and watched as Grandmother looked at baby outfits. On one occasion she raised her head long enough to shout, "You children mind yourself, you hear?" (They were now bouncing haphazardly around the store.) At no time during my entire observation did she pay significant attention to her grandson, either when he left or when he returned.

INTERPRETATION: I am particularly concerned when I see a young, energetic kid, barely noticed by anyone close to him, eagerly striking matches and watching the flame with fire in his eyes.

As puberty sets hormones in motion, preadolescents look for outlets for their strong drive for excitement. Fire has a frighteningly strong appeal to kids, especially for boys who have no masculine figure to help them channel their energies.

This kid was playing with fire out in the open, a sign that the deviance might soon pass. But if he turned to special hiding places in order to add mystery to his excitement, serious trouble could easily result.

RECOMMENDATION: Although sorely tempted, I didn't feel comfortable just walking up to the grandmother and telling her what to do. The kid needed more attention from a mature masculine figure (for example, a Big Brother) and less money to spend on trinkets.

Grandmothers and aunts who must assume the burden of raising a child often take the job less seriously than they should and let things slide when they should take disciplinary measures.

LESSON: Serious hell-raising can start with a small fire.

SITUATION: Eleven-year-old Mark lived with his parents and two younger sisters in an upper-middle-class neighborhood. He got a five-dollar allowance each week and had several household chores that needed daily attention. He did well in school and had many friends.

One evening around 11:00 P.M., Mark's father was awakened by the sound of rock music coming from Mark's room. He yelled at Mark to turn the music off and go to sleep. The next evening, Mark walked into the kitchen holding a blaring pocket radio to his ear. When asked where he'd got it, he said that he'd bought it from one of his friends.

Several weeks later, when she happened to run into Mark's friends, the mother casually asked which one had sold Mark the radio. They all denied knowledge of the transaction, unaware of the conclusion Mom would draw.

REACTION: Mom told Dad, and Dad confronted Mark. The boy persisted in his original story, but his stammering and blushful complexion convinced his father that something was wrong.

After several parental threats and considerable crying, Mark admitted that he had taken the radio from a local department store. It was three days later that Mark's father, fearful of legal reprisals and the continuation of his son's shoplifting, consulted me.

INTERPRETATION: This is typical of the first antisocial act of many preteens. It represents Level 4 trouble and the kind of behavior that can bring the immediate attention of the police. This particular act was not terribly serious, nor was cause for great alarm. But it had to be handled so that Mark would learn a lifelong lesson.

Mark had slipped into Level 4 trouble without passing through the first three levels. He was lucky that his parents took an interest in his activities and sought consultation before taking other action.

RECOMMENDATION: I gave the father three pieces of advice. First, he was to take Mark to the store manager and help Mark explain what had happened. Together they would be able to work out some type of agreement whereby Mark could pay the store back not only for the merchandise but also for the wrong that had been done (an "insult penalty").

Second, Mark's allowance was to be reduced by 20 percent for lying. He would be able to earn it back slowly by manifesting honesty and integrity.

Finally, Mark's father was to forget the entire issue as soon as possible and *never* bring it up again.

LESSON: It doesn't take spying to be aware of a child's possessions.

These cases are examples of Level 4 trouble. The kid who played with fire probably represented a steady progression of disruption through the first three levels of trouble, while Mark's shoplifting appeared to be the outcome of a momentary desire for excitement. The first kid seemed to have poor supervision and therefore was more easily enraptured by the activity of the street people who stand on corners covering their fear with a "bad rap" and a "fancy front" (talk and clothes). Mark, on the other hand, had parents who were present but slow to react. It took them time, but at least they were able to teach their son a valuable lesson.

These two different cases converge when one considers what would happen if Mark's father and mother pondered the long-term adjustment of their son. If they took a few moments to reflect, they might realize that Mark would inevitably come in contact with the sons and daughters of parents who were unable or unwilling to protect their children. Having a poor family life, these youngsters would become kids of the street, and these "street kids" could possibly exert a highly negative influence on Mark.

Mark's parents were the type who worried about their son coming in contact with the "trashy" kids in the world. Rather than stew and fret needlessly, they should speak out in favor of legislation and policies which would ensure that fewer children are faced with mothers and fathers who don't give a damn or don't know how to teach their children right from wrong. After all, the kid in the doorway playing with fire wasn't born that way.

We now turn to more typical examples of deviance at this age level, the kind found in the first three levels of trouble.

SITUATION: According to his mother, twelve-year-old Scott is constantly forgetting almost everything. He forgets to do his homework, forgets to take it with him if he does it, and forgets to remember he forgot it even when reminded that he has forgotten.

He forgets to bring home messages from the teacher and forgets to follow through on parental requests. He forgets reprimands and to complete a penalty for forgetting. Sometimes he forgets to remember what he forgot.

However, my in-depth investigation revealed that Scott had not forgotten a new friend's name, the time of baseball practice, or the cost of a Big Mac and fries at McDonald's.

REACTION: Scott's parents regularly became frustrated by his memory loss. They took him to a brain specialist who could find nothing wrong with him. They hounded him with questions about why he couldn't remember. He always answered, "I don't know." They usually responded, "I don't know what we're going to do with you."

No matter whom they talked to, they heard the same message: "He'll grow out of it someday." When they became particularly frustrated with him, they would say, "Scott, you'd better grow up before we have a collective nervous breakdown."

INTERPRETATION: Scott was really fooling his parents. He employed the "I-can't-remember" routine whenever he didn't want to do something. Scott's memory loss was willfully controlled as a slick method of avoiding responsibility. He avoided hassles yet received the goodies of life. He had a perfect game going.

RECOMMENDATION: The parents needed to teach Scott that not remembering important instructions and responsibilities would result in the loss of his favorite goodies. For example, if he couldn't remember his homework, he couldn't be trusted to attend school outings.

If he couldn't remember parental instructions, he couldn't be trusted with a weekly allowance or special treats. If he forgot to pay his penalties, he couldn't be allowed free access to the neighborhood (he'd be grounded). The key to making these changes was convincing the parents that Scott's memory loss was selective and voluntary.

LESSON: If a parent hears "I can't," substitute "won't" for "can't" and see if it sounds more accurate.

SITUATION: A middle-aged, austere, serious couple visited me one evening seeking advice about their eleven-year-old son, Dan. According to their story, Dan rejected his parents' authority and violated most of the rules and regulations at home. He had similar difficulties at school.

He constantly left the yard without permission, often lied concerning his whereabouts, and failed to follow through on household expectancies. They were most agitated by the fact that Dan had been caught smoking cigarettes in a neighbor's garage.

REACTION: They had tried all kinds of disciplinary measures, including grounding, suspension of privileges, spanking, loss of after-dinner treats, sending him to bed without the evening meal, and imposing extra chores each time he violated a rule. None of these efforts seemed to have any beneficial impact on Dan's behavior.

INTERPRETATION: Dan's deviance had a strong foothold early in his life. His disruptions were well established at home and in school. The neighbor's complaint about his smoking signaled the beginning of Level 3 trouble. If he didn't shape up immediately, it was inevitable that Dan would soon graduate to Level 4 trouble (for example, shoplifting or petty theft).

The parents' discipline was not effective because it represented what I call the "shotgun approach" to punishment. That is, parents, often out of desperation, hit the kid with every punishment they can think of without a particular pattern in mind. In turn, the child, thinking it is a game, tries new forms of disruption to see what the parents will think of next.

Most important, there was a dominant theme of "bad vibes" in the home. Discipline would not be effective as long as the parents saw Dan as a source of constant pain and deserving of punishment. Somewhere, Dan had to find an opportunity to practice respect and reponsibility.

RECOMMENDATION: Once they had stopped worrying that Dan would become a criminal, we were able to concentrate on effective control procedures. I explained that the shotgun approach was destined to backfire on them.

We discovered that Dan liked money more than he disliked punishment. That meant that he would work harder to get money than to be disruptive. Therefore, dollars could be an incentive both to practice responsibility and to avoid disruption.

I helped Dan's parents establish a Responsibility Checklist (see Steve's case in Chapter 9). It was designed to counteract four of Dan's major rule violations. With Dan's input, the responsibilities were outlined quite specifically, as was the potential reward of five dollars a week for 90 percent compliance. Punishment took the form of not getting the cash. The expectancies were of a higher level since Dan was older than Steve and more was expected of him.

I reminded the parents that the checklist was to be used as an *incentive, not a bribe*. That meant that Dan got money for acting responsibly (as adults do), *not* for ceasing his disruptive acitivity. He had to do something positive; this required more action than simply stopping a negative behavior.

LESSON: Parents should get a kid's attention by waving money, not a fist.

SITUATION: Twelve-year-old Eric's adoptive parents made an appointment with me to talk about their son's increasing disregard for household rules and regulations. The parents were confused by what seemed to be Eric's rather sudden rebellion against such expectancies as helping with household chores, coming home before dark, and following simple requests from his mother.

Two nights before our appointment, Eric's father had become angry when the boy arrived home well after sundown. He told Eric that if he didn't shape up, he would be punished. Eric's response was startling: "Go ahead and punish me, see if I care.

Anyway, you're not my real mom and dad, so I don't have to do what you say!''

REACTION: Dad turned to Mom with his mouth hanging open, and Mom stared off into space, overwhelmed by disbelief. In their shock and bewilderment, they said nothing.

INTERPRETATION: After speaking with Eric, I was fairly certain that his resentment and subsequent Ambush were the result of two distinct factors. First, he had a natural tendency to test parental authority, matching *his way* against that of his parents. Second, he had a generalized feeling of guilt, caused by his realization that all his friends loved their biological parents while he was ''stuck with'' adoptive parents.

Eric had somehow come to the conclusion that he was ''bad'' for not loving his real parents, even though he had never known their identity. Eric's adoptive parents had been honest with him about his birthright, but they were on the verge of regretting that honesty.

RECOMMENDATION: Once the parents got over their shock and identity crisis, they were able to implement my suggestions. First of all, I reminded them that Eric had neither the verbal skills nor the maturity to fully and candidly discuss his internal feelings. They would have to let him verbalize them as well as he was able.

I also recommended that they talk with Eric about the difference between biology and parenthood. They were to explain how they had loved him ever since they'd adopted him and had worked hard to be good parents. I also approved of their telling Eric that loving people has more to do with mutual respect, honesty, and trust than the fact of who gave birth to whom.

When they understood what I was saying and felt confident of not getting upset about Eric's inner confusion, we discussed the implementation of a Responsibility Checklist. They realized that Eric's personal feelings should not get in the way of his compliance with parental expectancies.

LESSON: Complaints of inner turmoil do not excuse a lack of compliance.

These three cases paint an accurate picture of how parents are confronted with the Three D's of deviance during the preteen years. Dan was setting a day-to-day pattern of disruptive behavior, hell-bent on doing things *his* way. Scott discovered the power of having a selectively poor memory and used it to excuse his laziness. He was demonstrating his detachment from the real world. Eric harnessed an internal pain and merged it with laziness in order to avoid compliance. He tried to get revenge on his parents for a painful misconception of his own making. His disrespect for his parents was actually a reflection of his feelings about himself.

Dan, Eric, and Scott were all disrespectful, disruptive, and detached. However, in each of the three situations, one of the Three D's dominated the others. Because they are so interdependent, it is impossible to isolate one from the others. Furthermore, for change to occur, it is unnecessary to do so.

All normal kids flirt with disruption, disrespect, and detachment once in a while, just as they experiment with the Three R's—respect, responsibility, and reciprocity. Being disruptive on occasion doesn't make a kid deviant; and one responsible act doesn't add up to creative conformity. It is the percentage of the whole picture that constitutes deviance and trouble or adulthood and creative conformity.

Even most well-adjusted adults haven't completely settled into a life-style of creative conformity. They still find themselves being deviant from time to time. They are disruptive of the Internal Revenue Service, disrespectful to their son's Little League umpire, and quite detached from their husband's or wife's criticism. While highly desirable, creative conformity is not 100 percent attainable in this life. Therefore, it could be compared to heaven. Heaven is a cherished goal, the pursuit of which causes most of us to watch our p's and q's. But despite our meditation, ministerial consultation, and behavioral review, we're never really sure we'll get there.

Being willing and able to look inside themselves to see shades of the past and understand that many children follow in their parents' footsteps is essential to parents' mental health during their child's adolescence. Here are two kids whose Ambushes would test anyone's sanity.

SITUATION: Robbie's father wanted my advice about his eleven-year-old son so I consented to give him my off-the-cuff opinion over lunch.

He explained that he was divorced and that Robbie lived with his ex-wife. He saw his son almost every weekend. He and his son enjoyed each other's company. They built model airplanes, played putt-putt golf, watched TV, and ate lunch together.

My companion admitted that he was a lousy cook. Each time he fixed a meal, Robbie would turn up his nose, give out a sickening bellow, and demand to be taken to McDonald's for a Big Mac and fries.

REACTION: When Dad tried to reason with Robbie, his son would only protest more, comparing his father's "yuk food" with Mommy's "yummy food." The father admitted that Robbie's comments really got to him. After lengthy discussions and repeated protestations, he would take Robbie to McDonald's.

INTERPRETATION: Robbie was obviously aware, at one level or another, of the delicate situation between his father and mother. He was playing it for all he could get. His father was adding to the Ambush by feeling guilty about his failure to serve his son the way he thought he should.

RECOMMENDATION: Since this didn't appear to be a serious situation, I Kissed the problem by suggesting to Robbie's father that he forget about being a good cook and concentrate on being a good companion when he was with his son.

His being phony by pretending to be a great and fearless cook when he actually wasn't reminded me of a captain of the Seventh Cavalry riding his great white horse across the plains of early America and acting as if he were invincible. Robbie's father was inviting an Ambush.

I recapped my recommendation by telling him to take his kid to McDonald's or else have him make his own sandwich.

LESSON: Parents do deserve a break today.

SITUATION: At a patio party, eleven-year-old Tyrone's father approached me in a bashful manner. He explained a very innovative Ambush. It seemed that his son was a very bright boy who understood more than he was willing or able to explain.

Each Sunday afternoon, Ty's mom and dad found themselves particularly interested in a romantic encounter. Because they spent so much time with their only child, Ty's father always felt it necessary to explain their disappearance into the bedroom.

Ty's dad would typically say something like, "Mommy is going to take a nap for a while." Before he could explain further, Ty would say, "I guess you're going to take a nap, too, huh?"

REACTION: Ty's dad admitted to being stumped by this remark. Instead of answering, he always got Ty to disappear and/or be quiet by giving him a candy bar.

INTERPRETATION: Ty's dad was not dealing with reality. He started out by lying to a bright eleven-year-old kid and then wondered why the kid Ambushed him so easily.

Chances are that Ty had some notions about his mom and dad's sexual activity in the first place. His father was insulting his intelligence with the old nap routine. Ty wasted no time in setting him up to get some goodies.

A treat given for the cessation of a bothersome behavior only leads to more disruption in anticipation of getting more treats. Ty was learning the fine art of bribery at an early age.

RECOMMENDATION: Ty's father would have been much better off if he had been honest. His son could handle as much of the truth as Dad cared to tell him. There was no excuse for lying.

He could have said something like, "Mom and I are going to be together, just the two of us, for a while. I'd appreciate it if you played by yourself and kept quiet."

I further suggested that, if he cared to, he could give Ty a candy bar *after* his son had been quiet and stayed out of the way. That's an incentive, not a bribe.

LESSON: Keep the warriors out of the bedroom with honesty, not bribery.

Robbie and Ty demonstrated the adolescent credo: "Get the goodies any way you can." They got the goodies by finding their parents' weak spots and playing them for all they were worth. Once again, we have seen how kids use parental weaknesses to initiate an Ambush. However, these two kids actually *planned* to get their parents absorbed in their own problems so that they would forget the issue at hand. This tactic is one reason I hear many seasoned parents say, "This generation is wise beyond its years."

Budding adolescents are usually smarter than they are given credit for being. They see weak spots hidden from younger children and thought by parents to be hidden from everyone. Robbie and Ty saw the guilt and embarrassment that their fathers were barely conscious of feeling. Instead of being defensive, the two fathers could have taken a long, hard look at themselves and learned something. If they're willing to learn, parents of such kids can grow old gracefully. If they start when their child is eleven or twelve and on the brink of adolescence, the parents will be younger than ever (between their ears) by the time their kid enters his or her third decade.

Being young in mind and spirit is essential for parental survival during the days of adolescence, which begin early and seem to last forever. Before looking at the teenage years, let's revisit carelessness one more time. After all, it's what helps each of us retain a spark of childhood.

SITUATION: Ted's mom complained that when her twelve-year-old son came home from junior-high football practice he used his six-year-old brother as a tackling dummy.

REACTION: Mom said that she usually heard about the problem when her youngest came running, screaming that his brother had hurt him. When confronted, Ted would just grin and protest his innocence by saying, "He's all right. I didn't hurt him."

Mom admitted to being very upset by Ted's attacks on his little brother. She wanted to know how deep-seated the resentment between the two children might be.

INTERPRETATION: Ted was being careless in showing off. His mother was jumping to conclusions without investigating the situation. She was the victim of an indirect Ambush. Ted defied rules about harmful physical contact with his brother and covered it with the football guise. In this way, he used his brother to Ambush his mother.

The little brother continued his participation in the Ambush since he got a special treat when hurt.

RECOMMENDATION: The mother was to take another approach—she had two Ambushes to deal with. Because the six-year-old was never seriously injured, I suggested the mother tell Ted to stop hitting his brother, no matter what his intentions. She was to advise him that hitting a young boy would be like a high-school player hitting him. She was then to warn him that any future hitting would result in grounding for one night.

As for the six-year-old, Mom was to ask some questions. A typical interchange might go like this:

MOM: Ted hurt you, huh?
BOY: Yeah.
MOM: How did he hurt you?
BOY: Hit me for no reason.
MOM: I guess he's mean, huh?
BOY: Yeah.
MOM: Well, I guess I can't let you two go to the zoo together this Saturday, can I?
BOY (to himself): *Ooops!*

LESSON: When in doubt, ask questions.

Examples of carelessness similar to Ted's could fill a book. In fact, every parent that ever was could write a story or two, telling about how his or her carelessness almost resulted in tragedy or misfortune. As we saw before and shall see again, it does little good to yell or scream at a child for unintentional recklessness. Sometimes a penalty might be appropriate, but, more often than not, the best lesson comes from an understanding smile and words of caution.

Besieged parents can find the patience necessary to smile and speak softly if they remember the theme of this chapter: Time and time again, parents are faced with the same old problems and must begin at the beginning, all over again.

12

Thirteen and Fourteen:
Rebels with a Cause

By the age of fourteen, adolescence is in full bloom for 99 percent of all normal kids. It's a time when bodies constantly change, emotions influence every move, and reason takes a holiday. Out of the blue, teachers are seen as "dumb," police officers are "pigs," and parents are suddenly visited with severe attacks of "stupidity." This rebellion against authority figures isn't a biological necessity (a few brave teenagers don't bother with it), but ninety-five out of a hundred high-school freshmen could be classified as "rebels." These poorly organized revolutionaries share a common belief: the world would be a better place without parents.

Added to this "cause" is the toll that sexism begins to take. Girls spend most of their time giggling, while boys stumble into everything in their path; girls have hundreds of secrets, while boys contrive endless dialects of the English language; girls spend hours on the phone, while boys dream of ways to become the leader of a gang; girls believe in the magic of makeup that allows the "natural you" to shine through, while boys try to devise ways of making pimples a status symbol. Girls have a different boyfriend every week, while boys pretend to ignore girls but masturbate three times a day. They often spout contempt for each other but find purpose and stability in their mutual displeasure.

Every rebel needs an opponent in order to make his or her cause come alive. Budding adolescents are no different. Parents who see the first signs of a revolution ("How could you ever understand what I'm going through?" "What do you mean, 'Is something wrong'? Of course *nothing is wrong!*") should back off, shut up, and remain steady during the storm. The rebellion will be tough enough without adding to it.

If parents can resist the temptation to demonstrate to a fourteen-year-old his or her immaturity, yet retain control over most of this age's erratic behavior, they will be better prepared for the worst storm of all: ages fifteen and sixteen. Early adolescence will pass quickly, and if Mom and Dad can hang together, this period can be used as a time for them to rediscover some of the wild irresponsibility that made their own adolescent years so exciting. Anyhow, ages thirteen and fourteen are a time span that, three or four years later, will be referred to by a kid as a time when "I was young and didn't know anything."

The struggles that surface during this stormy period have been seen before, but reemerge now in slightly different and more complicated forms. Carelessness, testing the limits, exploration, peer pressure, and deviance are old problems that dominate the scene. However, three features make them more complicated this time around. First, the Ambush takes on an even more mysterious nature as kids work to get around societal "No's," many of which are unstated or products of the kids' imaginations. Second, exploration and limit-testing take a new twist when put into a framework of experimentation. Kids believe that they can try any experience, dangerous or not, and emerge victorious. Finally, psychic struggles become so entangled with one another that each problem must be handled individually.

I have listened to many teenagers complain about parental dominance and/or indifference. Most of them share the strong conviction that parents usually get in the way. They also share a dedication to rebellion and the need to possess causes other than "parental irrelevance." However, I have concluded that, despite their voices to the contrary, kids don't possess causes, the causes possess them.

Kids who find a cause for rebellion are rarely in control of themselves. When they pledge allegiance to a cause, they throw caution to the winds and expend unlimited energy. Because they lack foresight, experience, and planning, much of their rebellious activity emanates from impulsiveness, the only purpose being the release of pent-up energy. When this happens, the act of rebelling becomes more important than the cause of the rebellion. Kids become addicted to a cause not because it yields solutions to social and personal problems but because it makes rebellion possible. Rather than a means to an end, rebellion becomes an end in itself. As a result, kids are "possessed" by a cause rather than the other way around.

When parents try to deal with this problem, they often bark up the wrong tree. They never get time to comprehend what's going on. Just when parents think they understand a particular cause, it changes. They fail to see that an adolescent cause, driven by impulse energy, has a short life span. It begins to die the moment it comes to life. The rebellion, not the cause, remains constant.

I've found that the best way to handle adolescent rebelliousness is to teach parents how to react to the battle cries that spearhead the rebellion. In the following cases, I've reviewed the six battle cries heard most often. They embody many causes, none directly related to "parental irrelevance." That particular one is held constantly in reserve, giving kids a cause to fall back on in case their rebellion temporarily runs out of steam.

The first battle cry reflects the timeless influence of peer pressure.

SITUATION: Fourteen-year-old Gary's father asked me about his son's potential for getting into trouble. He said that Gary was hanging around with three other kids, all of whom were on probation for shoplifting.

When the father first asked Gary about the situation, Gary denied any knowledge of the kids. When confronted with eyewitness accounts, Gary's only reaction was, "Oh, Dad, they're cool."

REACTION: The father attempted to talk with Gary about the potential dangers of associating with such kids. Gary dismissed him by saying, "Don't you want me to have any friends?" or "If you knew the kids, you'd realize they're cool."

Gary's dad finally forbade his son to see the kids. However, Gary began to sneak out at night to see the kids after his parents thought he was asleep. The situation blew up when his father caught Gary coming through his bedroom window at 1:00 A.M.

INTERPRETATION: Gary was clearly headed for Level 4 trouble. Not only might he break a law (I'm sure he already had), but also the gap between his father and himself was becoming so wide that Gary would soon stop listening to anything his father might say.

Gary's friends had cast a spell on him, and he was following them into practically anything just so that he could be with them. It was only a matter of time before he was with them at the probation office.

RECOMMENDATION: I told the father that trying to control Gary's friends would prove futile. He could control Gary's own comings and goings but not whom he saw when he was gone. I suggested a simple procedure by which Gary could demonstrate self-control and responsibility. Gary had to earn time out past 9:00 P.M. by getting B's in German (a difficult task for him). Once he had met that challenge, Dad could have more confidence in his independence.

Gary's dad had to listen to his son's desires for recognition and his chance to be an individual. He was to avoid getting caught up in Gary's talk about being "cool." Once he knew what his son was after, he could make some efforts to get closer to him. I suggested that they both start looking for satisfying activities that they could enjoy together.

If there had been no father in the picture (which is often the case in such situations), I would have advised Gary's mother to find an uncle, friend, or Big Brother to carry out this recommendation.

LESSON: When it comes to "bad" companions, two's a crowd, three's a disaster.

SITUATION: After a luncheon speech, I was approached by an exasperated mother who was embarrassed by her daughter's recently acquired habit. After making about a dozen excuses for why Stacey did it, her mom explained how the teenager expressed her displeasure with careless drivers, uncouth boyfriends, or anyone else who bothered her. When Stacey felt offended, she raised the second finger of her hand in a pronounced salute of disrespect. The mother's darling daughter was regularly giving people "the finger"!

REACTION: Stacey's mom protested that there was nothing she could do. She had tried to ignore the obscene gesture but found it too repulsive to tolerate. Eventually, she would yell, "Stacey, cut that out! Act your age." Stacey, undaunted, would say, "Mom, be cool; he deserved it."

INTERPRETATION: Since it occurred regularly, Stacey *was* acting her age. I don't believe such behavior should be ignored, especially when parents find it disgusting. However, rebukes and moralistic lectures fall on deaf ears when the ears are attached to a teenager.

The mother's best chance to get Stacey's attention was to point out the logical contradiction in her daughter's behavior. To do so, she needed more courage and less anxiety.

RECOMMENDATION: I told the mother that the next time Stacey "flipped the bird" to someone, she should say, "Oh, isn't that cute! You act vulgar and nasty to people and then go home to your room and splatter signs about *peace* and *love* all over your walls. You talk about love but spread hate."

I cautioned her to say these things in a firm but soft voice. If done in an instructional manner, such remarks could teach her daughter about the contradictions in her behavior and possibly shake her loose from some of her compulsiveness.

Besides, they would give Stacey a rap to use on her friends when they pressured her to be "cool" by engaging in this and other vulgar social responses.

LESSON: When kids "flip the bird," remind them it may represent their I.Q.

The cause that sparks kids like Gary and Stacey is best represented by the slogan "I gotta be cool." These two kids demonstrated that it was not *what* they did that counted, but that they *did* it. This made them victims of their compulsive desire to follow the crowd, no matter where it was going. "Gotta" was the key to their cause; "cool" had little or nothing to do with understanding what they did. "Cool" is simply an extension of "gotta," saying more about the prevailing pressures from a crowd of contemporaries than about its intrinsic meaning.

When parents hear the word "cool," they usually get sidetracked into an examination of what it means, hoping they can understand what their kid is doing. However, "cool" changes its meaning more often than a baby changes diapers. I've heard it applied to people in such diverse contexts as inciting to riot and trying to disperse a mob; attending church and militantly denying the existence of God; and pushing for good grades and making fun of others for going to school. "Cool" is a word that represents the direction in which any given crowd is heading. It reflects peer pressure at its zenith.

Most parents react to "cool" instead of dealing with the compulsion of "gotta." "Cool" can change its meaning before the parents know what's happening. But "gotta" becomes a guiding light for early adolescent behavior. It can easily lead a thirteen-year-old kid to try hard drugs, hang out with dangerous companions, or experiment with so-called spiritual cults, which are obsessed with deliverance but deliver only obsessions. "Gotta" has its roots in mindlessness, not in purpose or determination. It's a cause looking for a place to go.

When parents hear "I gotta be cool," they should concentrate on helping their kid face his or her own compulsiveness. General responses parents may find useful are "You *gotta* be? It sounds as though somebody else is controlling you," or "I can understand your wanting to be cool, but it sounds as though you don't have a choice," or, for more adventuresome parents, "You *gotta,* hell! Give me a reason that *you* thought of, or else I *gotta* say 'No'!"

These and other comments may put a dent in the "gotta" compulsion, but they will never completely stop it. Parents can take heart, though, in the fact that "gotta" can work in two opposite ways. If three or four kids get together and decide that being different is cool (which it usually is), then with a little help there's no reason that they can't be cool by being responsible or telling a drug pusher to go to hell.

Gary and Stacey believed they *had to* do certain things in order to be accepted by their friends and acquaintances. Another cause that can enrapture young adolescents sounds less serious than it really is.

SITUATION: I was standing in my backyard one day trying to figure out a way to avoid mowing the grass. A thirteen-year-old neighborhood boy was playing a unique game of "chicken" with several of his younger friends.

   While his father occasionally glanced his way, Gene was swinging a baseball bat around and around in a circle while the younger kids were seeing who could come closest to the bat without getting hit.

REACTION: Just about the time I was ready to intervene (although I didn't know whether to get after Gene or his father), Gene's dad yelled at him to be careful. When Gene didn't stop his bat-swinging, his dad went over to where he was playing, grabbed him by the nape of the neck, and popped him on the butt.

As Gene turned away from his father, I could hear him say to the other kids, "It ain't nothing."

INTERPRETATION: Several things were wrong with this backyard scene. Gene was being very reckless and disruptive. His father ignored him and finally overreacted (hitting Gene). Gene was forced to save face in front of the younger kids by pretending that his father's smack was insignificant.

Gene was obviously showing off. The younger kids, with no idea of potential disaster, were enjoying the excitement. This was a case in which the father didn't pay enough attention to his child, and, in the final analysis, the child practiced paying no attention to his father.

RECOMMENDATION: When Gene's father saw him acting so recklessly, he should have gone immediately to his son, called him aside, and explained that he should find a safer game to play. He should have avoided hitting him, especially in front of other kids.

He then could have engaged in a game with them, possibly a game of baseball. Or, even better, he could provide his son and his friends with two Batakas.

Batakas—or "aggression sticks," as I call them—are much like fat bats, two feet long, fifteen inches in circumference, made of foam rubber with a flannel covering and a handle. Many psychologists find them advertised in professional journals as instruments for expressing anger and frustration. I have found that parents as well as kids think of thousands of uses for "aggression sticks."

LESSON: Protective Parents must do more than just "keep an eye" on their gentle warriors.

SITUATION: During a marriage-counseling session, the wife explained that a lot of the tension in the home was due to the disrespect shown to herself and her husband by their thirteen-year-old son, Roger.

The tension resulted when Roger paid no attention to his mother's admonishments. When Roger came inside from playing, he usually threw his clothes on a dining-room chair, tossed pieces of athletic equipment on the table, heaved his shoes in opposite directions, and plopped in front of the TV, demanding some sort of snack.

REACTION: Each time this happened, Roger's mom demanded that he turn off the TV and pick up his things. He ignored these warnings until Mom threatened him with reprisals from his father. But Roger stalled by promising to comply during a commercial.

Within a few minutes, Roger's mother would dash into the family room and scream at Roger to move. She would then lecture him about his disrespect, bemoaning the fact that he was driving her to an "early grave." The father admitted that he, too, would join in the battle and criticize both Roger and his wife for his son's disrespect.

To both mother and father, Roger would say, "It don't matter; no big deal."

INTERPRETATION: Roger was making a shambles out of household regulations. I had the distinct impression that he didn't feel very good about himself and was simply spreading the misery around a little.

Mom's threats of punishment fell on deaf ears because Roger knew she was too upset to carry through on her threats. Father's infrequent punishments were no deterrent since most of Roger's buddies could brag about how they withstood the worst their own fathers had to offer. Anyway, these were the only times his dad paid any attention to him.

RECOMMENDATION: I told his parents to concentrate on Roger's misbehavior and not worry about his adolescent adjustment. I suggested that the next time he left things lying around, his mom or dad simply lock them away without saying a word.

When asked for one of his missing items, the parents were to say, "You've lost the use of [whatever was left out] until tomorrow evening because you didn't put it away last time you used it."

Roger may miss baseball practice once, wear an old pair of shoes, or do without his favorite blue jeans, but he'll learn very quickly that his mom and dad mean business when they make a request.

LESSON: "Don't do that" should really mean "Don't do that."

Kids like Gene and Roger could probably write a best-selling song entitled "It Don't Mean Nothin' to Me." It would represent their cause, but they probably lack the motivation to work hard enough to write it. However, if they got off their butts long enough to write a chorus, it might go like this:

> You can't hurt me, 'cause I don't care,
> You punish me here, I'll just go there.
> You have your rules, that's good to see,
> But what you don't understand
> Is that it don't mean nothin' to me.

Gene and Roger illustrated how disruption, disrespect, and detachment can get rolled into one big ball of deviance covered with a "who-cares" attitude. The careless and reckless nature of these two kids' behavior was not exactly chosen by them. They didn't actively seek deviance, but then they didn't avoid it, either.

Parents often find this cause to be the most frustrating. They watch helplessly as their bright, energetic kid turns into a lazy loaf, not caring enough to spend the energy necessary for the development of the Three R's. In a state of uncertainty and even panic, parents turn to punishment and screaming as their saviors. Instead of correcting the problem, punishment only adds fuel to the fire. Tolerating punishment often becomes a status symbol to teenagers—a reason to be "cool," if you will. They will brag, "Nobody can scream like my old lady, but it doesn't bother me 'cause I'm the coolest."

When parents react as if "It don't mean nothin' to me" indicates hostile rejection, they are knocking on the wrong door. The slogan should not be taken exactly as it sounds. Kids who sing this song are saying something very important. The message can be heard by paying attention to the word "it," instead of "nothin'."

"It," as a pronoun, does not signify parental authority, a parental request, or even the threat of punishment. When said in the manner noted above, "it" actually refers to the kid's soul. When teenagers lose their childhood identity and search for a new one, they get scared. Instead of becoming hysterical or depressed about how lousy they feel, many depersonalize their "self," calling the resultant psychic mass of emptiness *"it."*

Therefore, in the "It Don't Mean Nothin' to Me" song, "it" actually stands for "I." Thus, the real song title is *"I* Don't Mean Nothin' To Me," and that's a completely different tune.

Parents who want to change these lyrics must try to reverse the trend of deteriorating self-respect. Another two-edged sword is needed. One side must cut the kid loose from his or her lack of responsibility while the other must separate the kid from attachment to the emptiness inside.

The suspension of a highly desired privilege until the appropriate behavior results will most likely stimulate responsibility. The ugly self-concept can be wiped clean and the feeling of emptiness eased by giving the kid ample opportunities to talk about his or her search for importance.

If this combination is not implemented, parents might watch as their child enters the crucial years of middle adolescence behaving like a bump on a log. If that happens, parents should not be surprised if their kid acts as though he or she has a block of wood for a head.

We've seen two battle cries in which the listener can be misled by paying attention to the wrong word. Now we examine a cause whose slogan is an outright lie.

SITUATION: Rod's dad asked me to have lunch with him to discuss a school problem. Rod was thirteen years old and lived with his brother and sister in a middle-class neighborhood. Rod attended junior high and usually had a B average. He had never been in any trouble.

The day before our lunch, Rod and three of his buddies had been caught smoking cigarettes in a school bathroom.

REACTION: Mother and Father discussed the issue with each other and then with Rod. When asked why he had done it, Rod replied,

"All the guys do it. It's no big deal. What's everybody so upset about?"

His flippant attitude received a cold welcome from his father. "I told you no smoking—*no smoking,* got that?"

Rod countered, "No, you told me 'no smoking in this house.' That's what you told me."

As the father explained it, Rod's back talk resulted in a loud, name-calling argument. The madder Dad became, the more silent Rod grew. Finally, Dad told Rod that he was grounded for two weeks.

INTERPRETATION: By sneaking a smoke in the bathroom, Rod had engaged in a low-keyed Ambush. He knew he wasn't supposed to smoke, but the pressure of "everyone is doing it" was too great for his moral code. He gave in to the group consensus and then tried to squirm out of his misdeed by playing the word game with his father.

His father, on the other hand, never should have been suckered by the "everybody's-doing-it" routine. However, the father was susceptible to such an argument since he, too, judged much of his own behavior in terms of how the group viewed him. By using others as a major reference point, Dad had made himself an easy target for an Ambush.

The father's emotionalism, anger, and ill-conceived penalty set him up for future Ambushes. Such situations should be Kissed, as we've seen before, with the simplicity of "If you're gonna play, you gotta pay."

RECOMMENDATION: As I told Rod's dad, he should remain calm when his son breaks a minor rule. He can dismiss the "everyone" pressure by saying something like, "So how does that affect you?"

I suggested he call the principal, thank him for his concern, and agree with the four hours of after-school detention he had decreed as a penalty. Although he wanted to fight some of the school's rigid rules, I recommended that he could set a good example for his son if he did so through proper channels, not by yelling at the school administrators.

Rod should not receive a penalty at home. He should pay the

school penalty, but further punishment represented double jeopardy. He hadn't broken a rule at home and shouldn't have to pay two penalties for one violation. Following this course of action would teach Rod that different institutions have different rules and different sanctions, a lesson that will serve him well in the future.

LESSON: Where a parent sees smoke doesn't always mean there is a fire.

SITUATION: During a wedding reception, a mother cornered me to tell me about her thirteen-year-old daughter, Rhonda. She complained that Rhonda was "getting out of hand" and that her husband didn't understand the problems of a teenage girl.

She told of a recent blow-up in which arguing, complaining, and yelling had dominated the interaction. It had all started when Rhonda rather rudely asked for a larger allowance so that she could buy new clothes like her best friend, Kelly. She wanted ten dollars a week with special party allowances thrown in from time to time.

REACTION: I remember almost dropping my glass of booze as Rhonda's mother described the scene.

On one side of the room stood Dad, dead set against such a ridiculous sum of money. He could be heard yelling about the high cost of living and demanding to know why "these kids nowadays think they deserve so much."

On the other side of the room stood a sobbing Rhonda, protesting against her father's lack of understanding. "Everybody gets more than I do. *Everybody!*" Standing beside Rhonda was Mom, consoling her daughter and making sly remarks about her husband's "insensitivities."

As the mother went on, I could just see her patting her daughter and saying, "Men just don't understand what it's like to be seen in the same dress twice." As she continued her story, there was little doubt in my mind what the outcome would be.

Sure enough, after about fifteen minutes of the gory details, Rhonda's mother finally smiled and explained how Dad had backed down and promised the raise the forthcoming week.

INTERPRETATION: Rhonda was getting out of hand all right, and Mom was playing along. Rhonda had used "everybody" to support her moral values and then engaged her mother and father in a fight. It was three against one: "everybody," Mom, and Rhonda against Dad; Dad didn't stand a chance.

The issues involved didn't have to be so complicated. Rhonda wanted more money and clothes, and Dad didn't want to go along. Rhonda's antics should have been ignored. Mom could have been a mediator instead of a protagonist. Most important, the "everybody" argument should have fallen on deaf ears.

RECOMMENDATION: I told Rhonda's mother that I thought she should rescind the agreement, explaining it the following way: "I realize that you put the squeeze on me to side with you against your father, and I fell in line as you expected. But I'm going to undo what I did."

The mother agreed that ten dollars a week was too much and that Rhonda should not be able to con her parents with references to the pressures from her friends. She needed to tell her daughter this.

If Rhonda really wanted new clothes, she was bright enough to earn the money. I cautioned the mother not to get angry with Rhonda about the scene since Rhonda's talent for interpersonal manipulation could someday work in her favor.

LESSON: If parents act like money dispensers, their kids will treat them like machines.

It's pretty obvious that in a parade Rod and Rhonda could be found marching under a banner reading: "Everybody's doing it." This slogan represents a maneuver to weaken parental authority by using the group consensus to justify the morality of an act or request. Because "everybody's doing it," "it" is the correct thing to do. Parents who give credence to this standard of right and wrong could find themselves chasing their own tails.

"Well, who's everybody'?" Mom might ask.

"Just 'everybody,' " the daughter would answer.

Mom would persist, "Who's 'everybody'?"

The answer would remain unchanged. "Oh, c'mon, Mom, you know—'everybody.'"

If pushed further, the girl would probably list the names of her best friends. If Mom asked more questions, she'd just hear more versions of "Everybody's doing it."

Parents don't realize it, but when they try to find out who "everybody" is, they are searching for a ghost. "Everybody" doesn't exist. Each kid in a group of five or six will refer to the others as "everybody" because they don't have the courage or self-knowledge to say, "I want to do it." Sometimes they're not even sure that they *want* to do it. All their friends and all their friends' friends say "everybody," so they say "everybody." Since it usually works, it's no wonder they fall victim to the belief that "everybody" actually exists.

Parents find it difficult to dispel the "everybody" ghost because they used to believe in the teenage "everybody" and now have a grown-up "everybody" to contend with at the office, at the club, or at parties. The concept of "everybody" makes parents nervous. They forget about the issue at hand because they're too busy worrying about what "everybody" will think. "Everybody" is an age-old smoke screen used to carry out an effective Ambush.

Most kids know that their parents will have a tough time arguing with "everybody." Therefore, parents are well advised not to respond to this universal ego. Rather, they should forget about "everybody" and deal with their son or daughter directly. They might say, "So, 'everybody's' doing it. You're not 'everybody.' Tell me why *you* want to do it." If more parents did this, "everybody" would lose its strength and be less of a problem.

Now we move to a more serious cause, one that often results in parental heartache.

SITUATION: Lance's parents sought my advice after they had discovered that their fourteen-year-old son was having more than a few problems with school. Although they had been advised that Lance was regularly tardy and missed some classes, they had failed to take any action after hearing their son's excuses.

A week before our conference, the mother was called and told that Lance wasn't at school. Since he had left home that morning as usual, Mom found it hard to believe that Lance was a truant.

REACTION: Since Lance had never disappeared before, his mother was quite upset. She called her husband at work and was so distraught that he agreed to leave work and come home immediately.

A few phone calls later, Lance's father discovered that two of Lance's friends were also missing. He tried to convince himself and his wife that their son was just playing hooky and it was no big deal. He hid his agitation; his wife didn't.

At 3:15 P.M., Lance came strolling in with his books, acting as if nothing were wrong. In a cat-and-mouse manner, his father asked if he had had a good day at school. Lance's answering "Yes" and thinking he had fooled his parents only triggered an explosion.

Lance, caught and defenseless, spent his anger by spouting condemnations of the boredom at school, touching on the teachers, other students, academic subjects, and the principal. His father bellowed at him and told him that his punishment for the truancy would be the loss of a camping trip with friends, planned for two months ahead.

INTERPRETATION: Both parents became too upset too late. They should have realized that something was going wrong with Lance and school long before he skipped. They could have predicted this Ambush by watching the signs of rejection in Lance's tardiness and missing classes.

Even at this level of disruption, the situation wasn't too serious. Lance had the right to skip school, just as his parents had the right (and duty) to institute penalties for such disruptive activity. The blind acceptance of lame excuses and then emotional explosions made the situation more complicated than it needed to be.

Lance needed to talk about his fear of failure and his desire to do exciting things with his friends. He also would need help in catching up on schoolwork and learning how to find some interest in a couple of subjects that were taught by teachers who I knew had a knack for putting teenagers to sleep.

RECOMMENDATION: I strongly suggested a long talk in which Lance could be helped to air his complaints about school and to find some creative ways of dealing with the problem. I cautioned Lance's parents to have patience with their son as he fought an internal struggle to achieve.

I also recommended that they cancel the penalty and institute a more realistic one. However, he should be punished for lying about his activities, not for skipping school. The school would punish him for truancy; his parents should punish him for his deception when confronted with his lie.

I suggested that they ask Lance what penalty he thought he should pay for his lie. I reminded them that if coached correctly ("Think of a penalty that will hurt but will teach you a lesson"), a kid like Lance might come up with a penalty that would be more effective than one his parents could think of.

LESSON: If they keep their eyes and ears open, parents can often spot an Ambush before it hits.

SITUATION: Fourteen-year-old Tricia's mom complained that her daughter was terribly disrespectful. No matter what the request or problem, Tricia's first reaction was to "mouth off" with such comments as, "You can't make me. I don't have to do everything you say."

The mother admitted that she had learned to ignore these remarks, but Tricia's nastiness was spreading to school. The teachers were targets of considerable verbal abuse from her. Tricia would only comply with a request when she absolutely felt like it. Otherwise, she was practically intolerable.

REACTION: Tricia was an absolute tyrant at home. The mother was divorced, so Tricia had no discipline from a father figure. When the principal tried to talk with Tricia, she would say, "You run a stupid school, you know that?" Sometimes she would say nothing and just glare at him. She had been suspended on two different occasions.

INTERPRETATION: I saw this situation as potentially very dangerous. Tricia's disrespect had reached the level where she was a prime candidate for serious trouble. At quite a young age, she had been spoiled rotten through her mother's lack of discipline. Poor adjustment in school was quite predictable.

Tricia obviously had very little self-respect. She was dumping her fears and anger on any handy authority figure. When she looked at herself in the mirror, I'm sure she saw a "bad person" who would have to learn how to live in an ugly world. She was a rebel looking for a cause.

RECOMMENDATION: The mother had to reestablish herself as a strong authority in Tricia's life, and needed to do it immediately. I agreed to help the mother with her own lack of self-confidence, much of which was due to her guilt for failing in her marriage. Once she was able to talk the guilt out, we addressed ourselves to Tricia the tyrant.

The first time Mom told Tricia she couldn't go out, all hell broke loose. The mother actually had to physically restrain her daughter in order to prove she meant business. Tricia screamed and cursed at her mother, but Mom stuck to her guns ("You're not going out; that's *final!*"). Tricia sat in the living room sulking for the rest of the evening while Mom went about her business. The next night, the same thing happened, except that no body contact was necessary. Mom told Tricia, "When you act your age, we'll talk about your going out."

I told the mother not to be upset if Tricia tried to run away some evening. She must do what she could to stop her and then ground her one day for every hour she was gone.

The problem at school was just as tough. Mom enlisted the aid of a woman physical education teacher with whom Tricia had a fairly good relationship. She took Tricia out one evening (with Mom's approval) and was able to listen to her complaints about the "dumb" things happening at school. Furthermore, she got her involved in organizing a girls' volleyball team, which proved an outlet for her creativity and need for self-esteem as well as her physical energies.

FOLLOW-UP: Once Tricia realized the tolerance level in the home and who was boss, she calmed down considerably. She also found school more tolerable, especially since the volleyball team was a glowing success. She never tried to run away.

LESSON: Kids who fail to learn right from wrong will persecute their parents for the failure.

Although not always loud and clear, the battle cry of kids like Lance and Tricia is "School is dumb." They don't like to admit it, but what they're really saying is "I feel dumb, and it's all the school's fault."

Scapegoating the school because they feel bad about their own lack of success is a popular pastime for teenagers. Some do it because "everybody's doing it." But other kids, like Lance and Tricia, do it because there's more going on inside their heads than just the effects of peer pressure. Their emotional immaturity is such that the slightest hint of failure adds up to a catastrophe. These kids, like most, have an insatiable need for excitement. Besides these emotional aspects, adolescent thoughts easily stray into fantasies of adventure and intrigue, and, unfortunately, a class in world history can be pretty boring, especially if a kid never learned to read well.

Sometimes these situations can get so bad that kids will turn to destructive radicalism to compensate for academic failure. The mindlessness of destructive causes is surpassed only by the aggressive stupidity of their leaders. The so-called leaders of such movements are actually dummies in disguise. They had the insight to see the faults in the educational system but lacked the intelligence and courage to work from within for constructive change. Their pleas for revolution, rebellion, and rediscovery are music to the ears of disappointed and frustrated teenagers. These antiheroic drop-outs are idolized by kids who believe that "school is dumb," because their fancy words and promises of glory help hide their audience's lack of patience.

Thirteen- and fourteen-year-old kids who find more pain than pleasure in school will begin to look to such radicals for answers. Luckily they won't be convinced of the glory of revolution, at least at first. But if they listen long enough and receive no help or guidance from their parents, they could advance through the ranks to become leaders in a battle in which an enemy must be created in order to justify the need to fight.

About fifteen years ago, one of my professors, a distinguished Catholic priest, taught me a lesson in the folly of radicalism. He sat beside me during the rantings and ravings of a self-styled atheist. The young man had been invited to our campus to give his testimony concerning the nonexistence of God. When he'd finished pounding the podium, screaming about the opiate of the people and professing a new dawn of spiritual death, the wise old man to my left leaned forward in his seat and asked, "Tell me, young man, if there is no God, why do you protest His existence so strongly?"

If and when parents see their kids begin to look for an enemy upon which to dump their own self-doubt, they should be careful not to attack any cause or leader that may suddenly appear. Such attacks only make martyrs out of people and issues that don't merit the attention. Instead, they should turn their attention to the reason for the search—the self-doubt, lack of courage, fear of failure. Anything else is disrespectful to the kids' right to be confused. Furthermore, such disrespect might aid the kids in joining the deadheads who think they can attain peace and love by preaching war and violence.

Lance and Tricia centered their Ambush on school. Heather and Nancy concentrated on parental guilt.

SITUATION: Mindy's mom told me of a problem her best friend was having with her fourteen-year-old daughter, Heather. Since Heather's father didn't want any of his family seeing a "headshrinker," I agreed to give some secondhand advice.

The problem, according to Mindy's mom, was that Heather's mom couldn't understand or talk to her daughter. Friction between the two grew daily as Heather did some incomprehensible things and her mom regularly blew her stack.

The situation had come to a head when Heather brought home a rather atypical friend. The girl wore a pointy-cupped padded bra, tight blue jeans that "showed everything," heavy blue eye shadow, and a T-shirt that proclaimed: "I like sex best."

REACTION: According to the story, Heather's mom hit the ceiling after the girl had left. In no uncertain terms, she told her daughter that she must never associate with "that tramp" again.

Heather's reply was typical: "If you knew her better instead of being such a bitch, you'd like her, too." This comment only added fuel to an already raging fire.

INTERPRETATION: From what I could surmise at a distance, Heather had her mother right where she wanted her. Months of disrespectful language and disruptive behavior had enabled Heather to tie her mother in emotional knots any time she wished. The killer phrase was usually something like "If you really understood me, we'd get along better."

Heather was probably able to Ambush her mother regularly. Playing upon her mother's pride, Heather was able to bring up her mother's past "failures," constantly remind her of them in a guilt-provoking manner, and use the resultant guilt to get what she wanted.

I wouldn't be surprised to see Heather pull the following Ambush. Knowing she always had to double-date, and wanting to go out by herself, she might very well tell her mother that she was going to double with the friend who had come over. When Mom had finally come off the wall, Heather might say, "Well, fine. Since you feel that way, I'll just have to go by myself."

RECOMMENDATION: I told Mindy's mom to tell her friend not to get so upset. Rather, she should fight the fire with logic. The next time Heather tried to use "You don't understand" to get her way, the mother might say, "I don't understand? No, *you* don't understand. Blue eye shadow and a padded bra? I thought you liked the 'natural look.' "

The mother should hunt for other contradictions in Heather's reasoning and point them out gently but firmly. She could bet her

last dollar that Heather's accusations about her lack of understanding was a cover for some type of Ambush. Heather's mother
might also try relying on her daughter's good sense in knowing
when a friend was overdoing it.

LESSON: Understanding is a two-way street.

SITUATION: Nancy's parents came to me for advice. Their fourteen-
year-old daughter was gregarious, bright, and energetic. She had
always been a well-behaved child and never given them any
trouble. She wasn't too excited about going to church, but she
went every Sunday.

The problem had developed overnight. It had started when a
divorcée and her daughter had moved in three doors down. It
didn't take more than two days before Nancy and the girl were
friends. However, in that same time period, Nancy's mom discovered that the friend's mother had been arrested for possession
of marijuana. She promptly demanded that Nancy stop seeing the
girl.

REACTION: According to the parents, Nancy suddenly became defiant.
She said that she wasn't going to comply with their request and if
they didn't like it they could "shove it." Her mother threatened
to slap her, and her father reprimanded her strongly for her language.

A fight ensued in which Nancy accused her parents of never
trying to understand her. The parents, convinced that Nancy's
new friend had corrupted her already, grounded their daughter for
a week. They sought my advice the day after Nancy had slipped
out through her window in order to see her friend.

INTERPRETATION: Nancy had been somewhat overprotected by her
well-meaning parents. Her contact with the friend down the street
represented her first encounter with kids outside her church group
and private school. Her almost hysterical reaction was predictable.

The parents had to realize that Nancy's reaction was coming
from Nancy, not the girl down the street. She was experimenting
with some teenage Ambush strategies and her parents' emotionalism was only adding to the problem. Nancy was not aware

of all the elements of life, and the sooner her parents realized that, the better off everyone would be.

RECOMMENDATION: After helping them see the dynamics of my interpretation, I explained how they could be helpful to Nancy during the following months. First, they were not to forbid her to see the other girl—that would only make her want to do it even more. Second, without emotionalism, they were to express their love and concern to their daughter. Third, the mother was to pay a visit to the friend's mother to express her concerns openly. Fourth, they were to encourage Nancy to engage in activities that would take her outside the restricted circle of friends she had previously experienced. That way, they could monitor her development while they still had time. Finally, they were to rid themselves of the guilt they felt when their daughter said, "You don't try to understand me."

LESSON: "Bad" influences can be monitored, not eliminated.

Heather and Nancy would be first in line to see a movie entitled *But You Don't Understand.* The opening scene of the flick would have a mother who is saying, "Sissy dear, you know I love you. I just don't want you to get into trouble. It's not that I don't like your friends—some of them are fine. But that tramp down the street is no good for you. When you're older, you'll understand what I'm saying."

Sissy with an expression longer than her shoulder-length hair, would sigh, "But you don't understand."

A dialogue would ensue in which the mother would expound on her wisdom and reflect on her daughter's immaturity. The daughter would counter with all sorts of arguments, making a shambles out of simplicity. The movie would explore the relationship between kids in love, friends who reach across parents to touch one another, and parents who pull their hair out trying to understand where they went wrong. In the end, no one would kiss and make up. Everyone would live unhappily ever after.

The critics of the movie (including myself as producer) would determine that parental guilt was the lifeblood of the girl's disruption. Without the mother's guilt, the daughter would not be able to put her mother on the defensive for what she (the mother) thought was her failure to understand. Without the guilt, the cry of "But you don't understand" loses its effect, and the cause of rebellion fizzles out. Without the cause, the entire scene and movie flops (just as well—I hate sad endings).

Parents who attempt to act out their part in the cry of "But you don't understand" by feeling guilty and saying, "Why, of course I do" or "How can you say that after all I've done for you?" are foolish. In fact, I'm always suspicious of parents who say, "Oh, I always understand my teenager, don't you?" I've yet to meet anyone who fully understands a teenager, including the teenager!

No matter how dedicated they are, there are two things parents can't do for their kids. One is to understand everything they say or do, and the other is to control with whom they interact. If parents don't want their kid to see another kid, they would be much better off telling the kid the truth and then thinking of a way to compromise ("Give me a B in history instead of a C, and I won't hassle you about seeing that girl"). Parents might not be able to control who sees whom, but they can help their children realize that some privileges cost more than others.

We've seen the problem of "bad companions" before, and we'll see it again. There are no foolproof answers to this challenging problem. Locking doors and windows only sets the stage for revenge or sneakiness. There's enough of that without asking for it. The parent's best shot is to be honest ("You're right, I don't understand. But I love you, so I'll try to work with, not against you. Will you do the same?").

The two girls above wanted to be with "bad companions." Bernie just needed to be with *some* companions.

SITUATION: Thirteen-year-old Bernie was a black kid living in a white neighborhood. He regularly heard derogatory remarks aimed at him and was often threatened with physical violence by a group of white kids.

One night after dark, Bernie was walking home from a friend's house nearly four blocks away. Three white kids caught up with him half a block from his house and chased him home, throwing rocks at him. Later that night, Bernie slipped out through his window and threw bricks at the windows of the kids he thought had chased him.

REACTION: The police arrested Bernie and locked him in jail all night without notifying his parents. In the morning, when the parents finally were called, Bernie was petrified and his parents were boiling mad.

On the way home, Bernie sat frozen in the back seat of the car as his parents screamed about the horror of white racism and the need for revenge. The father threatened to beat up someone, while the mother kept repeating, "What a terrible thing they did to my baby."

INTERPRETATION: It was difficult to unravel the pieces of this situation. Bernie certainly Ambushed the kids who had made fun of him. In doing so, he violated social expectancies. Yet his reaction to ridicule and physical assault was not totally unwarranted.

Bernie had to be helped to find new ways to deal with bigotry. He must come to understand the meaning of living in a white-dominated society. In turn, he could use his ingenuity and creativity to equalize his footing in that society. Bernie's father did his son a disservice by complaining and teaching revenge while his son was experiencing the aftermath of spending a night in an iron-and-steel jungle.

RECOMMENDATION: The first priority was to allow Bernie to talk about his night in jail. This experience, more than any, could damage him for a lifetime. He needed to talk about the loneliness, the fears, the strange noises, and, most of all, the inhuman things that people do to one another in jail.

Despite the bigotry, Bernie's father was to help his son face up to the broken windows and make restitution for the damage. This would not only teach Bernie responsibility, it also would give him and his father a chance to confront the abuse to which Bernie had been exposed.

Bernie was to be encouraged to use sports, academic studies, politics, and other opportunities to find ways around prejudice. But he'd only find more iron and steel confining him if he again resorted to revenge to express his pain and displeasure.

LESSON: Black may be beautiful, white may mean might, but a broken window has got to be made right.

Bernie was angry. He had a right to be. What he didn't have a right to do was set himself up as judge, jury, and executioner (heavy on the executioner) and reap his own brand of revenge on those who had been cruel to him. Although the provocation was strong and the reaction understandable, Bernie would only hurt himself further if allowed to find credence in the precept that each person can seek justice according to his or her own beliefs.

Bernie is not alone in his "eye-for-an-eye" philosophy of social justice. Hundreds of kids Ambush others daily for the purpose of demonstrating their belief: "You can't do that to me!" This method of Ambush can assume countless forms during early adolescence. Here are a few:

Peggy and Melissa were friends. Peggy smiled at Melissa's boyfriend. Melissa spread the rumor that Peggy was pregnant.

George and Cary were junior-high basketball buddies. George had to go home early one night because his father had grounded him. Cary made fun of George by saying, "Can't control your old man, huh?" George, upon arriving home, punched his little brother across the room when the brother laughed at his shoes.

Betty and Andrea had three classes together. They were polite to one another. Betty told three other girls and two boys that Andrea had started her menstrual period. As soon as she had heard what happened, Andrea caught Betty alone in the locker room and banged her head against the lockers quite severely.

Shirley stole the neighbor girl's bicycle because the girl had told her (Shirley's) mother that Shirley wasn't at a slumber party she was supposed to be attending the week before, but out with a boy.

Stories of such revenge are endless. Other examples could be given in which kids simply roam around, like walking revenge machines, looking for someone or something to get even with. These kids usually have a chip on their shoulder and take it out on someone else's property. Street lights, automobile tires, bicycles, windows, and schools often suffer the consequences of kids' determination to prove "You can't to that to me!" The cause of the revenge—"you"—could be a father, mother, friend, enemy, teacher, or, more often than not, *life*.

What gives cause for grave concern is that these kids are usually not caught by the police and their parents are unaware of their actions. Allowed to continue, their actions can easily lead to tragic outcomes as their revenge becomes unsatisfied with materialistic targets and turns to people instead.

When parents suspect this type of behavior, they should bring the warfare out into the open. But, as I've cautioned before, parents should not be sidetracked by what appears to be the obvious problem. In the case of "You can't do that to me!," parents must not get hooked on the surface issue of whether the misdeed justifies revenge. They should simply make it clear that there is no justification for revenge—*period!*

A kid who feels offended and wants revenge needs to talk it out. Within limits, he or she should be allowed to complain, rant, rave, and scream about the inequities of life. The parent, keeping cool, must permit such outbursts, reminding a son or daughter that talking and complaining are permissible but a vengeful action is not. Despite the transgression, they must follow the law. Parents can find the patience to tolerate a little yelling from a wounded teenager once in a while if they consider that emotional catharsis is better than damaged goods or injured people. In the final analysis, parents should remember that someone must pay the cost of vandalism and other acts of thoughtless revenge, and it sure won't be the insurance companies.

The eleven kids and six battle cries discussed above only touch the tip of the iceberg of rebelliousness faced by the parents of budding teenagers. For every rebellious note heard, there are hundreds of potential causes just waiting to be discovered. With causes come mindless slogans, half-baked leaders, complementary fads, and other smoke screens designed to cover confusion and doubt. As was suggested, parents should not openly declare war on adolescent rebellion. If parents show themselves ready to do battle, they only add more fuel to the fire. In active retaliation, kids will scream even louder, "If Mom and Dad are against it, it must be good!"

Parents can become disheartened during the stormy period when youthful rebels with endless causes bounce around the house. When causes and battle cries lurk in every corner, familial contentment can be destroyed. As a result, it is sometimes difficult for parents to understand how they are relevant or needed around the house. To those who question parental relevance, I offer two facts. First, parents are relevant in that their very presence gives teenage rebels confidence that they'll never be left without a cause. Second, parents become relevant, although dumbfounded, when they listen to their kids' confusion and try to make sense out of it, a task that would stump a linguist. Only a parent would still love a son or daughter who said, "Everybody has gotta be cool, especially when so many things are dumb. But you won't understand that you can't do this to me, so you might as well forget it 'cause it don't mean nothin' to me."

13

Fifteen and Sixteen: Now or Never

QUESTION: What do you get when you put the seeds of independence in the fertile soil of the drive for immediate satisfaction and nourish it with the availability of fancy clothes, fast cars, booze, drugs, and popularity?

ANSWER: A sixteen-year-old.

QUESTION: What do you get when you rekindle the smoldering ashes of the adolescence that was by adding the fuel of worry about the adolescent that is and fan the flames with fear of the catastrophes that lie between today's adolescent and tomorrow's adult?

ANSWER: The parent of a sixteen-year old.

QUESTION: What do you get when you put a hedonistic sixteen-year-old in an environment full of fear and worry and controlled by an adult who wouldn't mind being an adolescent again?

ANSWER: The typical American home with a teenager.

The most critical stage of Protective Parenting comes with the ages fifteen and sixteen. That's when parents must start letting go the reins of external control, hoping they've done their job well and that the child can gradually take over. If there is an event in America that symbolizes this transfer of power, it's the day that Dad or Mom stops the car on a back street or country road and says, "All right, you drive."

If kids have been taught well, they will weave a little, babble a lot, and shake like hell. If they've learned the basics of control, they'll stay on the road; if not, they'll run into a ditch. Parents, with hearts jumping, must be willing to allow them to make or break it on their own. In most cases, if they do well, they get to drive more often; if not, they are subjected to more practice and continued observation.

Sixteen-year-old kids want to get behind the wheel and, without a moment's hesitation, pull into the mainstream of traffic. They fancy themselves to be Mario Andretti, A. J. Foyt, and Richard Petty all rolled into one. But in reality they wouldn't know the Indy 500 from the Ten Commandments. They want to be perfect at everything they do the first time they try it. All life's desires must be fulfilled immediately. *Now!* If not, they'll say, "I didn't want to do it, anyway."

Parents add to this all-or-nothing attitude by acting as if, once the kid slips into the driver's seat, they have no more control over his or her actions. They fail to realize that the teenager's partying, drinking, talking, dating, and other socializing can be handled the same way as driving. Give a little responsibility, see how it's handled—if it's well done, give more; if not, additional practice and supervision are in order. Parents of a sixteen-year-old can intervene slowly, giving a little, taking a little, always with a guiding hand.

While kids want what they want *now,* parents believe that they have to teach total self-reliance within a week or else they'll never get it done. Thus, at fifteen and sixteen, for both parents and kids, it seems to be *now or never.*

During this now-or-never phase, parents must concentrate on bringing reality home to roost. They must help their son or daughter reach a happy median between the simplicity of childhood temper tantrums and the overwhelming complexity of pointless rebellion. Parents can bring reality to the doorstep of each teenager's conscience by taking unequivocal stands on issues of public and private morality. They don't have to be *right* (I'm not even sure there is such an absolute), but they should be consistent in the application of their moral standards and willing to explain their position in a rational manner.

Because certain situations typically tie parents into knots, I have dedicated this chapter to giving parents mechanisms for getting themselves out of the corners into which teenagers can back them. In Chapter 12, I reviewed six slogans of rebellion. Now I shall look at six "coping comebacks" (as I call them) designed to help parents teach their teenagers about the real world and save some of their own sanity at the same time.

To make these coping comebacks work, parents must take a long, hard look at themselves. They must first reflect on their life and separate the adolescent that was from the parent that is. Then they must determine what, if any, adolescent frustrations remain from years long gone by. This is done by peeking into the closet of memories and dusting off the excitement, joy, pain, frustration, guilt, and shame that cover the trophies, pictures, and mementos of yesterday, always remembering what it was like to want everything *now*.

My recommended phrases will flop if parents fail to recognize the difference between the dreams of a perfect child and the harsh reality that trouble brings. The six handy phrases can give parents courage to face teenage warriors and help them envision the peace that comes with a job well done.

Parents can make my suggestions work only if they have the courage to take a stand, knowing that sometimes they will be off base and must compromise. Such give-and-take need not dampen the parents' authoritative position. Being fallible doesn't alter parents' ability to determine right from wrong—unless, of course, they have one moral code for their kids and another for themselves. In that case, fallibility is the rule rather than the exception.

If parents can be patient with the wobbling and weaving of

their sixteen-year-old and tolerant of the remnants of their own adolescence, they will find the coping comebacks effective. Keeping their hopes for the future in proper perspective, they will be able to prove to their kid, as well as to themselves, that there is a third alternative to the now-or-never dilemma—tomorrow.

Since this time period can be so confusing, I have outlined the first case in story form. Cindy did such a masterful job of playing her parents against one another that even I fell victim to her Ambush. However, Marlene's manipulation was easier to spot.

SITUATION: Sixteen-year-old Cindy was busted at a friend's party for smoking marijuana. Her father called me from the police station and asked me to mediate the crisis. When I arrived at their eighty-thousand-dollar upper-middle-class home, the mother was frantically pacing the floor, searching for a cigarette. The father was screaming at Cindy about being a "common criminal," and Cindy was curled up on the living-room couch, pulling at a string on her Levi's, making sure she didn't let her folks see that she was anxious to find out what had happened to the rest of her friends.

REACTION: I decided to try to get the three to communicate clearly and calmly, but every time I made a suggestion they just started yelling at each other again. I finally got Cindy's mother and father to present their side of the problem. Her father noted, "Her mother and I are very upset because our daughter has been arrested and almost locked in jail. Even worse, she doesn't seem to care."

Cindy's mother went on to discuss several situations in which Cindy had shown general disrespect and lack of family involvement. She assured me that Cindy's dope problem was only the "straw that broke the camel's back." I then asked Cindy for her response. I remember a few of the quotes; I also remember wanting to crawl into a hole.

"I'm a problem? That's bullshit! Mother, I remember when

Daddy said that you dressed like a whore, so don't criticize the way I look. Yeah, and Mom, you're always talking about whether or not Dad is fucking other women during his bowling night. And Dad, if there was more love and less bitching in the house, I could get more involved and study more, too. Anyway, marijuana isn't as bad for me as all that gin you drink is for you."

Cindy's ruthless attack on family secrets led to an hour of bickering, explanations, and shame-throwing between Cindy's mother and father. I remained silent as Cindy's parents talked about things that they had avoided saying for several years.

I finally interrupted. "Let's talk about where we go from here."

I felt like a miracle worker as everyone made some type of pledge to be more involved in the family. Cindy even offered to stay in two nights a week and not to fight with her sister unless she absolutely had to. Everyone was so happy with the resolution of bad feelings that nothing further was said regarding the marijuana arrest.

As everyone moved their separate ways, I asked Cindy's father about the arrest. He reassured me, "Oh, that. Well, I'll give the judge a call and everything will be okay. It's more important that we got all these things talked out here tonight. Thanks."

I was still shocked at the quick recovery as I stepped out into the late spring evening. As I got into my car, a young girl rode up on her bike and, brushing the long, stringy hair from her eyes, said, "Hi, I'm Patty. You Doc?"

Our short conversation proved that I still had much to learn about kids. "Yeah, I'm Doc. You're Cindy's sister, aren't you?"

"Yeah." She was bubbling. "How'd she do?"

She'd caught me by surprise, "Whaddaya mean?"

Patty's face brightened even further as she explained, "Cindy came into the bathroom right before you arrived and said that she had a neat way out of the dope rap. How'd she do?"

With my face half-hidden by my hand, trying to conceal my embarrassment, I replied, "Very well, Patty. Yes, indeed, Cindy did very well."

INTERPRETATION: This situation demonstrated how sophisticated the Ambush of a sixteen-year-old can be. Cindy remained in complete control of every thought and emotion while her mother and father lost *their* control. Then she struck at their most vulnerable spot: their lack of communication with each other.

Cindy had seen both sides and knew that her mother and father didn't talk honestly to one another. It was a perfect maneuver and very well timed.

Cindy's parents were genuinely concerned about her welfare, and there was a good chance that her trouble wouldn't get more serious. However, there probably would be more troublesome acts coming from her, and many of them would go unnoticed due to Cindy's sophistication and her parents' preoccupation with their own problems.

RECOMMENDATION: I told the mother and father to do more talking to each other and less to Cindy. If they insisted on sharing their marital difficulties with Cindy (which was likely), I cautioned them to expect to hear their secrets repeated during family conflicts.

In this particular situation, Cindy should have paid a rather stiff penalty (for example, loss of driving and dating privileges for at least two weeks) in addition to paying part of the fine and court costs. In fact, she paid none.

LESSON: Parents' weaknesses make perfect targets for an Ambush.

SITUATION: Fifteen-year-old Marlene lived with her divorced mother and younger sister. Her father lived about an hour's drive away. Marlene's father and mother harbored much resentment for each other and often argued about the mother's alleged inability to raise Marlene properly.

One night, Marlene came home at 3:00 A.M., disheveled and drunk.

REACTION: According to the mother, Marlene was not so drunk that she couldn't curse her mother's "stupidity." The mother screamed at Marlene, accusing her of trying to hurt her "just like your father does." In reaction, Marlene threw a vase across the kitchen and ran out of the house. Unknown to the mother, Marlene went to see her father.

Marlene's mother waited for an hour and then called the police. They put out a bulletin for a "runaway girl." When the police made a routine check of the father's house, he lied about his daughter's being there.

The next afternoon, after sobering up, Marlene went back home and told her mother what had happened. Her mother didn't mention the drunkenness, broken vase, or running away, preferring instead to make obscene remarks about her ex-husband.

INTERPRETATION: This situation was pretty much beyond help. There was such a backlog of hate, mistrust, and poor communication that any attempt to get the parents to cooperate in teaching Marlene parental respect would be futile.

Marlene had broken several rules and deserved to be punished. Instead, she manipulated her way around the real issues by playing on the pain between her parents. She had been caught in the middle during and after the divorce and was now doing an excellent job of getting revenge by destroying parental authority.

RECOMMENDATION: I told the lady to penalize Marlene the next time any of the infractions occurred. When Marlene tried to get out of the penalty by making references to her father, the mother was to say, "My problems with your father have nothing to do with your violation of the rules. You'll have to deal with me, not him."

The sooner Marlene got out of this vicious, backbiting situation, the better. The parents obviously weren't sensitive to how their fighting was affecting their daughter. A "cold-war" status was the best that could be hoped for.

LESSON: Using a child as a tool of revenge during or after a divorce should be considered a type of rape.

Cindy and Marlene played upon their parents' pain in order to make things go their way. Like many of their friends, they had learned that when parents are upset their ability to discipline their children is severely impaired. This Ambush strategy highlights the vindictive streak in most people that says, "Strike while the other guy isn't looking." When parents feel cornered by whatever pain is touching their hearts, they should relieve the pressure by saying, "Don't play with my pain."

If the parents in the cases above had said, "Don't play with my pain," things could have been cooled off a bit. Making such a request is an indirect admission that parents have personal problems, too. Furthermore, it is a statement that gives parents a moment to decide whether to proceed with a discussion or terminate it until they are better able to think things through. Although it can be misused, this coping comeback can alert a kid that using parental weaknesses to circumvent their authority is not going to work.

People in pain react to feelings, not the facts. Parents, being people (despite what teenage critics might say), find it hard to make rational decisions concerning their kids when the kids say or do something that stimulates their personal pain. "Don't play with my pain" can be a graceful exit for parents who are aware that their emotional unrest is too great to withstand their kid's antics. It therefore becomes a method of calling time-out.

Parents in pain should not try to be authority figures. The two don't mix well. However, if parents believe that they *must* do or say something, a qualifier should be added to their decision. For example, a parent under pressure to make a decision while feeling personal pain might say, "Since I have to make a decision and I don't feel too hot, we'll review it when I'm feeling better."

A response that says, "No decision for now," or, "No, but I'll reconsider later," respects the kid's request but lets him or her know that delaying action on the request is probably best in the long run. "Don't play with my pain" is a comeback that really contains a request for a compromise The proposed give-and-take might sound like, "Don't play with my pain, and I won't play with you when I'm in pain."

Cindy and Marlene got into trouble and played with parental pain in order to avoid negative consequences. The next two kids, while not inherently deviant, went too far in their experimentation and needed a loving rap on the head.

SITUATION: Sixteen-year-old Rick came home late one evening, apparently drunk. His father, realizing that Rick had always been a good kid, tried to talk with him. After five minutes of garbled nonsense, the father decided that his son was too far gone to make sense.

About two hours later, Rick had thrown up and was almost purple in color. He was having a difficult time breathing. His parents rushed him to the hospital, where he received oxygen and recovered. After intensive questioning, they learned that Rick, along with two other friends, had been sniffing an aerosol deodorant.

REACTION: The parents were absolutely dumbfounded. They had never expected such deviant behavior from their son. As their son lay moaning, the parents were overwhelmed with confusion and anxiety. I arrived when their pain was reaching hysterical proportions.

INTERPRETATION: The modern-day teenager will experiment with getting high just as his or her parents experimented with supposedly new and exciting things. Unfortunately, today's teenager is turning to extremely dangerous substances in order to find the "high."

I personally place marijuana and liquor in somewhat the same category in terms of seeking excitement. However, I am vehemently against the inhalation of such toxic substances as glue, paint, turpentine, deodorant, and other such vapors. I am convinced that they are lethal and their use must be severely punished.

Once his head cleared, Rick must be taught, by words and actions, that such behavior is clearly out of bounds!

RECOMMENDATION: The parents were correct to call me to get an opinion before taking any action. I agreed to return two nights later and help them put things straight. I reminded them that judicious action at this point could teach Rick a lifelong lesson about flirting with trouble.

I had a long discussion with Rick and his parents about the

brain damage that can result from inhaling such toxic substances. I told of several kids who had habitually sniffed such vapors and now were unable to control many of their actions. Once I got Rick's attention, he received a stiff penalty (no car for a month).

This was another example of using the lesson "If you're gonna play, you gotta pay."

LESSON: If a kid gets too high, he or she must be brought down to earth.

SITUATION: I was cornered one evening at a cocktail party by Carol's father. Carol was an attractive fifteen-year-old girl. She enjoyed parties, rock music, dancing, and the latest fads. She was pleasant, cooperative, and only occasionally challenged her parents' authority.

That morning, Carol had come to breakfast in a strange mood. She was sullen, grumpy, edgy. Her eyes were red, and her face pale.

REACTION: All parental attempts to find out what was wrong had been met with hostility. Her father told of how he had tried to ask leading questions. Carol had screamed at him for interfering in her life, and, after yelling at both parents about nearly everything, she had abruptly left the table, gone to her room, and locked herself inside.

The parents, thinking that Carol was "just going through a phase," might have forgotten the whole incident if it hadn't been for the suddenness and explosiveness of their daughter's reaction.

INTERPRETATION: From what I was able to ascertain, Carol might have taken some drugs (possibly speed) and was suffering withdrawal. She was strung out. Such an abrupt change from her normal pattern of behavior was cause for concern, but not panic.

Since he probably couldn't discover the truth, Carol's father couldn't do much about the incident. Punishment based on my supposition wasn't a good idea. However, he and his wife should work to prevent future such occurrences. They needed knowledge of the teenage drug scene. Also, they should talk to Carol about her involvement in that scene.

Whatever had happened, Carol's flirtation with trouble was a distinct possibility. Her parents should make perfectly clear to Carol where they stood concerning drugs. They needed knowledge in order to take that stand.

RECOMMENDATION: I suggested that the father and mother contact a local drug-abuse center and ask for all up-to-date information on the drugs being used by teenagers. Since they change from month to month, the parents had to get current information in order to take an intelligent position on the issue.

The father, being a firm believer that "such things don't happen in my home," was shocked by the overview I gave him of the teenage drug culture. In no uncertain terms, I told him that ignorance was his worst enemy. Unless he realized that no home was protected from the drug scene, he would have more Ambushes on his hands than he dared to imagine.

If Carol had messed with drugs, chances were that she was "chipping" in the drug scene; that is, trying out a little of this and a little of that in order to join her friends and acquaintances who were excited about getting a "buzzzzz."

LESSON: An ounce of knowledge is sometimes worth more than a pound of concern.

Because Rick and Carol were basically good kids, their parents didn't worry about their getting into trouble. They saw no reason to suspect that these kids would seriously violate any boundary of acceptable social behavior. Their ignorance could have proved to be their undoing. They confidently said, "My kid knows right from wrong. I trust him (her)." But trust and confidence are not enough when kids cross into dangerous territory seeking excitement. It wasn't too late for both sets of parents, aware of the teenager's propensity for experimenting with troublesome situations, to say, "Don't step over this line!"

"Don't step over this line!" represents a clearly drawn distinction between right and wrong. Setting such an absolute is beneficial in certain situations. I believe that the use of harmful drugs is one of them. However, in most situations drawing such a line prohibits the growth of reciprocity. Therefore, such a line should be drawn only when the parents believe that the behavior in question goes against the very fiber of the family's moral code. In Rick's and Carol's cases, "Don't step over this line!" was definitely in order in terms of avoiding a repeat performance of the behavior.

Parents must be willing to back up their statement of "Don't step over this line!" Convincing kids that parents mean business might call for locking them out of the house or calling the police for assistance. If parents aren't willing to go all the way, they should not draw the line in the first place.

"Don't step over this line!" is a nonnegotiable coping comeback. It reflects little or no understanding of a kid's desires. Such a dictatorial posture must be taken only rarely, and then only for the good of everyone concerned. If parents believe, "You shall not do that while living under this roof," then they must say, "Don't step over this line!"

If parents warn their kids about trouble by drawing clear lines between right and wrong and backing them up with whatever it takes, the kids will be less likely to bring trouble to the parents, society, and themselves in the future.

The ultimatum "Don't step over this line!" should be outweighed by the give-and-take inherent in another coping comeback, illustrated by the next two cases, "You do your thing and then I'll do mine."

SITUATION: I received a call at 6:00 A.M. from Patrick's father. His voice was a conglomeration of tension, anger, and relief as he explained how his sixteen-year-old son had left the house for a walk at 9:00 the previous evening and hadn't come home all night.

After a night of pacing the floor and exchanging fears and anxieties with his wife, the father was about to call the police when, at 5:50 A.M., Patrick staggered in, hung over and apologetic.

REACTION: Patrick's father was quite angry, but his mother was so relieved that she wasn't very upset. They wanted my input and guidance before taking any action. I told them to put the coffeepot on and I'd be right over.

INTERPRETATION: After a thirty-minute talk with Patrick, I learned that he had lost a battle with self-pity, taken a walk, met some friends, and spent the night drinking, smoking marijuana, and feeling sorry for himself.

He had violated house rules and society's regulations, not to mention having placed considerable stress on parents who cared deeply for him. His self-pity was understandable, but it didn't mitigate his violations.

After seeing his smile beneath the sorrow, I also determined that Patrick was testing the limits of family tolerance. He wanted to know how far his parents would let him go before yanking the chain.

RECOMMENDATION: I recommended a hard yank on the chain. This was one case where a suspension of privileges would not adequately define the boundaries of parental (ultimately societal) tolerance for deviance.

A stiff penalty was in order. Since Patrick was unable or unwilling to make a suggestion, I recommended that he pay back the seven hours of absence and agony threefold. Thus, he was "sentenced" to twenty-one hours of hard but meaningful labor.

His sentence was hard because he had to clean up the bathroom, garbage cans, and toilets with a toothbrush. It was meaningful because these chores had to be done for the good of the home, and the number of hours represented his infraction of the rules.

He was given five days to complete the assignment and was to have no recreation until the job was finished. Possibly the worst outcome for Patrick was that I insisted that his parents send him to school, hangover and all.

While I helped the parents understand the devastating effects of self-pity, this didn't alter the fact that Patrick had done his thing and now the parents must do theirs.

LESSON: If you do the crime, you gotta pay the time.

SITUATION: After a lecture to a church group, a dignified middle-aged man approached me with what he called a "minor problem." He explained that his fifteen-year-old daughter seemed to be dominating the home. He was genuinely amazed that his "little Lucy" had become a tyrant so quickly.

Lucy got up when she wanted, helped with chores when it was convenient (which was rare), and was regularly sassy and disrespectful, saying such things as "Who's gonna make me?" and "Quit trying to run my life." She would also threaten reprisals (for example, "If you keep hassling me, I won't go to church with you anymore").

The father had realized that the entire situation was getting out of hand one evening when he had asked her whether she was running around with a twenty-year-old guy. Lucy, without batting an eye, had blurted, "Stay the fuck out of my life!"

REACTION: Lucy's dad said that he had been dumbfounded and stunned. He had remained silent for a few moments. His wife, overhearing the obscenity, had run into the room and confronted her husband about his lack of disciplinary action. He admitted not having known what to do and therefore had done nothing.

He added that on several occasions he had grounded Lucy but that hadn't seemed to work. During her punishment, he told me, Lucy would stay in her room and listen to records or talk on her phone.

INTERPRETATION: This was definitely *not* a "minor problem." Lucy was out of control and heading for trouble. Her parents had made an error by seeing her behavior as a necessary part of growing up. The onset wasn't sudden; the word "fuck" just finally forced the parents to look at what was happening.

It was past time for intervention, but probably not too late. Lucy needed to learn that her actions caused *reactions* in others. Disrespect was deeply rooted, and it would take a lot of work before respect was established. She needed to learn about realistic limits, and confinement to her room where she could enjoy the latest rock 'n' roll and secretive conversations with her friends was not the way to get the job done.

RECOMMENDATION: After we had agreed to meet again, I gave the father a recommendation I rarely give. I told him that he must first get Lucy's attention. Because he was a mild-mannered, gentle sort of fellow, I suggested that a well-placed yell, significantly loud, would shake his daughter into reality.

If ever there was a time for a parent to yell at a kid, now was the time. Not a wild, emotional, overreactive scream, but a well-toned, loud yell, designed to let Lucy know who was boss.

As I always like to do, I role-played how he might do it. When Lucy screamed, "Stay out of my life," he could shock the hell out of her by yelling, "If you'd act like a young woman, then I might be able to."

After getting her attention, he was to calmly but firmly point out the parental expectancies and what would happen if she violated them (leaving out the room-confinement and taking away phone privileges instead).

I explained to him that he was to use this recommendation only under my continued guidance. I wanted to make sure he didn't abuse my suggestion and that he compensated the girl for the verbal spanking.

LESSON: Rational or not, parents will occasionally follow Kiley's law: If you truly love your kids, sometimes you just gotta yell at them.

Patrick's and Lucy's parents were more than a little shocked by their kids' behavior. In both cases, it was evident that the kids were lacking in respect and self-control. However, they were not beyond help. A lot of parents wake up one day and realize that their teenagers are quite disruptive. When they finally realize, "It *can* happen in my family," many parents are so numb that they don't know what to do. In most cases, they continue to do what they've always done: nothing. For parents who find themselves in such a state, I strongly recommend the use of the coping comeback "You do your thing and then I'll do mine."

This vernacular expression can take different forms. For example, "There's different strokes for different folks. Each person must choose the way that is best for him or her." When said by parents to their kids, the expression means two things: first, the parents have respect for their kids' freedom to be disruptive, disrespectful, and detached; second, the parents are assuming an authoritative posture in which they let it be known that they will choose their course of action *after* the kids have chosen theirs.

"You do your thing and then I'll do mine" provides kids with a choice-situation. By saying this, parents are telling their offspring that their (the parents') reaction will depend upon what the kids decide to do. This puts the pressure on the kids to weigh all factors carefully before making a determination of which direction they will go. It also introduces the possibility of compromise in case the parents react more strongly to the proposed action than the kids had anticipated. If kids realize that what they're getting won't be worth the price they will have to pay, they can change their minds before acting.

When parents use "You do your thing and then I'll do mine," they are giving recognition to their kids' desires. They are saying, in effect, "I see that your thing is very important to you. So tell me what you're going to do and then I'll let you know whether I can live with it." This is the opposite of the dictatorial stance of "Don't step over this line!" and is preferred as the most frequent course of action.

The "you-first" stance of this comeback is very helpful for parents in allowing kids to make a mistake, rethink the problem, and change their minds without looking foolish or "uncool." However, some might misuse this comeback as a mechanism of entrapment. They speak of tolerance but are really saying, "You tell me your thing and then I'll make fun of or punish you." This is not a coping comeback. Rather, it is an ugly way to dump personal hate on kids and invites revenge.

A very effective way to see how this comeback works and how it differs from the hard-line approach is to consider the following case review.

I met Vivian shortly after she had been declared a ward of the court and put into a foster home. The sixteen-year-old girl had run away from her natural parents at least ten times, and everyone involved agreed she'd be better off in a new environment.

Vivian had numerous complaints about her natural parents. She listed seven or eight social activities that were prohibited by her parents' religion. Strangely enough, one of the more explosive issues came to the fore because Vivian refused to hide her affection for her eighteen-year-old boyfriend. When confronted by her mother, she did not hesitate to admit that she regularly had intercourse with "the man I love."

The mother had basically said, "Not as long as you live in this house" (which can be taken as another version of "Don't step over this line!"). Vivian absolutely refused to live within that restriction, and when the pressure became too great, she would run away. The mother was very honest about her moral standards and said that if Vivian couldn't live within her guidelines, she no longer wanted her as a daughter. Although suffering some rejection pains, Vivian chose to move in with foster parents rather than continue to fight with her mother.

The foster mother wasn't too thrilled with the idea that Vivian was having intercourse with her boyfriend, either. However, she had a different moral code and was willing to tolerate Vivian's "thing," provided Vivian would compromise. Thus, before Vivian moved in with the foster parents, the following agreement was reached. Vivian would not be hassled about her sexual activity, provided that it took place away from the home, didn't interfere with Vivian's responsibilities (school, curfew, chores), and she agreed to take birth-control pills and have a Pap smear once a year.

Vivian was going to do "her thing" come hell or high water. Drawing an absolute line just didn't work. The compromise of "You do your thing and then I'll do mine" helped make an unfortunate situation somewhat better.

This didn't exactly represent a happy ending, but at least Vivian was living in a family environment, abiding by the household regulations. Things might have been better if both Vivian and her natural mother hadn't been so stubborn.

From the complexity of compromise, we move to the relative simplicity of free enterprise.

SITUATION: Fifteen-year-old Brad ran with a bunch of older guys, all of whom were well known to the police as shoplifters, vandals, and curfew-violators. When his father found out about it, he warned Brad to stay away from the kids because they were "bad influences" on him.

REACTION: Brad tried to argue about his friends' "coolness" and how much fun he had with them. His back talk was the cause of his parents' yelling—at him as well as at each other. His father told him that he *had to mind* or else he would call the police. His mother criticized her husband for threatening such a ridiculous thing. Everybody yelled at everybody, and nobody did anything about the situation—except Brad. He regularly sneaked out to see his buddies.

INTERPRETATION: I determined that Brad was so busy rebelling against his father that he didn't realize the trouble he was heading for. Hanging around guys who support each other's deviance is not a good idea. These kids often get into trouble because there's nothing better to do.

Brad needed to recognize the kind of problem he was asking for by seeking this type of friendship. His father's labeling of his friends as "bad influences" only strengthened Brad's rebellion. Typical of such situations, Brad's father was spending less time with his son just when he needed him the most.

Brad's father couldn't control his son's friends. To try to do so would only make a bad situation worse. However, the father could inform Brad what might happen if he continued his thoughtless rebellion.

RECOMMENDATION: I suggested a police contact, but not the type the father originally had in mind. I put him in touch with the local juvenile officer, whom I knew to be willing to do preventative work. The officer consented to try to get Brad's attention.

Two days later, in a parking lot outside a record shop, the officer and his partner stopped Brad as he was walking with three other guys. The officer separated Brad from the rest and gave him a short lecture, the gist of which went something like this:

"Hey, Brad, haven't you got anything better to do? You know what these guys like to do, don't you? So do I. It's just a matter of time before I catch them in the act. If you're with them, I'll have to use these [he pulled out his handcuffs] on you. Don't make me do that—okay?"

Brad's father, who knew of the encounter with the juvenile officer, took his son bowling later that evening. Brad told his father what had happened and that he was scared. As per my instructions, the father listened to his son and talked about doing more things with him. They joined the bowling league that evening, giving Brad a ready-made excuse for the guys in case they pressured him: "I'm going bowling with my dad."

LESSON: The policeman can be a parent's best friend.

SITUATION: Sixteen-year-old Frank lived with his mother and three sisters in a well-to-do home. Frank's father had died when he was four, leaving him a substantial sum of money in the form of allowances controlled by Frank's mother.

According to the mother, Frank usually got what he wanted. When he didn't, he cried or threatened to hurt one of his sisters. Whenever he threw such a tantrum, his mother gave in. One night, Frank was told that he could not stay overnight at a friend's house.

REACTION: Frank whined, cried, and fussed for over twenty minutes, rambling on about how unfair life was and how he would get even with somebody. Finally, his mother gave in and let Frank go. During his night out, Frank and three other kids broke into a house and were arrested.

INTERPRETATION: Frank's mother and sisters were spoiling Frank beyond belief. Operating from a deep sense of love, respect, and remorse, they felt that without a father Frank was "owed" some special breaks in life. The result was that Frank never learned how to give and take, just how to take.

The excitement of breaking into a house was just an extension of getting a new toy. Frank had no ability to control the excitement in his life. If he wanted something, he got it. He had no idea how to earn something by being responsible. This was a good example of how the lack of self-control can result in a geometric expansion of the desire for excitement and how that desire can lead to serious trouble.

RECOMMENDATION: As I saw the situation, Frank's mother and sisters had plenty of opportunity to teach him self-control. After the arrest, they had the one missing ingredient: the motivation to do it.

If they ignored his inappropriate and childish behavior and rewarded his self-control with money and privileges, Frank could still be taught that excitement has a limit *and* a price. Minding the rules would get Frank money, privileges, and attention. Whining, crying, screaming, and fussing would get him grounded and broke.

LESSON: A spoiled kid will spoil much.

SITUATION: Fifteen-year-old John had a case of chronic laziness. At least that's the way his good-natured mother saw it. No matter what was requested of him, whether taking out the garbage or getting out of the house to have some fun, John stayed in his room, sleeping and listening to records. When told to do something, John would grunt, "Yeah," and that was it.

REACTION: The mother complained about his laziness but didn't seem to want to do anything about it. John's father would yell at him, but he didn't back up his yelling with any consequences. No matter how they approached him, John stayed in his room, except to go to school and eat.

INTERPRETATION: After several informal conferences with the family, I determined that John had learned that he didn't have to exert any energy in order to have life pretty much as he wanted it. His mom waited on him hand and foot, and his father, although loud in his criticism, never took any negative action toward him.

While John was enjoying the good life, his laziness was beginning to dominate his life to the exclusion of responsibility. He was being disruptive lying on his bed!

Lying around the house, sleeping, eating, and doing little else was damaging John more than anyone realized. If and when he left home, he would be subject to a rude awakening in terms of what life expected of him. He wouldn't be the first kid to react with revenge to such a realization.

RECOMMENDATION: I suggested that the parents have regular conferences with John to talk about the reasoning behind their requests. They were to make sure that they clearly explained how they had failed to teach him responsibility and exactly what they expected of him in the future. He was to know that things were going to change.

John didn't seem to pay attention until his mother said that she wouldn't cook for him if he didn't start doing his chores, studying, and finding other things to do besides sleep. I assured her that if John went hungry a couple of times, things would start changing. (*Note:* Within a month, John was doing his chores and had tried out for the golf team at school.)

LESSON: To get some kids' attention, one has to enter their heads through their stomachs.

John, Frank, and Brad were living as if the world were theirs for the taking. They demonstrated that they didn't have to conform to regulations in order to get what they wanted. In some ways, they were acting as if they were still five years old, waiting for Mommy to fix breakfast and whining, "I don't want mine fixed like that, I want it turned over."

John thought, "If I can get it by lying around, why should I exert myself?" Frank realized, "If I can get it by screaming and fussing, why should I learn to be responsible?" Brad theorized, "If I can get it by hanging around the 'cool dudes,' why should I force myself to make new friends?"

These kids should "get it," all right—exactly what they deserve. The way their parents could start to give them what they were asking for was to use the coping comeback "Life's not a free ride; you get what you earn." Using this approach, John would get no food for no work, Frank no money for screaming and threatening, and Brad no freedom for sneakiness. Since "earning what you get" is a two-way street, John could get food and money for working around the house, Frank could get money and privileges for compliance, and Brad could get attention and freedom by finding new, more responsible things to do.

"Life's not a free ride; you get what you earn" may be one of the most important lessons Protective Parents can teach their children. This comeback reflects the struggle between creative conformity and deviance. It confronts the detachment, disruption, and disrespect so clearly evident in the three cases above. It brings reality to the kid's attention in the form of two messages. First, good actions bring good consequences, and bad actions bring bad consequences. Second, the comeback teaches that parents are the ones who define "good" and "bad," and they must be dealt with—there is *no way* around it.

If kids learn that what they earn is what they get, they'll realize that they can control much of what happens to them. Furthermore, the control mechanism is located between their ears. If they know how to use their free will to make good things happen to them, they will have the Three R's well in hand and will be able to survive on their own. With self-survival skills mastered, the final objective of Protective Parenting—turning to one's "self" when trouble comes—is assured.

Living with the stresses, strains, trials, and tribulations of everyday life demands that kids know the scope of their power, including its limitations. If, by ages fifteen and sixteen, kids understand that life is good, bad, and ugly and that they have some ability to up the percentage of good, they'll be better able to exorcise the curse of hedonism, which ultimately catches up with all of us. To me, this curse warns, "If you take all you want when you want it, tomorrow you'll wish you hadn't."

My personal experiences tell me that this curse is lifelong and each person must find some incantation that will help reduce the grip hedonism can hold on a body. After many black-and-blue marks, my ballad still reminds me that earning my way slowly is not always easy.

> Ego, I, self, and me,
> We live together in harmony.
> No fussing, no fighting, no complaining, no strife,
> We'd have no trouble if it weren't for life.

The next coping comeback also gives the parent the opportunity to convey several messages in one simple sentence.

SITUATION: During breakfast, a colleague described some recent changes in his sixteen-year-old daughter, Ginger, that greatly concerned his wife and himself. As he saw it, the changes had come out of the blue and been growing more disruptive for about two or three months.

Within the time span of a week, more or less, it was not uncommon for Ginger to scream at the slightest hint of parental authority, talk in secretive riddles with old friends, refuse to accompany her parents on favorite outings, fail to follow simple directions from her mother, and accuse her mom of searching through her personal belongings as a "spying" maneuver.

REACTION: My friend described how he and his wife had tried to be tolerant of their daughter's "growing pains." Ginger's distress seemed more intense around her mother. While she complained or pouted around her father, she was accusatory, sarcastic, and hostile toward her mom.

My buddy was scratching his head in bewilderment. In the space of a few months, his sweet little daughter had turned into a monster and his self-confident wife was hiding from the family. When Ginger's father tried to get some answers, his daughter would blurt out one of the following: "You're treating me like a child." "I'm a woman now, you know."

INTERPRETATION: A psychoanalyst would have concluded that Ginger had finally reached that stage in life in which daughters vie with their mothers for their fathers' attention. While such an interpretation has some validity, the reason for the change was not so important as the change itself.

After asking a few questions about Ginger's dating experiences and her steady boyfriend, I made some assumptions about what was going on. From my own experiences with teenage girls, I tentatively concluded that Ginger had had some type of serious sexual encounter with her boyfriend (possibly intercourse). As a result, she now saw herself as forever changed and ready to assume a new role in her family.

Ginger didn't know what to do with the realization that she was somehow "different" from before. She was upset with her mom because she (mom) served as a reminder that not only is there but one "mature woman" per household, but also that she (Ginger) probably wasn't sure of her new identity. Hence, anxiety and tension were directed at Mom as the projected cause of the unrest.

RECOMMENDATION: There was a good chance that Mom and Dad would not hear about Ginger's sexual experiences, if and when she had them. Therefore, my conjecture as to the reason behind the change had little or nothing to do with dealing with the problem.

I suggested that my friend keep things as simple as possible. He and his wife were to verbally praise Ginger for assuming a more independent role in the home, punish any extreme violation of house rules, and ignore the crap she was handing out.

In the event either of them (especially Mom) got fed up with Ginger's caustic remarks, a well-timed and carefully controlled verbal assault was in order (for example, "I'm getting sick and tired of your crap. I don't want to be your punching bag anymore. So *cut it out!*").

In addition, Mom and Dad were to be slow to do Ginger any special favors as long as she was so hostile, but they were to be quick to listen to any "growing pains" she might want to discuss.

LESSON: Understand the struggle of *"Treat me like a woman (man)—please, Mommy."*

SITUATION: Sixteen-year-old Joe was driving his mother wacky. At least that's what Joe's dad said during our first consultation session. He explained that his son's school grades had been going steadily downhill for several months. Parent-teacher conferences had done little to alleviate the problem.

When questioned about his poor showing, Joe would say, "I don't care; it doesn't mean anything, anyway. What can good grades get you?" This attitude was terribly upsetting to Joe's mother. She had challenged him about his plans to go to college, barking at him about his deteriorating performance.

He had answered, "*You* want me to go to college; I don't want to go. If you want good grades, *you* get 'em; I'm sick of school."

REACTION: Joe's father wasn't too worried about the reason behind his son's rejection of college. However, he was concerned about Joe's math scores, realizing that failure in such a crucial area could spell trouble later on, no matter what he did for a living. He had already hired a tutor, but Joe continued to fail.

The major hassle for Joe's father was the bickering between Joe and his mother. Accompanying Joe's "don't-give-a-damn" attitude was the wife's constant badgering about her son being a "nobody." She also confronted her husband regularly about his failure to change Joe's behavior.

INTERPRETATION: Joe evidently had some bad feelings inside. They were somehow related to his mother's pushing and labeling him a "nobody" for not liking school. In reaction to this pressure, he continued to fail, despite plenty of help. In this way, he got revenge on his mother for her attitude.

Joe's rebellion was spilling into areas other than school. Although the parents didn't realize it, he complied with their requests less than 50 percent of the time. Some more serious type of trouble was not far off.

Joe was capable of getting C's in most subjects, if not better. Instead, he did nothing as a handy way of upsetting his mother. His plan was working well for the present, but in the long run it would hurt him more than he realized.

RECOMMENDATION: In order to relieve some of the pressure, I recommended that Joe's mom leave her son alone unless they could do something fun together. I encouraged his father to continue with the tutor and employ the following strategies:

1. When Joe criticized education, the father was to ask him if he wanted to talk about it. If he did, he was to discuss the importance of having power through knowledge and "something to fall back on." If he didn't, he wasn't to pursue it.
2. For every daily grade below C, Joe was to be grounded for an hour a week. This penalty was to start slowly and increase in hours if it proved ineffective. It had to be based on daily grades in order to allow Joe to improve quickly.
3. For every grade above C, Joe was to be given an extra hour out or a small bonus in his weekly allowance.
4. For any attempt to do makeup work, Joe was to be given a larger bonus of some type.

In order for this plan to work, I cautioned the father to employ all of it, not just one or two parts, *and* keep his wife out of it.

FOLLOW-UP: This was a case in which I had a chance to find out how things went after my recommendations were implemented. At my last contact, Joe and his mom were both breaking a hundred on the golf course, and Joe was getting B's in math.

LESSON: If parents can't find the right answer, maybe they're working on the wrong problem.

Emotional pain is a legitimate human experience. It happens all the time. Unfortunately, moms, dads, and kids often ignore their emotional pain, believing it unimportant or shameful. Just as parents shouldn't discipline if they're too upset, kids should not test parental authority while they're feeling bad. Since kids usually express their emotional discomfort with disruption and disrespect, parents can best react to their lack of self-control by saying, "Have your pain, but mind the rules."

With this coping comeback, parents tell their children, "Emotional pain is understandable, but it cannot be used as an excuse for breaking the rules." This gives the kids the counterpart of "Don't play with my pain." Parents are saying, in effect, "I won't discipline you when I'm feeling bad. In turn, don't you break any rules when you're feeling down."

Parents will have an easier time with this complicated situation if they make it very clear to their kids that excuses do not release them from responsibility. I've heard countless kids spout the belief that getting into trouble is "no big deal" as long as they have a good excuse for why it happened. I try to convince them and their parents that there is no such thing as an excuse for getting into trouble, only explanations of *how* it happened. However, many parents go for the excuse "bait" because they don't want to face the fact that their kids can be deviant.

Parents can use "Have your pain, but mind the rules" to separate two overlapping elements, emotional pain and rule infractions. They can listen to their kids' pain without allowing them to continue their Ambushes. Ginger had pain; so did Joe. Both fathers knew that somehow their teenagers were using emotional pain as an excuse for failing to follow the rules and/or justifying their rebelliousness. They both heard, "Don't expect me to follow the rules when I feel so bad," and knew it wasn't a good thing. They were correct.

If kids believe that emotional unrest is a license to throw away their moral standards, there's a good chance an iron-and-steel door will slam shut on them as a result of their judgment. Much too often I've talked with kids who were arrested for an offense for which they had a "perfect" excuse. They didn't understand why the judge hadn't excused them as they had excused themselves. "After all," they explain, "Mom and Dad did."

I offer one more coping comeback to cornered parents. This one is delicate and must be handled with care.

SITUATION: Barry was the oldest of four children and because of his status was the only child with his own room. He had lots of graffiti on the walls and a mess on the floor. One day, during a routine "search-and-destroy" mission, Barry's mom found stacks of pornographic literature in her son's closet and "dirty" films in his dresser drawer.

REACTION: According to Barry's father, his wife hit the ceiling. She ripped the books into shreds and placed them in a trashy heap on Barry's unmade bed. She took the films, promotional material and all, and burned them in the kitchen sink.

That evening, a monumental fight ensued in which Barry was accused of being every type of pervert known to mankind. He countered by accusing his parents of employing a double standard, pointing out that they gambled but he couldn't show a few films to his friends.

The comment about showing films to his buddies slipped out in the heat of battle, and Barry could have bitten off his tongue. His double-standard argument went nowhere as his mother led the charge to get him grounded for a year.

Throughout the foray, the father remained fairly passive. He centered his remarks on the fact that Barry had left the materials where his mother could easily find them. After everyone had run out of anger and hostility, the entire matter melted away.

INTERPRETATION: I had an opportunity to shoot some pool with Barry and informally discuss the situation. As I approached the subject delicately, Barry laughed, saying, "You shoulda seen the old lady's face. She damn near had a stroke." At that moment, I realized that Barry had turned the entire situation into an Ambush, at least in his own head.

Barry knew that his mother had some hang-ups about explicit sex, and his natural interest in such matters became a tool with which he could undermine his mother's authority. He knew how to yank her chain and make her holler. He obviously enjoyed it.

Since Barry took such delight in seeing his mother upset, I concluded that his self-confidence, especially in the area of sex, wasn't exactly 100 percent perfect. He seemed to mask his anger behind a grin while his disappointment was cloaked in revenge.

RECOMMENDATION: I suggested to the father that he counsel his wife about digging into Barry's room, especially when she was unable to control some of her emotions. I also recommended that he play middleman in attempting to resolve some of the contempt that Barry felt toward his mother.

Then I recommended that the father have a little talk with his son about his accumulation of pornography, especially in light of the fact that he was obviously showing his collection off to friends. The fact of having pornography wasn't so important as the manner in which Barry was using it. It was more than an exploration into sexual fantasies; it was a tool of revenge against his mother, a tool that could lead to other trouble. If a friend let the story about the films slip at the wrong time, the police might suspect Barry of peddling pornography.

LESSON: Parents should put their noses into their kids' private business only when they can put their feet into their kids' shoes.

SITUATION: Tom's parents consulted me after their fifteen-year-old son had come home high from a friend's party. They said he was wearing a plastic smile and acted "spacy," moving slowly about the house singing a love song and telling his parents how "groovy" he thought they were. His eyes looked like road maps.

They knew something was wrong when he gently patted his seventeen-year-old sister on the head and said, "Sis, you are a far-out lady." He hadn't said anything nice to her for at least eight years.

REACTION: After recovering from the initial shock, Tom's father tried to find out if he had taken drugs and who had been at the party. Tom's mother quizzed him about where his friend's parents had been and why he had allowed himself to lose control. Tom made light of their questions, preferring instead to turn on the record player and float around the family room.

The next day, when confronted with the same questions, Tom denied any wrongdoing, saying only that he had tasted a marijuana cigarette but had not inhaled it. His parents wanted to believe him, but, as they sat in my office, it was clear that they weren't sure what to believe.

INTERPRETATION: Although I never had a chance to talk to the kid, I know that nobody gets a buzz like Tom's by sniffing a marijuana cigarette. Off the top of my head I'd say Tom probably had thirty or forty "hits" from six to eight joints within a two-hour time period.

Given the fact that most kids don't smoke dope for the maximum effect (by holding the inhalant until the drug has been absorbed into the lungs) and that the friend's dope was cut with parsley (a fact I found out later), it was logical to assume that some of Tom's high was self-induced.

Parental fears of drug addiction, irresponsible, drug-induced behavior, and impending catastrophe were unfounded *in this instance*. Tom demonstrated his need to have someone teach him how to respect drugs and their effect so that he could protect himself better.

RECOMMENDATION: I cautioned the parents against delivering long-winded, moralistic lectures or other forms of intimidation. Rather, I suggested that they invite a colleague of mine (a very experienced drug counselor) over to their house for the purpose of learning about the teenage drug scene.

During the course of the visit, Tom was to be asked to join the conversation. My friend would get him interested, and I was sure Tom would learn a lot about the world of drugs. Reliable data that Tom could trust were more important than all the lectures in the world.

In addition, I suggested that they ground Tom for two weeks for being so foolish in his violation of society's rules.

LESSON: If kids smoke a joint, they need the straight dope.

Barry and Tom represent a piece of teenage reality that is particularly difficult for parents to accept, especially when it exists in their own home. Like it or not, no matter how many warnings are given, discussions held, penalties imposed, or tantrums ignored, kids are going to experiment with Level 4 trouble. Eventually they are going to raise hell with somebody or something, and, in the process, most of them will break a law. By definition, they are in trouble. However, their troublesome behavior will not become known to society because they probably won't be caught. Nonetheless, if parents are concerned about crime, damaged property, and injured persons, such actions must be taken very seriously. When parents see trouble or its signs, they can start to confront the problem by very cautiously adopting the coping comeback "If I can catch you, they can, too."

This comeback recognizes that everyone has a streak of deviance. The deviance must not be condemned or ignored, but accepted and controlled. The reality is there; denying it won't make it disappear. Parents gamble, so do kids; parents drive after drinking, so do kids; a lot of parents are sexually promiscuous, so are many kids; many parents "shoplift" from the Internal Revenue Service, kids rip off stores. The major difference between the deviance of parents and that of kids is that parents have strengths that offset their weaknesses. Status in the community, money, maturity of judgment (in some cases), and a good lawyer are a few assets that parents have that kids usually don't. This is why more kids than parents are caught.

In addition to this general condition, there is another important reason kids get caught. Not only do they break a law, but they also do it in such a manner as to attract the attention of authority figures. Since there are more authority figures watching kids' behavior than parents' actions, parents should make a special effort to catch their kids before someone else does.

When kids are caught by parents breaking the law or definitely heading in that direction, they should first hear, "If I catch you, they can, too." Then the kids should learn who "they" are and what "they" can do. Next, kids should hear about how the criminal justice system makes kids worse the longer they are in custody. (Two of the best books to brief parents are Ken Wooden's *Weeping in the Playtime of Others* and Patrick Murphy's *Our Kindly Parent—the State*.) [1]

When they understand more of the realities of getting caught

1. K. Wooden, *Weeping in the Playtime of Others* (New York: McGraw-Hill Book Company, 1976); and P. Murphy, *Our Kindly Parent—the State* (New York: Viking Press, 1975).

by law-enforcement agencies, they should receive a constructive penalty that will teach them to be more careful in the future. Then comes the tricky part. Parents should graphically describe how they knew something was going on. Usually, silliness, atypical secretiveness or nervousness, goofy mannerisms, and sudden changes in habits or personality are among the behaviors that tip parents off that something is wrong. The final step of action associated with "If I can catch you, they can, too" is taken by teaching kids how to avoid getting caught.

The last time I came to that conclusion, an angry father got up from the audience and accused me of being some type of subversive social element. "You're just teaching kids how to do naughty things and not get caught!" he bellowed.

I answered him as I always do. "That's incorrect, sir. While I advocate the Three R's of creative conformity, I am not blind to the fact that kids will engage in deviance. My purpose is to help parents teach their kids to cover their tracks by being mature, knowing when it's time to say 'stop,' avoiding damage to property and person, and increasing their knowledge of what they are getting themselves into. These things represent respect, responsibility, and reciprocity, not deviance. I do not deal with whether breaking a law is right or wrong—it is *wrong,* there can be no question about that. I prefer to address myself to the fact that kids are the underdogs when it comes to deviance. They don't have the skills in their bag of tricks to compensate for their troublesomeness that their parents do. They must therefore work harder to cover their tracks than their parents do because they have less to work with. It may not be pretty, but it's real!"

People like the man in the audience don't understand the complexity of my position until I give an example of what I'm talking about. I typically use the case of parents who wish to teach their son about alcohol within the confines of their home, and want to use actual experience instead of just talk.

Parents who do this must have an educational scheme in mind that does more than get the kid drunk and help him throw up.

The son must learn to respect alcohol for the poison it is and what it can do to human behavior. Parental motivation for this educational effort must begin and end with the fervent desire to avoid seeing their son or daughter lying dead at the scene of a bloody accident caused by drunken teenagers who thought they were indestructible.

Parents who allow kids to drink in their home venture into shaky territory. They must be very careful about using such an "experiential" technique since they are actually breaking the law (contributing to the delinquency of a minor). Therefore, they, too, have to cover their tracks. Most parents explain their actions by saying, "I'm his (her) father (mother), and I can do as I wish." Fortunately (as in child-abuse situations), the law does not agree.

Family law must never supersede social law. Juvenile laws in most states are laws of spirit rather than of hard-line letters. They are designed to give parents leeway in seeking to improve the child-rearing atmosphere of the home. Parents who wish to teach their kids to respect alcohol by allowing them to drink must be prepared to back up their educational program with more than platitudes about parenthood.

Parents can cover their tracks by making sure that they can prove to a judge, if they have to, that their efforts were in the best interests of the child. The best alternative I can suggest is that whenever an educational program violates the letter of juvenile and family law, it should be carried out under the supervision and guidance of a reputable professional. In this way, parents can meet the test of having the child's best interests at heart and, therefore, their actions are compatible with the spirit, if not the letter, of society's law.

It is under these stringent conditions that I approve and even encourage parents to carry out demonstration projects within the home. There's no greater teaching experience regarding the effects of alcohol than letting kids get smashed and then making them walk, talk, play intellectual games, and discuss serious subjects, playing it all back to them on a tape recording the next day after the headache and nausea have subsided.

When all's said and done, if in their daily course of activity (with intense spying kept off limits) parents can't catch their sons and daughters in illegal or otherwise troublesome behavior, they can relax somewhat, content with the realization that their kids are actually chips off the old block. The only problem left is whether the block is part of an ethically sound social foundation.

The thirteen cases reviewed in this chapter bring more meaning to the concept of trouble. Promiscuous sex, drugs, curfew violations, and general incorrigibility are the types of trouble that challenge the protective role most. These things are dangerous to kids' satisfactory entry into adulthood. The development of these troublesome behaviors reaches a critical point during middle adolescence. It is during this time that they become entrenched or begin to die out.

In their Ambushes, fifteen- and sixteen-year-old kids are playing for keeps. *Now or never!* Through the judicious use of the coping comebacks noted, parents can buy the time necessary to teach kids how to protect themselves. They can say, in effect, "Let's wait until tomorrow."

The longer erratic behavior can be delayed, the better the chances for the growth of compromise and conformity. If kids suspend their "now-or-never" ultimatum for a few minutes or hours, the very action of waiting is a compromise and sets the stage for other compromises. If a string of several compromises can be put together, reciprocity results. If reciprocity remains active, it will continually support the crucial attributes of respect and responsibility. Thus, if kids learn to wait (count to ten if they must), they have taken a giant step toward creative conformity.

Parents can avoid the heartache of entrenched deviance and Level 5 trouble by implementing these comebacks (in modified versions) as early as ages one or two. The earlier children hear these messages, the less likely it is that they will take delight in backing parents into a corner in order to watch them squirm. If there is less competition between parents and teenagers to see who can control whom, more attention can be paid to avoiding trouble.

Parents need not squirm too much when their kids say, "Everybody fails to understand my need to be cool, but it doesn't mean nothin' to me 'cause you're all dumb, anyway."

Instead of getting bent out of shape, parents can Kiss their kids by replying, "Here are three lines. If you step over this one, I'll catch you, and you'll be in trouble. Cross this one, and emotions will clash in one helluva fight. Test this one, and your thing will earn my thing."

Since there are usually four lines that define the limits of a struggle, parents must not forget about the final boundary. However, the fourth line isn't exactly predictable, or, for that matter, describable. Unfortunately, parents have to wait for kids to cross it to know it exists. It has to be experienced to be understood. This fourth line is drawn when parents, faced with deviance, trouble, emotional pain, uncertainties, and strife, take a long, hard look at themselves and say, "I don't have the foggiest notion what to do. *Help!*"

14

Seventeen and Eighteen: Shape Up or Ship Out

If parents are convinced that nothing could be harder to understand than a sixteen-year-old, they should wait a couple of years and think again. The confusion of adolescence climaxes somewhere around the age of seventeen or eighteen. Although they can't do much about it, the pain of being the parent of an adolescent also climaxes at approximately the same time. Internal pressures build as adolescent fads fail to answer deeply rooted questions. Issues such as true love, career choice, trustworthy friendship, parental respect, and self-confidence dominate kids' inner thoughts. Their flippant, off-the-wall comments just don't work anymore.

Some kids give up searching for answers and slowly lapse into the troubled life of aimless wandering or irresponsible cavorting. For those who press onward, the tension mounts. The hedonism that engulfed their heart and soul two years earlier is forced outward by an influx of endless soul-searching and emotional unrest. Thus, the eighteen-year-old still looks good on the outside but starts to feel terrible on the inside.

The result is the emergence of two worlds: one in which kids want to maintain the image of being cool, the other in which they are besieged by unanswered questions. When they are alone at night with the lights out, this is what a dialogue between the two worlds might sound like:

CONSCIENCE: Who are you, anyway?

EGO: I am Joe cool, dy-no-mite, and outta sight. I gotta fancy front, a bad-ass act, a foxy chick, and some wheels. I'm your man, Stan.

CONSCIENCE: Huh?

EGO: What I mean to say is that I have nice clothes, good friends, plenty of money, a good-looking girl friend, and a nice car.

CONSCIENCE: Yes, but are you happy with your soul?

EGO: What kind of jive talk is that?

CONSCIENCE: I'm trying to say that you don't have inner peace.

EGO: Hey, wow! I'm the guy on the sly. The man with the plan!

CONSCIENCE: Yes, but where are you going?

EGO: What do you mean?

CONSCIENCE: I simply mean—where are you going?

EGO: Oh, I dig it! Where am I going? To sleep, man. I'm going to sleep.

The ego, or the person "up front," represents the adolescent who's been "groovy" for several years; the conscience embodies that spark of wisdom that says, "There's got to be more to life than always being cool." These two live together in the same mind, unable to communicate and each pretending that the other doesn't exist. They try to ignore one another but are pulling in opposite directions. As the pressure increases, something eventually has to give. Drinking, smoking dope, picking fights, and complaining become occasional methods of blowing off steam. Some kids lose control, hurt someone, and get into serious trouble. Most kids, however, release their tension by Ambushing anything or anyone that represents a "No."

When parents become the dumping ground of pent-up emotions, they are used as a mental punching bag. The only strategy

I've seen work under these circumstances is for parents to clearly and fairly draw the line between tolerable and intolerable behavior. If the kid wishes to continue living under the parents' roof, he or she must operate within defined limits; if not, the parents must be willing to kick the kid out of the house.

Thus, in all his or her confusion, the kid hears one message loud and clear: *"Shape up or ship out!"* If they shape up, the parents have performed a minor miracle; if they ship out, they take with them the realization that some limits are unyielding. Kicking a kid out of the house can be the best thing a parent ever did. The strength it takes to do this might be translated by the kid as, "Hey, Mom and Dad really care about me. Their love is worth living with some rules I don't like."

This age level represents the parents' last stand against the Ambushes of their gentle warriors. Following in the footsteps of the most famous last-stander of them all, parents must rally to the cause in the final hours as General Custer might have. Despite past failures, poorly conceived plans, inappropriate strategies, or errors in judgment, parents can pursue their protective cause down to the last man or woman. Even if parents face insurmountable odds, there is cause to struggle until the last arrow has been launched.

Thus far, I've sat atop the ridge overlooking the battleground watching gentle warriors Ambush their parents with disruption, disrespect, detachment, or a combination thereof. My reaction has taken the form of professional consultation intended to give parents the courage and skills necessary for survival. Like a good scout, I've tried to give warnings ("Watch out! Behind that rock . . . Look out from above! No, no . . . the *other* way"). For the most part, I've said, "If you want to keep children out of trouble, you should. . . ."

I feel confident in my recommendations because I've seen them work time and time again. However, there is one thing missing from this book that parents often receive when seeking my advice. That one thing is my personal involvement in the lives of parents who ask for my help. I usually "feel" their problem and sometimes give more than just a recommendation. My personal involvement occurs after parents ask, "You're a parent; what would you do if you were in my shoes—not as a shrink, but as a parent?"

During the commentaries on groups of cases in this chapter, I shall get personally involved in each family's life, pretending that one of the parents asked, "Well, Doc, what would you do if it were your kid?" In response, I will get off the ridge, put on my battle armor, and demonstrate *my way*.

I've grouped fifteen typical cases into the five problem areas that seem to dominate the trouble of this age level. I begin by reviewing an old problem, peer pressure.

SITUATION: I received a call one evening from Paula's mother. Her seventeen-year-old daughter had just arrived home from a date with her twenty-two-year-old boyfriend. Paula was a mess. Her boyfriend, who apparently was on the verge of becoming an alcoholic, had hit her, leaving a red mark over her eye.

After brief questioning, I discovered that such occurrences were quite typical. Her mother said that Paula had refused to talk about the fight and became hysterical when her mom suggested that they call the police.

REACTION: At the time of the phone call, Paula was crying, Mother was absorbed in pity for her daughter, and Father was sitting in his easy chair reading the paper, aware that his daughter was having more "love problems." Every time I tried to determine what was going on, Paula's mother moaned about her daughter's misfortune of being "in love with a drunk."

INTERPRETATION: In this highly sophisticated Ambush, Paula had fallen into a pattern of associating with a drunk, unaware of the long-term, negative consequences. She had adopted the role of martyr, which gave her three types of satisfaction: a mechanism for making her mother squirm, a source of self-pity, and special status among her friends.

Paula was one of those kids who put pressure on friends by

saying, "If only you knew what it's *really* like to be grown up and facing the *real* world of adulthood."

She was also using her "terrible" position to barter for a new car and clothes (so that she would "feel better").

It was my guarded opinion that it wouldn't be long before Paula got into more serious trouble. If and when it occurred, Paula and her family would be shocked, unable to understand how it had happened.

RECOMMENDATION: After a couple of individual sessions, I saw the three of them together. In a no-nonsense manner, I covered the following topics:

It was fruitless to try to rehabilitate a drunk who wouldn't admit that he had a problem. Giving pity for martyrdom was disrespectful and only asked for more problems. Father needed to be involved more in Paula's life, and Mother needed to stop the pity routine.

I spent extra time pointing out the disasters that could occur. I paid close attention to erasing the family's assumption that *it* (serious trouble) couldn't happen to them.

LESSON: Serious trouble can be hidden by many things, even "love."

SITUATION: One evening I received a long-distance call from a college buddy who had moved to New York City. After exchanging stories about our small-town heritage, he outlined a very sticky problem. It was actually too difficult to handle over the phone, but I gave it my best shot.

The long story made short was this. The gang milieu was moving rapidly into my friend's neighborhood. His seventeen-year-old son, Bob, was being pressured into joining the gang. Bob didn't want to join, but it had reached the point where his life was in danger as long as he delayed his entrance. The situation had been brought to a head when three gang members cornered Bob and, showing him a knife, said, "You want to carry one of these in your pocket or your stomach?"

REACTION: At the time of my friend's call, Bob was determined to join the gang. My mild-mannered buddy was aghast at his son's decision. Bob was even starting to spout the gangland theme, "We know what's happenin'; we're cool."

INTERPRETATION: Bob was in the middle of the worst possible effects of peer pressure. Many kids like Bob start out conforming to gangland morality and then become addicted to its protection and easy answers for every problem.

Gang activity, like other social phenomena, seems to be most severe when it starts; then it ebbs in intensity, but it always remains. My association with gangs has suggested that gang kids are willing to die (and do) to preserve their culture.

Talking with gangs doesn't work; extreme measures are called for. I have learned that, given the primitive conditions under which gangs operate, their pressure must be dealt with by mixing guerrilla-type survival skills with a refined sense of self-control.

RECOMMENDATION: Bob's father couldn't get directly involved, so I suggested he concentrate on preparing his son. I told my friend to search out a master of kung fu and ask that Bob be taken as a student. I thought Bob could use his study of the martial arts as an avenue away from the gang and toward a new peer group.

Such an association not only would give him new self-defense skills but a new way of life—diet, friends, self-control, and so on. With dedication to such a life-style, Bob could more easily command respect from friends, new and old.

This drastic change seemed warranted in light of the peer pressure on Bob and the fact that the self-control practiced by masters of kung fu is usually respected by a broad spectrum of people.

LESSON: One way to relieve the pressure of peers is to find new peers.

The troubles associated with peer pressure seem to lose some of their intensity during later adolescence. While kids between the ages of twelve and sixteen live or die by what their friends think, seventeen- and eighteen-year-olds are more settled in their reaction to peers. Peer pressure still operates during this time, but these teenagers are less likely to be victimized by it. Instead, they are often the ones who set the standards by which kids put pressure on one another. Paula was setting the pace for others to follow, while Bob's predicament was an obvious exception to the rule.

As for what I would have done:

If I had been sitting and reading the paper when Paula came in, crying and carrying the marks of drunken violence, I would have taken immediate action. Without hesitation and paying little attention to hysterics, I would have called the police and informed them of the incident, requesting that they arrest the young man.

Paula could have screamed all she wanted. However, I would have warned her that the more she screamed, the harder I would press the charges. I would have attempted to explain that when drunken people hit a person I love, they've stepped over a line that means *war*. I would have talked with her about love, alcohol, violence, or anything else, but only if she asked my opinion. I would also have supported leniency for the young man if he sought counseling.

The next time Paula and her friends were sitting around gabbing, I would have interrupted them and calmly said, "Paula thinks she's being 'grown-up' because she has love problems with a drunk. I have news for all of you. If it's grown-up to lose control and hit people you supposedly love, then I don't want to be grown-up anymore."

As for Bob and his gangland problems, I would have been more directly involved. Since gangs are a direct threat to me, Bob's problem would quickly have become my problem, also. I would have responded by forming my own gang. Using every means available, I would have gathered the names of the gang members. Then I would have paid a visit to their mothers, fathers, aunts, uncles, cousins, and anyone else who gave a damn about the kids. With legal guidance, I and my gang would have harassed the other gang. We would have broken up their meetings, trailed them constantly, reported their activities to the police, painted slogans (such as "Gangs Are for Girls" or "Little Boys Join Gangs") on their jackets, and threatened them and made their life miserable until they left the gang. I would have demanded that at least one member of every kid's family join my gang. If not, I'd have brought suit against them for contributing to the delinquency of a minor.

Paula and Bob were playing with fire. I wouldn't have burned them so much as I would have shut off the source of the fuel.

Peer pressure is not so big an issue during this period as rebelliousness, which can take many forms.

SITUATION: Eighteen-year-old Stan was a freshman at a state university. One Saturday in early autumn, his parents called me, saying that Stan had been arrested in a campus disturbance. He had called them from jail, told them of the situation, and sheepishly suggested that the nature of their impending visit would have to change.

It seemed that Stan had been arrested as one of the leaders of S.L.O.P. (Students Liberating Others of Ptomaine). The S.L.O.P. organization, fed up with the university food, had staged a sit-in at the university food service. They had dramatized their cause by placing a hundred pounds of fresh cow manure in the central cafeteria.

REACTION: The father was quite upset. He had called his lawyer to arrange immediate bail and then called me to see what else he could do. Stan was his only child, and he and wife were very upset.

INTERPRETATION: Upon reviewing the situation, I discovered that Stan had been pampered and overprotected during his years at home. He was spoiled rotten.

His involvement with S.L.O.P. reflected his need to rebel against authority figures, something he had learned on his daddy's lap, so to speak. He was going to extremes in order to find the limits of his ability to disrupt the world. Stan needed to learn that the world was not *his* to do with as he wanted.

RECOMMENDATION: I told them to cancel the bail effort by their attorney and to take their time driving the 120 miles to the university. In fact, I suggested they delay their visit. The idea of getting tough was difficult for them to accept.

I told them that Stan had to start earning his own way. His free ride should be over. I recommended that Stan get a part-time job at the university food service in order to make things better (if that's what he wanted). Any earnings must first be used to pay off legal fees and court costs and then be applied against his tuition.

I tried to get the parents' attention by telling them that if they didn't want to see their son in jail again, they'd better force him to start paying his own way.

LESSON: When a kid finally hears *"No!"* it can be a stinky mess.

SITUATION: Seventeen-year-old Linda had slowly slipped into the habit of using disrespectful language toward her aunt, with whom she lived. Her parents had died when she was quite young, and her aunt had taken over as surrogate mother.

One evening, Linda's aunt warned her about keeping company with a girl who had the reputation of being "a whore." Linda, after thumping her fingers on the coffee table, suddenly jumped to her feet and started to leave the room. As she neared the door, she wheeled around and, looking her aunt square in the eye, said, "Aunt Helen, fuck off!"

REACTION: According to Aunt Helen, she almost had a heart attack. Her mouth flopped open as Linda disappeared out the door. The incident brought no negative consequences to Linda.

INTERPRETATION: Certain words (especially "fuck") have an overwhelming shock value when used on authority figures. Most older kids know exactly when and where to use them in order to weaken authoritative controls.

Linda obviously believed that she had a "right to rage" and expressed it with obscene words to her aunt. Linda's self-pity about not having a mom and dad and her resultant rebellion had gone far enough. Aunt Helen had better get on the ball.

RECOMMENDATION: I told Helen to draw a clear line in terms of tolerance for "bad" language. She didn't need to argue with Linda about whether or not "fuck" was a bad word; she just needed to make it clear that she didn't want to hear the word in her house.

With my help, Helen drew up a list of words that she didn't want used in her house and told Linda to follow the guidelines or find somewhere else to live. Helen gave the harsh alternative to her niece because she didn't think Linda would take her seriously if she didn't.

LESSON: The intent behind a word is sometimes more important than the word itself.

SITUATION: Walt's parents consulted me about what they considered to be strange behavior in their eighteen-year-old son. In the preceding three or four months, they had observed the following:

Walt had become sloppy and unkempt in his appearance, developing stringy hair, dirty blue jeans, and that certain unwashed odor. He talked of revolution and read books on the Manson family and communal living. Midnight meditation sessions were regular, and Yoga and health foods suddenly became popular with him.

REACTION: Since Walt's parents believed in talking, not punishing, they tried to make their son explain what had come over him. They begged him to return to his "old self." When this approach didn't work, they started making fun of his opinions and criticizing his reading material.

His father was particularly vehement in his attacks upon the "lazy hippies who live off of others." His mother was convinced that some dire catastrophe was only days away. However, the more they attacked his behavior, the more dedicated Walt became to his beliefs.

INTERPRETATION: Walt's parents had good reason to be concerned. However, their fear of catastrophe was premature. Walt was examining a different side of life. His rebellion against the typical teenage image was obvious. His rebellion was not harmful—at least, not yet.

The most distressing element in Walt's behavior was his budding identification with the Manson cult, a group of people whose life-style was founded on loneliness and was devoid of personal warmth, bounded by years of failure, revenge, and self-pity. It was a life-style characterized by the inability to harness knowledge for constructive purposes and, most of all, an overwhelming lack of self-respect and appreciation for the beauty life can hold.

Walt's behavior was most likely due to his search for answers to many unresolved issues. He had found a cause that fitted his confusion. He was experimenting with a low-grade revolution, one that centered on personal change. Parental castigation and retribution would only force these experimental behaviors to become solidified.

RECOMMENDATION: The most important thing I told his parents was *not* to belittle Walt's exploration. Since dealing with his motives, fears, and inquisitiveness would do them no good, I encouraged his parents to react solely to Walt's behavior.

Walt's parents were to allow their son to explore the wilds of his imagination but to make sure he continued to deal with reality. That meant, if he didn't keep clean, he wasn't to be allowed to eat at home (*at all*); if he met his daily expectancies, his meditation was acceptable (in fact, it might do him some good).

Walt had the right to express his political views, such as they were, but he had to realize that accompanying his right to speak was the right of others to challenge those beliefs. As long as Walt conformed to the basic house rules, there was no way his parents could control what he read. They were not to try.

LESSON: Unfettered exploration by youth, when monitored by reasonable adults, is the key to freedom and truth.

Rebellion can take as many forms as there are persons who are dissatisfied with what they see and want something different. Scientists rebel, as do athletes, business people, and housewives. Kids' rebellion draws adverse reaction from authority figures because it lacks conformity to commonly accepted standards and doesn't appear to be heading anywhere. As I've noted before, parents are far ahead if they react to the need to rebel rather than to the rebellion itself. And since for every rebel there are ten reasons supporting rebellion, the best way to deal with rebellion is to unclog the auditory canals and *listen*.

I would have listened *after* I had got the kids' attention.

If I were suddenly confronted with a spoiled eighteen-year-old, I'd have to take drastic action. In Stan's case, I would have left him in jail one night *after* making sure, through my attorney, that he would be assigned to an individual cell and hence be safe from homosexual rape. Before going to court, I would have sought an arrangement with a livestock farmer and the judge to "sentence" Stan to the hard labor of shoveling manure two hours a day for two weeks. I would have asked that a court order restrict his movements during that time to classes, to eating, and to the farm.

During his sentence, I would have made several trips to the campus to discuss with Stan the problems he was having with life. I would have vowed not to support him any more if he did not tell me how he was going to learn that life didn't owe him a living. Finally, I would have apologized to him for letting him push me around for so damn long.

If Linda had said "Fuck off!" to me as she was darting out a door, I would have run after her, grabbed her by the arm, and set her firmly in a chair. Then, in a growling voice, I would have said, "Listen, young lady, use whatever words you want when you're mad at me, but remember two things: first, I expect you to mind the rules, no exceptions at all; second, have the guts to give me a chance to yell back at you. I don't like people who scream obscenities at me and then duck out before I have a chance to say my piece."

In general, Linda could have used whatever language she wanted around the house *as long as* I never heard that she used it in front of people who would be seriously offended, such as her grandparents, aunt, teachers, ministers, salespersons, and others who might have an impact on her life. If she had uttered obscenities to offend someone important in her life, I would have penalized such language in the home for about two weeks or until I thought she knew how to control herself better.

Once she understood my position, I would have tried to convince her that no words have an intrinsically "bad" meaning, *but* some words constitute bad public relations and could hurt her in more ways than she realized.

As for Walt, I would have employed the professional recommendations given but taken further action. I would have taken time to confide in Walt some of my own searches for personal meaning when I was his age, complete with some of the goofy mistakes I made. I would have hoped but not demanded that he return my confidences. I would have listened extra carefully to his thoughts about the Manson cult and gently challenged him to explain how people can actually enjoy hurting other people without feeling remorse or regret.

I would have insinuated myself into his meditative life, aware that such a thing might be beneficial to me, too. I would have asked him to help me learn Yoga and teach me about health foods in hopes of improving my sagging waistline. Most important, I wouldn't have pushed him to change, realizing that the combination of the recommendations and my honest desire to share in his search would have worked, all in good time.

From rebellion, our attention now shifts to the drug scene, an area that makes my professional and personal blood boil.

SITUATION: Seventeen-year-old Mike and his best friend, Bob, were at Mike's house smoking marijuana in the kitchen. They took their time because they thought Mike's mom would be shopping all day. However, Mom showed up and caught them right in the middle of their second joint.

REACTION: According to Mike's father, his wife came unglued. Since Mike was a lousy liar, he admitted to smoking marijuana, and his mother promptly belted him across his face with her hand. She then told Mike's friend to "get out" and Mike to go to his room. She called her husband at work and hysterically recounted what had happened.

INTERPRETATION: Mike and his buddy were doing a fairly typical thing. Mike was being careful insofar as he smoked at home with his best friend.

Smoking marijuana in the privacy of one's home is not the worst thing that kids (or adults, for that matter) can do. However, it is a clear violation of the law and must be considered as troublesome.

Mike's mother overreacted; her slap proved that she didn't have much understanding of her son's needs and desires. Hitting a seventeen-year-old is as ridiculous as ignoring a two-year-old who is playing in the street.

RECOMMENDATION: I told the father to handle the situation and keep his wife calm. Mike was to be told the good and bad sides of his actions. It was good that he had protected himself by smoking at home and with a trusted friend. It was bad that he had jeopardized the family's home, his own career, his crime-free record, and his placement in school.

Mike was to impose his own penalty with his father's approval, but it should not be less than one week of limited freedom.

LESSON: Kids must learn that they are never completely protected from trouble—even at home.

SITUATION: Seventeen-year-old Al came to see me at his parents' insistence. Although he had had difficulties following some house rules, the incident that had precipitated his visit had occurred in church. One Sunday during the sermon, Al reached into his pocket for a handkerchief and his money clip fell onto the pew.

His father's head jerked from the Bible as a wad of bills an inch thick plopped to Al's side. Al knew he was in trouble because his only source of money was a part-time job at a neighborhood hamburger stand where he cleared about twenty-five dollars a week.

REACTION: Al's father accosted him as soon as they had shaken hands with the minister. After accusation and denial, counteraccusation and counterdenial, Al admitted to selling a little marijuana to a few close friends.

His father called him all sorts of derogatory names, threatened to call the police, and demanded that Al reveal the name of his suppliers to the authorities.

Al was too frightened not to comply with his father's demands. With his dad at his side, Al told his story to the police. Because of his honesty and his father's pledge to be more observant, Al received only a warning from the police. Several nights later, at his favorite pool hall, Al was beaten up by several strangers who advised him against being a "trick."

INTERPRETATION: Al had unknowingly stumbled into a dangerous part-time racket. Although he professed never to give drugs to kids under sixteen, he didn't have the character (or lack of it) to be in the drug business. He was playing a very dirty game with guys who have "cold hearts."

Although he was playing for extremely low stakes, he was still playing and therefore subject to the rules, the most wicked of which is that "tricks" (people who give the police information) must be eliminated. Al didn't have the meanness to play. He gave too much marijuana to his friends and didn't push them to pay him. He was quite lucky to be alive.

RECOMMENDATION: I told Al's father that he should have been a little more cautious in allowing Al to link himself directly to the pushers. I suggested that the police could have been given more clues and fewer names.

Al had learned a lesson, especially after I told him what could have happened. Instead of punishing him, I recommended that he attend weekly group sessions at a local drug-counseling center for a month. His father agreed to the plan, provided Al continued good behavior at home.

LESSON: Kids have no business in the drug business.

SITUATION: Verle's parents cornered me during a cocktail party, bemoaning their son's propensity for trouble. They gave me the "he-has-had-everything" routine and then outlined their present situation.

Their eighteen-year-old son had returned home from an exclusive military school after graduating with honors. He had spent the summer lounging around the family's summer home in northern Wisconsin while his father confirmed his entry into an Ivy League college. That fall, instead of preparing for college, he had shown up at the family estate with his Japanese girl friend and told his parents that he wanted to move into one of their apartments.

Although secretly distressed (mostly about the girl friend), they had relented. A few nights later, the apartment had been raided and Verle arrested for possession of hard drugs (speed and cocaine) and suspicion of pushing. He was sitting at home with his girl friend awaiting court action.

REACTION: Verle's father had called the family lawyer, who thought he could clear everything with the court. Although they had supposedly wanted my reaction, it was clear that his parents wanted to complain about the burden they were carrying more than change it.

INTERPRETATION: Verle was too rich for his own good. He didn't realize that money couldn't protect him from the law. He obviously had reason to believe that nothing bad would come from his arrest. From what I'd heard, he was probably correct.

When I spoke with Verle, it became obvious that he enjoyed "shaking his parents up" with behavior they didn't like. I came to understand that his girl friend was a symbol of rebellion and disrespect for his parents' wishes. She was being used as a weapon in Verle's Ambush.

Verle's arrest on drug charges was an indication that he was in serious trouble. Not only was his life messed up, but he had also been instrumental in helping other kids get into trouble. He had to be stopped.

RECOMMENDATION: I recommended that the lawyer not make any special deal with the court. Rather, I suggested that Verle be forced through court proceedings and be given a choice between a jail sentence and entry into a residential drug-treatment program.

FOLLOW-UP: The parents agreed to this course of action, but before it could be implemented Verle jumped bail and disappeared. We found out later that his grandmother had given him several hundred dollars and he had set up a drug business. He shot another man in an argument over nonpayment for contraband drugs. He was sentenced to five to thirty years in a penitentiary.

LESSON: Money does not protect kids from trouble.

Drugs, including alcohol, do more than just destroy rational behavior. The circumstances surrounding their consumption promote deviance while eroding respect, responsibility, and reciprocity. The act of sniffing, inhaling, swallowing, snorting, or mainlining is only part of the problem. Secret meetings, exchange of "dirty money," negative peer pressure, lying, and a perverted sense of excitement can become more addictive than some drugs.

Much of the "high" obtained from a drug is associated with the conditions under which it is taken rather than the neurochemical effects of the drug itself. When parents say, "I'm not so worried about one marijuana cigarette as I am about what it could lead to," they should be concerned about lying, cheating, and stealing—not sniffing, snorting, or swallowing.

Honest, open communication and an understanding of what kids are up to are the best ways for parents to fight drug addiction. And, as I firmly believe, if parents don't do it, it won't get done.

As one might guess, if I had been in Mike's parents' shoes, I would have concentrated my energies on the circumstances surrounding the act of taking drugs, rather than the drugs themselves.

If I had caught Mike smoking marijuana in my kitchen, I would first have sniffed the air and then said, "Hey, man, you've been smoking dope."

Mike would have responded vaguely, "Huh? Yeah."

Then, without much emotion, I'd have said, "I caught you smoking dope, and you're hereby grounded until you and I can discuss an appropriate penalty. Air out the house because your mother and I don't like the furniture to smell like smoke."

After calmly explaining the situation to my wife, I would have repeated my instructions to Mike, once he had returned to reality. At no time would I have asked him where he'd got the grass, how he'd got it, how often he smoked it, or why he smoked it. If I hadn't known about the ready availability of cheap marijuana and its popular use, I would have talked to someone else before asking Mike to give me the details.

After Mike and I had agreed on his penalty, I would have taken two courses of action:

First, after checking with the other father, I would have supervised the two getting high. (Supervision would mean staying with them all the time and taking nothing that would impair my judgment.) I would have encouraged them to talk about girls, football, music, or anything else they wanted to discuss. I would have tried to get them to play a game with me (Scrabble, Monopoly, cards, and so on). I would have tape-recorded the entire evening's activity and played it back the next evening, discussing with the two of them how the marijuana had altered their personality and judgment.

Second, I would have gone on record as being opposed to marijuana and let Mike know that if I caught him, he would pay a "fine" in terms of the loss of freedom. Any response from Mike that said, "That's not fair; if you can drink alcohol at home, I should be able to smoke dope because dope is not as bad for you as booze," would have got this double-edged answer from me: "Dope is illegal; booze isn't. If the law changes, then I will, too. As for fairness, who told you that life is always supposed to be fair?"

If Al's profits had dropped onto the church pew when I was reading about Moses and the law, I would have put him out of business with as much fire and brimstone as I could muster. I would have tried to take a couple of his suppliers with him. Once I had the names of his suppliers and customers, I would have paid a visit to the police and to some parents. Realizing that I had more protection than my son did, I would have left Al in the car when I talked to the police.

I would have given the names of the pushers and as much information about their activities as I knew to the police. If they asked my source, I would have said, "Concerned parents have more sources than chickens have feathers."

When talking with Al's friends and their parents, I would have attempted to share with them what I had learned so that they would be more aware of what was going on. I would have rejected any accusations about my son's corrupting their sons, pointing out that the corrupter one day is very likely the corruptee the next.

Al would have had to regain my trust gradually. After his penalty was complete he would once again have had to demonstrate that he could drive safely. I would have imposed a 9:00 P.M. curfew; with responsible conduct, he could slowly have earned the privilege of staying out until the hour prescribed by the local laws. Finally, my wife and I would have tried to determine how we had missed the cues that Al had sent out about his financial condition. I would have made sure that we spent more time with him, even if it meant less time with the Bible.

Verle was probably too far gone, but I would have tried my best to save him. When he approached me with the request for a free apartment after all the arrangements had been made for college, I would have slapped myself into consciousness and wondered, "What in hell is going on?"

Then I would have consulted a professional I could trust to help me sort out the pieces of the puzzle as well as give me the strength to employ the "shape-up-or-ship-out" strategy. There was a good chance I would lose my son, and, after thinking everything was beautiful, I would be in great pain and need a trusted confidant.

After settling on a course of action, I would have told Verle very bluntly, "There will be no apartment, no money, no free ride, no *nothing* until you get a job and start making your own life."

After the drug arrest, I would have requested that Verle receive a one-year probation with the stipulation that he see a counselor of his choice once a week for at least six months. Any action demonstrating Verle's willingness to "shape up" would have been rewarded by a pat on the back and a little money.

I would have continued seeing my own professional consultant every month to make sure I wasn't repressing anger, disappointment, or revenge against Verle for a situation for which I was at least half responsible.

From the explosive issue of drug abuse, I now turn to the nagging condition of general irresponsibility.

SITUATION: Seventeen-year-old Brett's mother complained that her son was making jokes when she wanted him to be serious. This usually occurred when she asked him to do something around the house. One occasion stood out as particularly frustrating.

The night before his final semester exams, Brett was reminded several times to study. Each time his mother pressured him to comply, Brett told her a joke. Two of his funniest were: "There's this kid at school who's so ugly, tears roll down the back of his head. This same kid is so ugly that when he was a baby, his dad had to tie a pork chop around his neck so that his dog would play with him."

REACTION: The mother admitted that she had laughed at Brett's jokes and hadn't pursued her request. She felt somewhat responsible when Brett flunked one test and failed to complete another.

INTERPRETATION: Brett was using his sense of humor as an Ambush strategy. He replaced compliant responses with humorous ones, thereby avoiding what he didn't want to do. He received the reward of his mother's laughter and therefore kept it up.

If and when he used his jokes to avoid conforming to society's guidelines, he might have the opportunity to try laughing off a serious legal violation.

RECOMMENDATION: I told the mother to enjoy Brett's jokes and then make sure that he complied with her original directive.

LESSON: If kids can joke their way out of complying, trouble may turn their laughter to tears.

SITUATION: Denny's father complained that his seventeen-year-old son looked like "a warmed-over pile of manure." He rarely showered, had holes and patches on his dilapidated blue jeans, and hair that stuck out like a stack of flea-infested straw. All in all, his dad said he looked like a walking disaster area.

REACTION: When his parents complained about his appearance and personal hygiene, Denny said, "I'm just doing my thing." His mother continued to nag him about cleaning up, and his father threatened grave reprisals if he didn't improve his appearance. Denny said, "It don't mean nothin' to me." He was right; nothing happened.

INTERPRETATION: Denny was taking the rebel phrase "Don't mean nothin' to me" and using it as an excuse to be sloppy. He demonstrated poor personal hygiene and obviously saw it when he looked in the mirror.

The major problem with Denny was that he was the type of kid who might accompany other, more deviant kids in breaking the law and be the first one caught because he was too lazy to run.

RECOMMENDATION: The coping comeback "You do your thing and then I'll do mine" was to be used in this case. Free food, free board, free TV, free laundry, free money, and free living were to be suspended until Denny compromised *his thing* with his *parents' thing*.

LESSON: If kids look in a mirror and see an animal, expect them to act like one.

SITUATION: Eighteen-year-old Mac came home drunk two or three nights a week. He was doing poorly in his last three months of school. When he was not out drinking and carousing, he was at home watching TV. He received money from his mom, his girl friend, and an occasional odd job.

REACTION: Since his mother ran the show in the home, Dad's anger went unnoticed. Mother's reaction, according to the father, was, "He'll be leaving us soon enough. Leave him alone. It's just a stage."

INTERPRETATION: Whether or not the mother realized it, Mac had already "left home." He was living on easy street doing what he damn well pleased. He was supported by a father who was too scared to do anything and a mother who didn't want to lose her "baby." The idea of a "stage" accounting for his irresponsibility was just an excuse not to take action.

RECOMMENDATION: This was another case in which "Shape up or ship out" was to be employed. If Mac wanted to follow house rules, earn his keep, and even pay for some of his room and board, then he could stay; if not, he was to be thrown out. I warned the mother that Mac was headed for trouble unless they took action. There was a slim chance she might take some action; the father certainly wouldn't.

LESSON: If a "stage" accounts for trouble, maybe the kid should get on one that takes him or her out of the home.

Brett, Denny, and Mac exhibited various degrees of incorrigibility. Incorrigibility is actually irresponsibility that has spread from kids to their parents. Irresponsibility turns to incorrigibility when kids who act irresponsibly fail to correct their behavior and parents are unable to find a strategy that works. While irresponsibility applies to one person's actions, incorrigibility represents an interaction.

Kids become incorrigible when their irresponsibility gets so far out of hand that parents can't change it, no matter what they do or say. The kid is militantly deviant, and the parent is stumped. While it takes one to be irresponsible, it takes at least two to be incorrigible. Thus, when parents think of their kids as incorrigible and even have legal records to back them up, they are talking about themselves as well as their kids.

I would have made sure that I shaped up my half of the responsibility before giving Brett, Denny, and Mac any ultimatums.

As for the joking son, Brett, I would have laughed quite loudly. Then I would have told him *my* story. It would have gone like this: "There was this kid who thought he could get out of studying by making his dad laugh. He was a nice kid and meant no harm. However, nobody laughed when this kid didn't get his allowance on Friday and lost the car for *this* Saturday night." Naturally, I would have followed through on my threat if he had failed to return to his studies immediately.

I might have softened the seriousness of my story by asking Brett to write his stories down so that I could remember them.

The aspiring goon, Denny, would have incurred my strongest wrath. I wouldn't have hesitated to impose my own personal standards of cleanliness on him, making it very clear that if he didn't get *with it* immediately, I would kick him out. If he had tried to argue about shades of cleanliness or degrees of personal hygiene, I would have said, "The standards of personal appearance to be followed in this home are what I say they are, nothing more, nothing less. So don't hassle yourself about whether or not my values stand the test of the mutterings of some dropout who thinks he can change the moral standards of this home by babbling nonsense about personal freedom. You're free to do your thing, and I'm free to do mine. If your thing is to stink, my thing is to lock you out. I can't make it simpler than that."

If there was any love in me at all, I could have said these things in such a way that Denny would know I cared for him but would no longer tolerate his irresponsibility. I'd have worried like hell, but I'd have locked the door if I'd had to.

If my son were coming home drunk, raising hell, and doing little or nothing to earn his keep, I'd have been seriously tempted to hit him. However, hitting him would only make matters worse. So I wouldn't have talked to him until I had calmed down. Then I would take "shape-up-or-ship-out" action.

One morning after he had been out late and come home drunk, I'd have pulled him out of bed and thrown water in his face at about 6:30 A.M. I'd then have told him to get dressed because I wanted to talk with him. When he came to the kitchen, I'd have given him a written list of the guidelines of my "shape-up-or-ship-out" demands. I wouldn't have negotiated or discussed the demands, just made sure he was awake enough to understand them.

Somewhere in my speech I'd have been sure to include a statement acknowledging my awareness of having some share of his irresponsibility because I'd been too fearful to confront him sooner. I'd have finished by saying, "I've corrected my half; now you correct yours. If you don't do so within one week, the locks will be changed and you won't have a key."

The last four cases reviewed in this book include the issues of disruption, disrespect, detachment, doing one's thing, Ambush, sneakiness, potential trouble, lack of understanding, need to be cool, peer pressure, and adolescents' need for excitement. There is only one issue that could bring so much complexity to a discussion of protective parenting: sex. You see, I saved the best for last.

SITUATION: Carl was seventeen years old and lived with his father. Carl's parents had been divorced after fifteen years of a rocky marriage filled with too much booze and too little love.

Carl's father called me after he'd found out that Carl's girl friend was pregnant and that Carl, contrary to his father's wishes, was planning to drop out of school and get married.

REACTION: By the time I was able to see Carl, he and his father had had several arguments about Carl's decision. His father vehemently protested his son's judgment, saying, "You're throwing your life away for some tramp." Carl continually defied his father on every point.

Carl made it very clear that nothing would stop him from marrying the girl. He wanted to "give the child a legal name." His father threatened to throw Carl out. Carl, in turn, threatened to leave if his father didn't quiet down.

INTERPRETATION: Here were a father and son at each other's throats, neither one listening to the other. Their threats were empty and their anger pointless. They would never solve the problem by dumping hate on each other.

After several hours of probing, I was able to see that Carl's unwavering desire to marry his girl friend rested solely on his own frustration and hurt at "not being wanted by my parents."

He realized that he couldn't get a good enough job to support a family adequately and his chances of making the marriage work were about 1 in 100. Nevertheless, any kind of protest only deepened his commitment to his cause.

RECOMMENDATION: I tried to get Carl to see two overlapping issues: his pain and frustration and an unborn baby's chance to grow up in a mature family. At no point did I push him to make any particular decision.

I told Carl's father to leave him alone but be available in case Carl wanted to talk to him. I cautioned the father that calling his son's girl friend nasty names was an error for which he should apologize.

FOLLOW-UP: One year later, Carl was married, had a son, and had reduced his chances of failure to 1 in 50.

LESSON: Often parents must end the relationship with their kids the way it began—by giving them unconditional love.

SITUATION: Cathy was a gregarious, good-looking girl who dated frequently. At 2:00 A.M. one morning, Cathy's father, worrying because his daughter was not yet home, walked downstairs to wait up for her. Half-asleep, he wandered into the living room, turned on the lights, and found Cathy lying on the couch, partially undressed, with her boyfriend.

REACTION: Cathy jumped up, pulled her blouse on, and ran to the bathroom. Her father curtly asked the boy to leave. When Cathy came out of the bathroom, her father gave her a stern lecture about "letting boys into her pants and acting like a slut." He told her, "Boys who are decent won't like you or give you a second look." He then told her that she couldn't date for two months.

INTERPRETATION: Dad overreacted just a little. Cathy was a typical teenager: she was seventeen, liked boys, craved attention and excitement, was somewhat naive and a little scatterbrained. Dad's moralistic labels would hurt more than help.

RECOMMENDATION: I told Cathy's dad that he should be glad that he had caught his daughter on the living-room sofa—at least this was preferable to some disturbed man's interrupting the kids on a lonely road. Now he had a chance to talk with her.

I cautioned him to cool his reactions to such emotional situations in the future. He'd been angry and shouldn't have said anything while in such a state. I suggested that he back off the penalty and ask Cathy to talk with him.

If he could get her attention, he was to talk with her about the potential consequences of spontaneous lovemaking: the many types of sexually transmitted diseases, the possible pregnancies, bad reputations, and other social complications that accompany sexual activity.

The standards he wanted his daughter to live up to were filled with strict moral injunctions and not tempered with enough understanding.

LESSON: Sex isn't dirty, but ignorance can make it hurt.

SITUATION: Seventeen-year-old Becky lived with her mom, dad, and younger brother in a middle-class neighborhood. Becky dated regularly, but didn't go steady. When she woke up one morning vomiting, her mother forced her to go to the doctor. Becky was pregnant.

REACTION: Becky's mother was so stunned and horrified that she had to be sedated by the family physician. Becky's father was madder 'n hell. He demanded to know the boy's name. When Becky said it could be either of two boys, her father blew his lid. He called her every name in the book and passionately told her he would send her to the probation office as a delinquent.

INTERPRETATION: After a long talk, Becky abandoned her "I-don't-care" attitude and broke down in tears. She told of how she had gotten into the habit of having intercourse, sometimes on the first date. She'd believed it would make her popular. The pressure to "go all the way" was overwhelming.

It became apparent that Becky was probably known as an "easy lay" and therefore the pressure would mount on every date. Like so many girls her age, she had a strong desire to be liked but lacked reliable information concerning sexual activity. The peer pressure plus that little streak of deviance plus her need for excitement plus her lack of knowledge had equaled trouble.

RECOMMENDATION: This particular family finally calmed down, and we were able to make sensible plans for the future. The parents decided that Becky was to have an abortion. Since I always let the family make the choice, I concurred. My only input was that Becky was not to be faced with an unwanted baby.

Becky and I had a little conversation in which I gave her a strategy for undoing her reputation without losing sight of the positive aspects of sex. I recommended that she use the following "rap" the next time a boy propositioned her: "Hey, thanks for the offer; I'll take it as a compliment. But not right now." If the guy kept pushing her, she could say, "Hey, my head is not there right now. I'd rather just talk. Check me later."

LESSON: One of the literal aspects of Protective Parenting is teaching teenagers about birth control.

SITUATION: Eighteen-year-old Candy was an attractive, well-built young lady. She had just graduated from high school and was spending the summer working prior to entering college. Candy was a well-adjusted girl and liked to think of herself as "liberated."

One sunny afternoon, Candy was lying on the enclosed patio of her house and decided to sunbathe in the nude. A neighbor lady saw the spectacle from her upstairs window and called the police, complaining of indecent exposure.

REACTION: When the police arrived, Candy was indignant at their intrusion and began calling them names ("pigs") and yelling obscene remarks. Meanwhile, her mother, overwhelmed with shock, explained the situation and apologized for Candy's rudeness. The police, satisfied that everything was under control, left and went next door to calm the neighbor down.

Candy's mother criticized her daughter for her nudity, bemoaning the anticipated reaction from the "gossip circle." Candy's reaction was simply, "Oh, mother, don't be so old-fashioned!"

INTERPRETATION: I thought both mother and daughter had been a little off base in this one. Candy should have been aware of the consequences of being liberated with a busybody living next door; the mother, on the other hand, should have been dealing more with her daughter and less with what other people might say.

Understanding the potential hassles coming from other people would be a good lesson for Candy before going off to college. She had to understand that not everyone agreed with her liberated views and her thing could earn her more bad feelings than she wanted.

RECOMMENDATION: I suggested that the mother and daughter sit down together and spend a lot of time discussing my interpretation.

LESSON: Liberation is no excuse for stupidity.

Pregnancy, petting, forced marriages, and nudity are only a few of the problems confronting parents when they deal with their kids' sexuality. Since ultimatums, demands, and accusations only cause more hard feelings, parents must Kiss their seventeen- and eighteen-year-olds more than ever. Reducing the issues involved in a sexual conflict to the bare minimum can be a sanity-saver. This also gives parents more time to ensure that their kids have an ample supply of the single most important ingredient in a healthy sex life: knowledge.

Eventually parents must ask themselves: "When it comes right down to the wire, what am I willing to tolerate in order to enjoy the pleasures of having my kid around?" In Vivian's case (see Chapter 13), her mother was convinced that if her daughter wanted premarital sexual intercourse, she didn't want her daughter at all. Because sexuality is such an emotionally laden topic, there never will be any easy answers. Only through compromise can parents and kids reach a point where they each get a little of what they want, a little of what they don't want, and learn to tolerate the rest.

I would have Kissed all the situations as quickly and firmly as possible.

If Carl had been my son, I would have obtained a court order prohibiting his marriage. He was under age, and I would have refused to sign a permit for him to marry in order to bring a baby into the world; in fact, I would have done everything possible to stop him. The father in this case didn't have the strength to get in his son's way. However, there would be no way I would condone bringing a child into the world with three strikes against the infant to begin with.

I would have sat down with Carl and the girl's parents to determine which was the better alternative: abortion or adoption. I might have been willing to let Carl get married after the issue of the baby had been resolved. However, this probably wouldn't have occurred since Carl was getting married partially as an act of revenge against what he believed were injustices committed against him by his divorced parents.

If I had been Cathy's father and walked in on a passionate love scene, I'm convinced that, in a state of sleepiness, I'd have moaned, "Oh, hell, not here!" I'd have growled and returned to bed, plagued for the rest of the night by visions of my daughter's promiscuity. The next day I'd have sat down with Cathy and said, "I'm sorry I interrupted your petting last night. I didn't do it on purpose. It's hard for me to adjust to the fact that my daughter is becoming a woman. I obviously can't control your sex life. However, in order for me not to hassle you about your dating, I want you to prove to me that you're mature enough to be above average in responsibility. Thus, I propose a compromise: I won't hassle you about sex if you'll take the responsibility for making an appointment with our family doctor, get a thorough examination, and start taking the Pill."

Knowing that such actions by a teenager call for exceptional maturity, I'd have relaxed somewhat, realizing that not only would Cathy be protected against pregnancy, but that she had also demonstrated adult behaviors. Because I would probably dominate this household, I'd then have told my wife to be supportive of my position and make herself available to Cathy for mother-daughter talks.

If I were Becky's father and a physician had told me that my seventeen-year-old was pregnant, I'd have felt many things at once—sorrow, fear, remorse, and anger the major emotions. After pacing a bit, I'd have made arrangements to see a shrink as soon as possible. With Becky and my wife present, I'd have aired my feelings and asked them to do the same. Then, with professional help, I'd have drawn up a plan of action.

First, I'd have determined what was to be done about the pregnancy. I'd have suggested abortion but allowed Becky to choose between that alternative and adoption. Under no circumstances would I have allowed Becky to keep the child. If she hadn't been able to make up her mind, I'd have called in an abortion counselor to talk with her and help her make a decision.

Assuming that Becky decided on abortion, as in the case above, I'd have made arrangements for her to receive continued abortion counseling while a highly reputable physician performed the necessary procedures. I'd have made sure she had complete birth control information plus the Pill. I'd have spoken with her about the pressure she felt and given her the same suggestions noted above.

Then, still under the guidance of my shrink, I'd have stated firmly that Becky had to regain my trust and confidence. I'd have said that in order to do this, she had to submit to my control of her dating. That is, during the first month following the abortion, all dates would take place in my home and under my supervision. If there were no hassles with this, the second month she could date but had to be home by 10:00 P.M. I'd have explained that I was not trying to control her sex life (which I couldn't do) but wanted a demonstration that she was willing to earn back my trust.

If she'd conformed to these guidelines without error, I'd have extended the curfew to 11:00 P.M. during the third month of dating. If all had gone well, I'd have restored full dating privileges during the fourth month, content with the fact that she'd proved she could obey regulations.

All these suggestions would have been open to modification, depending upon the input of my wife, Becky, and the shrink. If my emotions had been dominated by my reasoning (that's what my shrink would be for), I'd finally have suggested that Becky pay 25 percent of the costs incurred in this whole process, except for the shrink's fee. Once everyone had agreed, I'd have implemented the program, monitored it closely, and once four months had passed, I'd have put the memory of the entire event in the closet of broken dreams.

If my good-looking daughter had been sunbathing in the nude, I'd first have realized what a woman she had become and done everything I could to help her realize the impact that a beautiful woman has on the world. Then I'd have concentrated my attention on the issue of Candy's "liberation," seeing how much of it was real and how much of it was her attempt to shock people into losing their cool.

I'd have challenged her liberated viewpoints by asking her to pay a visit to the nosy neighbor for the purpose of exchanging ideas and explaining her position to someone who obviously didn't understand.

If she'd consented to do it, I'd have role-played with her what I thought she should say. I'd have suggested that she say, "Mrs. Johnson, it's unfortunate that you felt it necessary to call the police about my nude sunbathing. It's also unfortunate that I lost my cool with the police. But I came here to tell you that I see nothing wrong with nude sunbathing as long as I take the precautions that I took [doing it in an enclosed patio]. I also want to tell you that I may very well do it again, and I suggest that you not look out your window. I don't mean you any harm, but I won't take responsibility for the obvious fact that you do not like your body and are dumping your resentment on me."

As soon as I'd heard myself say the last sentence of the role play, I'd have recognized my own dislike for people who try to make beautiful things ugly. I'd have told Candy to skip the last comment because I wanted to give the neighbor that piece of *my* mind. If Candy had been able to say the other things to the lady without getting angry, then I'd have had more confidence that she could "cover her tracks" when she went away to college.

These fifteen cases only scratch the surface of the problems parents face when they realize that their kids, who look in the streets to find themselves, may be forced to live there. Despite their anger and pain, they usually realize that they can't allow their seventeen- or eighteen-year-old kid to continue to destroy the integrity of their home. If kids must be "shipped out," parents must understand that even the act of kicking a kid out can be protective—if not for the kid, then for the rest of the family.

When faced with the do-or-die Ambushes of older adolescents, parents must remember to limit themselves to realistic controls. They can control only what happens under their own roof. If they succeed there, they may have an outside chance of influencing other spheres of the kid's life. It's a slim chance, but better than none.

Trying to convince parents that they must take a last stand against the ruthless attack of not-so-gentle warriors is an extremely emotional experience. The last parent I helped to take such a stand was a woman whose tired face was overshadowed by two deep creases in her skin that curved a path from her glassy eyes down to her quivering lips.

These "tear canals" spoke of deeply entrenched pain. "What if my son ships out?" she protested. "He doesn't know how to live on the streets. What if he gets hurt? I could hold on a little longer."

I gave the mother the best advice I could. "You know you don't want to keep going. It's not good for your other children. You know things can only get worse. You've got one last shot. If you're lucky, you'll be a miracle worker; if not, you can rest assured that you tried your best. Anyhow, someday your kid will return and make up for his bad judgment."

The lady's last comment was more pointed than most. "Can you assure me that he will return? I'm sure you can't. I know you're right, and I'll do my best. I just hope you never have to face this."

The lady left, and I sat there with her thoughts bouncing around inside my head. I mused, "No, I couldn't assure her that her son would return. In fact, I've heard of many kids who lose their lives on the streets before they have a chance to say, 'I'm sorry.' "

That particular evening, I found more apprehension than usual creeping into my guts as I left my office. By the time I reached my car, my head was spinning with my own worry. "Will *my* son end up in some type of serious trouble? I help other kids; am I doing all I possibly can for my own, even given my limitations? Will my son experiment with trouble and get badly burned? Would I ever have the heart to actually kick him out? Maybe his mother could do more. Maybe he'll be all right in spite of his father. Maybe . . . maybe . . ."

On and on the uncertainties flowed. Such bouts with myself are not uncommon. Each time the murmurings drown out my professionalism, I come to the same conclusion. The uncertainties about my son's life are in me, not in him. He loves life, new toys, football, arithmetic, new friends, his mother, me, and the many special people who love him. He is facing his world and doing fine. I have to do the same.

I recently shared these thoughts and feelings with the husband of one of my co-workers. We'd bellied up to a bar, and eventually our conversation centered on exchanging stories and gripes about how kids manage to do stupid things, despite their intelligence.

He pounded the bar adamantly as he made a climactic point: "Sex, dope, alcohol, irresponsibility—what in hell are these kids thinking about? Won't they ever learn? That's no way to live. They have to quit sometime."

I was pretty mellow and didn't mind his ranting. "Doesn't seem like they do, though. In fact, I'm not sure they ever quit."

"You gotta be kidding me," he said sarcastically. "These kids better quit or else they'll be left out. Why, this country couldn't survive for one day if these blind-headed kids tried to run it. All they think about is booze, dope, and girls."

He beamed with pride at his patriotic stance and brilliant insight while I furrowed my brow in bewilderment at his pompous attitude.

Before I had a chance to comment, my bar buddy grabbed another cigarette, took a long drink of his double martini, and said, "Boy, look at that chick over there! I'll bet she's hot to trot."

A time bomb went off inside my head. I remember screaming to myself, "Why you hypocritical s.o.b.! You criticize kids' hell-raising while ignoring your own rudeness and self-indulgence. What's worse, there's too damn many 'adults' like you."

I smiled meekly on the outside as I inhibited my desire to pour a beer over his head.

15

After Eighteen: Success or Failure

Parents cannot be absolutely certain about their success or failure at Protective Parenting until the job is finished. The Protective Parenting Potential (P.P.P.) score, derived in Chapter 3 from the Protective Parenting Questionnaire (P.P.Q.), is not wholly reliable. Even the ABC Assessment is subject to human error or misapplication. Predicting success from the P.P.Q. or the ABC's is not as accurate as many parents would like. Added to this deficiency is the uncertainty derived from the fact that many parents are unwilling to admit that age nineteen marks the end of their job.

Once kids reach their nineteenth birthday, patterns of troublesome behavior should be easy to spot. For the most part, kids this age are either in trouble or they're not. Unless there is a special set of circumstances, parents should be able at this time to make a decision about their success or failure at Protective Parenting.

This final chapter is dedicated to helping parents make that decision. To make this possible, I've developed a three-step procedure that adds more reliability to self-evaluation. This procedure is a mixture of objective and subjective strategies. It is designed to evaluate the self-protective skills of kids past the age of eighteen.

When combined with the P.P.P. score and the ABC's, this procedure yields a more perfect assessment. The combination permits parents to more completely understand *one part* of their parenting. When completed by prospective parents or parents with kids younger than eighteen, this procedure opens the door to the future and gives parents a peek at the target they should be shooting for.

Some parents may find themselves stopping after Step 2, content with their evaluation. Still others will find the three-step procedure and the P.P.P. score incomplete. Others, never satisfied, will use the combined assessment as a stepping-off point for an evaluation that continues daily.

Before beginning the evaluation process, parents must cast aside any guilt concerning possible failure. Guilt represents needless self-recrimination and adds confusion and anxiety to a difficult situation. Therefore, thoughts about the "horror" of failure have no place in the following evaluation.

Step 1: Put the Nineteen- to Twenty-two-Year-Old in Perspective

For the most part, these kids stay out of—or talk their way out of—trouble. They still don't have the answers to the conflicts that haunted them at ages seventeen and eighteen, but they're getting closer to workable solutions. The two worlds that once tore them apart begin to merge into some type of conglomeration. It's usually clumsy, changeable, and confusing, but they possess the foundation of an adult personality.

Step 2: Examine Their Behavior

This step is sometimes very difficult, so I shall once again employ the Kiss method. Many of these kids are in college or trade school, but some go to work and live across town and others are marking time at odd jobs until they find out what they want to do. A few are bumming around, looking for booze, dope, sex, and a free ride. Since a full-scale analysis of their daily behavior is practically impossible, their behavior can best be evaluated if the parents answer these two questions:

1. If in college or trade school, is the kid getting passing grades? If not in school, is the kid gainfully employed at least twenty-five hours per week? (This includes activity in the armed forces, Peace Corps, VISTA, and so on.)
2. Has the kid avoided spending more than one night in jail?

If parents answered "Yes" to both questions, they may consider themselves successful at Protective Parenting. If one answer was "Yes" and the other "No," they have been minimally successful at Protective Parenting. If parents answered both questions "No," they most likely have failed at Protective Parenting.

If parents determine from these two questions that they have failed, they may wish to seek the cause of failure. The three most frequent causes are: the kid was smarter than the parents; the parents had too many problems of their own; or the process was started too late. More specific causes might be found by reexamining the discussions associated with the P.P.Q. Also, rechecking some of the case studies might shed light on the reasons. No matter what the cause, parents can rest assured that the kid used a series of strategies and techniques to undermine parental authority and continue to make noncompliance a way of life.

Just because parents have failed at Protective Parenting does *not* mean that they or their kids are total failures. Nor does it mean that parents did everything wrong. It means that they failed at *one* aspect of parenting: keeping kids out of trouble. There are many adults who demonstrate that such failure is not forever. They overcome parental failure and become successful in their own right. Thus, even though parents may fail at Protective Parenting, it doesn't mean that their kids are stuck with a life full of failure.

No matter how old, kids still have a chance to use their will-power and mental resources to "get their heads together." It may mean a trip or two to a shrink, but it can be done.

Step 3: Subjective Evaluation

If parents still don't know whether they've succeeded or failed at Protective Parenting (even though they answered both questions "Yes"), it may mean they don't know if their job is finished yet. In order to clear this hurdle, parents need to take a subjective look at the day-to-day relationship between them-selves and their kids. This is best done by placing themselves somewhere between two extremes.

Overprotection The following are frequent signs of the af-termath of overprotection: Kids take parents' money and give grunts of disrespect in return. They spend most of their time drinking or smoking dope instead of working. Kids accuse their parents of not loving them as they demand that parents stay out of their lives. Kids still have a bed in the parents' home where they occasionally "crash" free of charge.

If these things are happening, parents have very likely over-protected their kids. They have failed to transfer control of their kids' lives from themselves to their kids. In other words, they never really gave their kids the chance to run their own lives.

Underprotection The following are frequent signs of the af-termath of underprotection: Parents don't have the foggiest no-tion where their kids live. Kids are confined in prison or some other detention facility. Parents don't care where their kids are or what they're doing. Kids come and go, but parents don't know when or where and couldn't care less.

If these things are happening, parents have most likely un-derprotected their kids. Such parents will probably never realize or admit it. They never really cared about controlling their kids or just didn't have the strength to keep up with them.

If parents can place themselves somewhere between the two extremes and still don't know whether or not they have been successful at Protective Parenting, an accurate assessment is probably not possible. If this is the case, parents should suspend attempts to evaluate their parenting and take a look at what another mother and father went through.

Stepping into other parents' shoes breeds compassion. Com-passion permits parents, whether successes or failures, to give love to a kid in trouble. And, after age eighteen, love is the most valuable thing parents can give to their kids.

I was called by a well-to-do businessman who expressed con-cern about his twenty-two-year-old daughter, Alice. He outlined the problem this way:

Alice went to college when she was eighteen. She was fas-cinated by African studies. She was exceptionally bright, win-ning a nationally competitive scholarship. Not only did her father support her expensive college pursuits, but he also footed the bill for two summers of work with poor tribes in an African state. By the end of her sophomore year in college, Alice could speak several native languages, fully understood the history of American blacks, and had written scholarly works unraveling the "black plight in America." By the start of her third year in college, she was on the verge of attaining national, if not inter-national, recognition. Then, within three months, her entire world collapsed.

As our phone conversation continued, I could almost see her father's head shaking in disbelief as he detailed what had hap-pened in the past year or so. First came a lessening of contact—

no letters, no calls, and finally no weekend visits at home. Then came the estrangement that her mom and dad had felt during visits they made to her campus. It became apparent that Alice didn't want to talk with them. When she did, her voice was bleak, her interests dulled, and her face filled with anguish. The spark was gone.

Her father's voice quivered as he told of how he and his wife had begged Alice for an explanation. She had given none. She answered their questions with meaningless phrases and impersonal stares. She displayed emotion only when she made a couple of unintelligible remarks about her father's wealth, power, and influence.

Three months into her junior year, Alice showed up at her parents' house with her possessions in the back of an old, broken-down convertible and her arm around the shoulder of a bearded, long-haired young man. At this point in the conversation I could hear her father reliving the nightmare he and his wife had experienced. He went on to say that Alice dumped her possessions in her old bedroom and blandly informed her mother that she was moving in with her boyfriend. Her father's voice began to crack as he attempted to convince me that he and his wife were not responsible for their daughter's "conversion." He was vehement in his belief that "the freak had poisoned her mind with dope." I assured him that I would see Alice and give her my best shot.

I met Alice in the fountain area of a local "head shop." We had agreed to meet at 5:00 P.M. She strolled in and approached my booth at 6:10. She was a quietly attractive girl, five feet three inches tall, with sandy hair, tired green eyes, and a lightly freckled complexion. She wasn't very happy about meeting me and let me know it.

As she sat down, she muttered, "Whaddaya wanna talk about?"

I was disappointed that she placed total responsibility for the meeting on my shoulders. After all, she had agreed to meet me.

I had difficulty concentrating on my original purpose, not only because she'd caught me off balance but also because I was startled by the lifelessness of the human being facing me. I gazed into her eyes, captivated by the exhaustion that seemed to dominate her inner self. I thought to myself, "This girl is tired. Tired of pain, tired of not knowing who she is, tired of hurting, tired of emptiness, tired of living." I did the best I could.

"Your father suggested that it might be a good idea for you and me to talk. He thought maybe I had an idea or two about how to help you get along better."

"I don't really need to 'get along better.' "

"Well, he just thought you were having some troubles."

She wasn't interested in talking to me and continued to let me know it. But at least she told me why she'd shown up: "Just tell my father I'm okay and he'll get off my back."

"He's on your back, huh?" (I hoped this remark would get the counseling session off the ground. But I was wrong again.)

"Yeah."

She said nothing further, so I tried to go elsewhere.

"I hear you're interested in African studies."

"Long time ago."

"That's very interesting. Can you tell me about it?"

"Not interesting anymore."

She continued to stare right past me, even though our noses couldn't have been more than three feet apart. I decided to take still another approach.

"Where are you living these days?"

"Was living with a guy, but I moved back home. Ran out of money."

"What do you do at home?"

"Oh, just hang around. Mostly stay in my room."

"What do you do to keep busy?"

"Nothing much."

Since I thought I had the beginnings of a good conversation, I thought it would be a good idea to let her know that I was understanding.

"Do much dope?"

"Used to."

"Working?"

"Oh, here and there. I get tired of things easily."

"What kind of work do you like best?"

"It doesn't make much difference. Housework. Waitressing."

I was running out of patience, let alone inane topics. I was also becoming frustrated with Alice's spacy attitude, don't-give-a-damn responses, and militant avoidance of engaging me in meaningful conversation. I finally pushed her as far as I thought I could without her getting up and walking out.

"You have a helluva lot of pain in your life, don't you?"

Her eyes glazed up even more. "Oh, yeah, I guess."

"But you seem dead inside. Not willing to deal with life."

"You get that way after a while."

I pushed onward, not sure where I was going. "What happened to your life, Alice? Why did it go down the tubes so quickly?"

"I don't know. Just changed." She paused, but I could sense something close to the surface, so I remained quiet for a minute or two. Finally she let me have a little peek inside her head.

"Some people have money and power and no pain; others have nothing but empty lives and frustrated dreams. People have it nice—sometimes they don't know what they want other times. Some people don't know what other people die for; some people don't care."

Her words didn't make much sense the first time I heard them, so I quickly replayed them in my head. *Bango!* The light began to dawn. As she finished her Coke, I finally put two and two together. I think I got four. Bright, upper-middle-class girl, money, deep feelings, the best of everything plus sudden painful exposure to a rotten side of life equals painful identity crisis.

"So you figure your father has somehow caused the oppression and pain of the people you used to care for."

She focused her eyes on mine for the first time. For a split second I saw the glaze disappear and the hatred burning deep within her. When she quickly shrugged her shoulders and gave me that "you-don't-really-understand-me" look, I knew that I had hit home. She tried to conceal it.

"That doesn't matter anymore."

I continued looking deep into her eyes as I once again talked to myself. "This lady is suffering for the sins of her father! She is offering herself as a pure white sacrifice to the god of racial justice in hopes of making up for the pain and torment that she feels she has indirectly caused. She was just a clean, naive little girl who was suddenly thrust into the cesspool of racism and bigotry. Her pain was so overwhelming that she simply burned herself out. And now she's just a shell of a human being, deeply engulfed in self-pity and unresolved conflicts."

I had all these conclusions flashing through my head faster than I could understand them, at least at that moment. I wanted to reach out and grab that spark of fire left in her soul and bring her back to life. I extended my hand toward hers, gently stroking her fingers. Her hands were clammy and devoid of any warmth.

"I want you to know that I think I understand part of your pain and that I would be willing to help you as much as humanly possible."

She looked longingly at me, then refocused her eyes into outer space and murmured, "I'd sure appreciate some type of waitress job if you know of any."

My mouth dropped open in painful disbelief.

She had slapped me down, and I got mad. There was fire in my eyes as I leaned back in the booth and gave her a sneer of disapproval and contempt. "You don't want to do anything but

sit on your butt and feel sorry for yourself while you expect
your father to take care of you. You are a bummer!''

With the same spacy stare and a sneer of her own, she
grunted, ''Care? Huh!''

I continued my challenge, not sure where it would lead.
''What do you mean, 'huh'? Can't you see their love?''

''What love? They think of money and possessions, not
love.''

She was as hooked as I would ever get her, so I tried to communicate something that might get her attention and stay with
her during her hours of emptiness. ''They think of you. They
worry about you. They love you. They've given you a lot.''

''*A lot!* What did they ever give me?''

The interaction was hot and heavy and wouldn't last long.
''They gave you morals, an education, and protection from
harm.''

''They didn't protect me from shit!''

''Hey, what in hell do you want? Perfect parents all the time
in all ways?''

''No, but they failed at everything. They didn't do anything
like they should have.''

''That's what you say now. They gave you lots of things in
the past. Can't you remember those things?''

Her indignation sounded the beginning of the end of our conversation. ''Remember what things? What things? *Name one!*''

''They gave you life.''

She took her last shot: ''Ha! That's a failure, too!''

I took mine: ''Yeah, but who's responsibility is that now?''

She glared at me, and I could feel chills run up my back.
There was little else I could say. It was up to her now. She had
to face her lack of responsibility or find a way to discredit what
I had said. The forces of her badly damaged ego clashed with
the logic of my argument and offer to help.

She rose slowly from the table as her eyes pronounced the

verdict. She looked past me to the wall and said, "I have to go now. Hope I didn't keep you. Charge the Coke to my father, he has plenty of money."

She walked listlessly away, and I sat looking at her half-empty glass. The condensation running down the side of the glass reflected my own tears of remorse for a girl who had refused to face the hard facts of life.

Alice was typical of so many kids who wander around the world with fire in their eyes and ice in their hearts hoping somebody will take responsibility for their actions and magically transform them into adults. Alice wanted to be full of life but didn't want to work for it.

I watched her as she disappeared out the door and moved across the street, walking as though living in the world had grown too painful. I remember thinking out loud, "Nobody said it would be easy."

I paid the bill and walked out into the cool fall evening. I approached a crosswalk where a lady was having trouble with her five-year-old daughter. The little girl was screaming and demanding to be carried across the street. The mother kept saying "No," and the girl kept screaming louder and louder. Finally the mother picked the little girl up and carried her across the street. I shook my head in despair and thought to myself, "Wonder if that girl's name is Alice?"

Appendix

Lessons in Protective Parenting

The lessons included in each case study have been grouped below in such a manner as to give new life to old clichés.

Spare the rod and spoil revenge.

> Punishment does not have to be abusive or harsh to be effective.
> Physical punishment and idle threats make a parent feel better but rarely help a child.
> If punishment is the parents' first choice, a kid will make them wish it had been their last.
> Hitting kids because of a sweet tooth will turn them sour.
> Parents should hit their kids with an "or else," not their hand.
> Parents should get a kid's attention by waving money, not a fist.
> Parents should compensate for verbal spanking before kids decide to strike back.

Creative discipline is 1 percent perspiration and 99 percent inspiration.

> When push comes to shove, a child should be Kissed.
> Parents must use their head when a child abuses his.
> Wise parents can help nature take its course.
> Every Ambush has a key behavior; think of a constructive manner in which the child can engage in the behavior.

If a gentle warrior is smarter than a parent, the parent should dull the tip of his (her) arrow.

If a parent hears "I can't," substitute "won't" for "can't" and see if it sounds more accurate.

When kids "flip the bird," remind them it may represent their I.Q.

To get some kids' attention, one has to enter their heads through their stomachs.

The policeman can be a parent's best friend.

Feed compliance, starve a tantrum.

Be cautious with the obvious; things aren't always what they seem.

Parents sometimes make a molehill out of a mountain.

Don't judge a problem by the size of the tears.

> There once was a girl, oh so sweet,
> Dad's lap was her fav'rit retreat.
> When Mom got mad
> She ran to Dad,
> But now she's pursued by the heat.

A child's need for attention is often difficult to hear.

Where a parent sees smoke doesn't always mean there is a fire.

If parents can't find the right answer, maybe they're working on the wrong problem.

Serious trouble can be hidden by many things—even love.

Liberation is no excuse for stupidity.

The school of hard knocks can teach many lessons.

Teach a child that screaming for attention only gets him or her a sore throat.

A smile can open many doors, but one of them may lead to trouble.

Some kids can turn a "touch-and-smile" neighborhood into a "shove-and-smirk" jungle.

Someone has to teach children that life is not a continuous merry-go-round; it's sad, but true.

Black may be beautiful and white may mean might, but a broken window has got to be made right.

Kids must learn that they are never completely protected from trouble—not even at home.

Money does not protect kids from trouble.

The road to trouble is paved with good intentions and needless worry.

Worry about mental disturbance *after* a kid follows the rules.

Investing too much worry will result in overdone interest that can yield problems that are compounded daily.

Protective Parents must do more than just "keep an eye" on their gentle warriors.

An ounce of knowledge is sometimes worth more than a pound of concern.

Giving is part of receiving.

Cooperative play is a giant step toward reciprocity.

The golden rule of Protective Parenting is: If you do unto me what hurts, I shall refuse to do unto you what feels good.

If kids are gonna play, then they gotta pay.

Understanding is a two-way street.

If you do the crime, you gotta pay the time.

Parenting is a play in which there are many roles.

If parents really want a "break," take the kids to Grandma's and go out for a steak.

Parents must respect their kids more than any material object; if they don't, kids will use materialistic means to make them wish they had.

If parents lose sight of their kids, the kids may get lost forever.

Parents should not forget that they did dumb things when they were young.

There are some parents who shouldn't be.

Parents should covet their kid's respect more than a neighbor's praise.

Some parents get kissed one minute and Ambushed the next.

Parents do deserve a break today.

If parents act like a money-dispenser, their kids will treat them like a machine.

Parents should put their noses into their kids' private business only when they can put their feet into their kids' shoes.

Parent's weaknesses are perfect targets for Ambushes.

Hell-raisers can burn a lot of people.

To a four-year-old, raising hell is sometimes more important than ice cream or pizza.

If more couples could see a five-year-old's reaction to the word "No" before they became parents, they would demand protection lessons.
Serious hell-raising can start with a small fire.
A spoiled kid will spoil much.
When a kid finally hears "No," it can be a stinky mess.

Both maturity and trouble develop one step at a time.

The stairway to trouble is steep; most kids take their first step up when they learn to walk.
Responsibility each day will keep the policeman away.
One small step for a child can be a giant leap for society.
Unfettered exploration by youth, when monitored by reasonable adults, is the key to freedom and truth.

Like all things, words have their place.

If a two-year-old can drive the neighborhood crazy with words, think what he or she will eventually do with actions.
Talking to yourself is not only fun but also psychologically healthy since in a world filled with poor communication, misunderstandings, and lack of empathy, you are probably the only one who really understands you.
Parents should not teach their children that certain words have magical powers.
Kids' sexual problems often get started when they listen to their parents.
Believe it or not, a nine-year-old can "talk it all out."
Complaints of inner turmoil do not excuse a lack of compliance.
Understand the struggle of, *"Treat me like a woman (man)*—please, Mommy."
The intent behind a word is sometimes more important than the word itself.
One action is worth a thousand reprimands.

Too much of a thing can ruin it.

Limits must be imposed on "bad-mouthing" others.
The more a kid watches the tube, the more likely he'll be a boob.
Overindulgence can be addictive.
If a kid gets too high, he or she must be brought down to earth.
Rational or not, parents will occasionally follow Kiley's law: If you truly love your kids, sometimes you just gotta yell at them.

If kids can joke their way out of complying, trouble may turn their laughter to tears.

If a "stage" accounts for trouble, maybe the kid should get on one that takes him out of the home.

With eyes and ears open, parents should remember that a minute of thought is worth more than an hour of talk.

Parents' words sometimes come back to haunt them.

Parents must have a kid's attention before ignoring works.

Hearing the wrong thing can be worse than not listening at all.

It doesn't take spying to be aware of a child's possessions.

An "or else" without follow-through gives a child live ammunition.

When in doubt, ask questions.

"Don't do that" should really mean "Don't do that."

If they keep their eyes and ears open, parents can often spot an Ambush before it hits.

Often parents must end the relationship with their kids the way it began: by giving unconditional love.

Beware the four marks of serious trouble:
violence, sexual ignorance, drugs, and negative peer pressure.

It takes two to kill—guns and people.

A "right" is a privilege to be spoken for, not something to be used to hit another person with.

Use extreme caution before advising a child to hit someone.

When it comes to "bad" companions, two's a crowd, three's disaster.

"Bad" influences can be monitored, not eliminated.

If kids smoke a joint, they need the straight dope.

One way to relieve the pressure of peers is to find new peers.

Kids have no business in the drug business.

Sex isn't dirty, but ignorance can make it hurt.

One of the literal aspects of Protective Parenting is teaching teenagers about birth control.

Children belong wherever there is a home for their heart.

If everything in a home is "to be seen, not touched," the home is actually a house where children don't belong.

In a fascinating world that is often out of reach, children need to be lifted up, not beaten down.

Honesty may not always be the best policy, but every kid should know how it's done.

There are some places where children should be neither seen nor heard.

A child has a right to his or her own problems. If parents try to make their child's problem their problem, they're going to have even more problems than they already have; and that's a problem.

Keep the warriors out of the bedroom with honesty, not bribery.

Kids who fail to learn right from wrong will persecute their parents for the failure.

Using a child as a tool of revenge during or after a divorce should be considered a type of rape.

If kids look in a mirror and see an animal, expect them to act like one.

Index

About the Author

Dan Kiley received his B.A. from St. Ambrose College, Davenport, Iowa, in 1964. He was granted a master's and a doctorate in counseling/clinical psychology from the University of Illinois in 1966 and 1969, respectively. After being exposed to a full spectrum of clinical cases, he narrowed his work to children and adolescents.

Acting as psychologist and administrator, Dr. Kiley inaugurated the VAST (*V*ocational *A*cademic *S*ocial *T*raining) Program. During his five-year tenure as director, this Illinois Department of Corrections program grew to house an average of seventeen juveniles at a time from throughout the state, who are exposed to six months of intensive reeducational programming. An independent study found that 87 percent of VAST "graduates" are successful at staying out of trouble. VAST has attracted national attention and is the subject of ongoing study by professionals.

Dr. Kiley's writings have been included in both professional and trade publications. He holds memberships in the American Psychological Association, the Illinois Psychological Association, and the Association for the Advancement of Psychology. He was recently listed in Who's Who in America, 1976–1977. He has maintained a private practice throughout his professional career.

Dr. Kiley is married. His son, Patrick, is ten years old.